World's Top Terrorist Organisation and their Major Notorious Acts

World's Top Terrorist Organisation and their Major Notorious Acts

Capt. S.L. Soni (Redt.)

Col. C.P. Bhargav (Retd.)

PRASHANT PUBLISHING HOUSE
DELHI-110094

Published by :
Prashant Publishing House
C-34, 28 Foota Road, Gali-3,
West Karwal Nagar, Delhi-110094
Phone : 011-22963970, Mob. : 9810396373
e-mail.: prashantpublishinghouse@gmail.com

World's Top Terrorist Organisation and their Major Notorious Acts

First Published 2015

ISBN 978-93-80565-56-9

PRINTED IN INDIA
Published by Mr. R.K. Jha M/s Prashant Publishing House and Published at H.S. Offset House Press, Delhi.

Preface

Common definitions of terrorism refer only to those violent acts that are intended to create fear (terror); are perpetrated for a religious, political, or ideological goal; and deliberately target or disregard the safety of non-combatants (e.g., neutral military personnel or civilians). Another common definition is political or religious violence by non-state actors. Some definitions now include acts of unlawful violence and war. The use of similar tactics by criminal organizations for protection rackets or to enforce a code of silence is usually not labeled terrorism, though these same actions may be labeled terrorism when done by a politically motivated group. Usage of the term has also been criticized for its frequent undue equating with Islamism or jihadism, while ignoring non-Islamic organizations or individuals.

Al Qaeda is a brand name, but Islamic State is the devil itself. Officially known as ISIL or ISIS (Islamic State of Iraq and the Levant/Syria), the Islamic State controls northern parts of Iraq and the Western parts of Syria, within which it has formed its own government.

Derived from the Pashto word for "students", Taliban is well-known for being one of the few militant organisations to have been in charge of a country – Afghanistan from 1996 to 2001. Founded by Mullah Mohammed Omar, the Taliban took Afghanistan back into the middle ages with their strict imposition of Sharia and Islamic laws. It received active support of the Al-Qaeda, and was overthrown in the US-led invasion of Afghanistan.

—*Sunjoy K. Singh*

Contents

1

Al-Qaeda

Founded by Osama Bin Laden, Abdullah Azzam and other militants, the al-Qaeda's objective is to unite the Muslims across the world in global jihad and a strict interpretation of the Sharia law. The al-Qaeda is a Wahhabi organization. The al-Qaeda had a role to play in the Spetember 11 attacks, the 1998 US embassy bombings and the 2002 Bali bombings. Although the death of Osama Bin Laden has proven to be a setback to their operations, they are still the deadliest among all such groups in the world. Their characteristic way of carrying out missions is to employ suicide bombers or execute suicide missions. Their attacks are also known to be sectarian in nature. The Ashoura massacre and the April 2007 Baghdad bombings are testimony to that fact. The 1993 bombing of the World Trade Center was also carried out by al-Qaeda. They are known to be extremely influential and have been alleged to own several aircrafts including Boeing 727s and executive jets.

Al-Qaeda, alternatively spelled al-Qaida and sometimes al-Qa'ida, is an international Sunni Islamist movement founded in 1988. Al-Qaeda have attacked civilian and military targets in various countries, the most notable being the September 11 attacks in 2001. These actions were followed by the US government launching a military and intelligence campaign against al-Qaeda called the *War on Terror*.

Characteristic techniques include suicide attacks and simultaneous bombings of different targets. Activities ascribed to it may involve members of the organization, who have taken a pledge of loyalty to Osama bin Laden, or the much more numerous "al-Qaeda-linked" individuals who have undergone training in one of its camps in Afghanistan or Sudan but not taken any pledge. Al-Qaeda's objectives include the end of foreign influence in Muslim countries and the creation of a new Islamic caliphate. Reported beliefs include that a Christian-Jewish alliance is conspiring to destroy Islam, and that the killing of bystanders and civilians is Islamically justified in jihad. Its management philosophy has been described as "centralization of decision and decentralization of execution." Following 9/11 and the launching of the War on Terrorism, it is thought al-Qaeda's leadership has "become geographically isolated", leading to the "emergence of decentralized leadership" of regional groups using the al-Qaeda "brand name."

Al-Qaeda has been labelled a *terrorist organization* by the United Nations Security Council, the North Atlantic Treaty Organization Secretary General, the Commission of the European Communities of the European Union, the United States Department of State, the Australian Government, Government of India, Public Safety Canada, the Israel Ministry of Foreign Affairs, Japan's Diplomatic Bluebook, South Korean Foreign Ministry, the Dutch Military Intelligence and Security Service, the United Kingdom Home Office, Russia, the Swedish Ministry for Foreign Affairs, and the Swiss Government.

HISTORY

Jihad in Afghanistan

The origins of the group can be traced to the Soviet war in Afghanistan. The United States viewed the conflict in Afghanistan, with the Afghan Marxists and allied Soviet troops on one side and the native Afghan mujahedeen on the other, as a blatant case of Soviet expansionism and aggression. The U.S. channelled funds through Pakistan's Inter-Services Intelligence agency to the native Afghan mujahedeen fighting the Soviet occupation in a CIA program called Operation Cyclone.

At the same time, a growing number of foreign Arab mujahedeen (also called Afghan Arabs) joined the jihad against the Afghan Marxist regime, facilitated by international Muslim organizations, particularly the Maktab al-Khidamat, whose funds came from some of the $600 million a year donated to the jihad by the Saudi Arabia government and individual Muslims-particularly wealthy Saudis who were approached by Osama bin Laden. Maktab al-Khidamat was established by Abdullah Azzam and Bin Laden in Peshawar, Pakistan, in 1984. From 1986 it began to set up a network of recruiting offices in the United States, the hub of which was the Al Kifah Refugee Centre at the Farouq Mosque in Brooklyn's Atlantic Avenue. Among notable figures at the Brooklyn centre were "double agent" Ali Mohamed, whom FBI special agent Jack Cloonan called "bin Laden's first trainer," and "Blind Sheikh" Omar Abdel-Rahman, a leading recruiter of mujahideen for Afghanistan.

The Afghan Mujahedeen of the 1980s have been alleged to be the inspiration for terrorist groups in nations such as Indonesia, the Philippines, Egypt, Saudi Arabia, Algeria, Chechnya, and the former Yugoslavia. According to Russian sources, the perpetrators of the first World Trade Centre bombing in 1993 allegedly used a manual allegedly written by the CIA for the Mujihadeen fighters in Afghanistan on how to make explosives.

Al-Qaeda evolved from the Maktab al-Khidamat (Services Office), a Muslim organization founded in 1980 to raise and channel funds and recruit foreign mujahadeen for the war against the Soviets in Afghanistan. It was founded by Abdullah Yusuf Azzam, a Palestinian Islamic scholar and member of the Muslim Brotherhood.

Maktab al-Khadamat organized guest houses in Peshawar, in Pakistan, near the Afghan border, and paramilitary training camps in Afghanistan to prepare international non-Afghan recruits for the Afghan war front. Azzam persuaded Bin Laden to join MAK, to use his own money and use his connections with "the Saudi royal family and the petro-billionaires of the Gulf" to raise more to help the mujahideen.

The role played by MAK and foreign Muslim volunteers, or "Afghan Arabs", in the war was not a major one. While 250,000 Afghan Mujahideen fought the Soviets and the communist Afghan government, it is estimated that were never more than 2000 foreign mujahideen in the field at any one time. Nonetheless, foreign mujahedeen volunteers came from 43 countries and the number that participated in the Afghan movement between 1982 and 1992 is reported to have been 35,000. The Soviet Union finally withdrew from Afghanistan in 1989. To the surprise of many, Mohammed Najibullah's communist Afghan government hung on for three more years before being overrun by elements of the mujahedeen. With mujahedeen leaders unable to agree on a structure for governance, chaos ensued, with constantly reorganizing alliances fighting for control of ill-defined territories, leaving the country devastated.

Refuge in Afghanistan

After the Soviet withdrawal, Afghanistan was effectively ungoverned for seven years and plagued by constant infighting between former allies and various mujahedeen groups. Throughout the 1990s, a new force began to emerge. The origins of the Taliban (literally "students") lay in the children of Afghanistan, many of them orphaned by the war, and many of whom had been educated in the rapidly expanding network of Islamic schools (madrassas) either in Kandahar or in the refugee camps on the Afghan-Pakistani border.

According to Ahmed Rashid, five leaders of the Taliban were graduates of a single madrassa, Darul Uloom Haqqania (also known as "the University of Jihad",) in the small town of Akora Khattak near Peshawar, situated in Pakistan but largely attended by Afghan refugees. This institution reflected Salafi beliefs in its teachings, and much of its funding came from private donations from wealthy Arabs, for whom bin Laden provided conduit. A further four leading figures (including the perceived Taliban leader Mullah Mohammed Omar Mujahed) attended a similarly funded and influenced madrassa in Kandahar, Afghanistan.

Many of the mujahedeen who later joined the Taliban fought alongside Afghan warlord Mohammad Nabi Mohammadi's Harkat i Inqilabi group at the time of the Russian invasion. This group also enjoyed the loyalty of most Afghan Arab fighters.

The continuing internecine strife between various factions, and accompanying lawlessness following the Soviet withdrawal, enabled the growing and well-disciplined Taliban to expand their control over territory in Afghanistan, and they came to establish an enclave which it called the Islamic Emirate of Afghanistan. In 1994, they captured the regional centre of Kandahar, and after making rapid territorial gains thereafter, conquered the capital city Kabul in September 1996.

After Sudan made it clear that bin Laden and his group were no longer welcome that year, Taliban-controlled Afghanistan—with previously established connections between the groups, a similar outlook on world affairs and largely isolated from American political influence and military power—provided a perfect location for al-Qaeda to establish its headquarters. Al-Qaeda enjoyed the Taliban's protection and a measure of legitimacy as part of their Ministry of Defence, although only Pakistan, Saudi Arabia, and the United Arab Emirates recognized the Taliban as the legitimate government of Afghanistan.

Al-Qaeda training camps in Afghanistan and the Pakistani border regions are alleged to have trained militant Muslims from around the world. Despite the perception of some people, al-Qaeda members are ethnically diverse and connected by their radical version of Islam.

An ever-expanding network of supporters thus enjoyed a safe haven in Taliban-controlled Afghanistan until the Taliban were defeated by a combination of local forces and United States air power in 2001. Osama bin Laden and other al-Qaeda leaders are still believed to be located in areas where the population is sympathetic to the Taliban in Afghanistan or the border Tribal Areas of Pakistan.

Fatwas

In 1996, al-Qaeda announced its jihad to expel foreign troops and interests from what they felt were Islamic lands. Bin Laden issued a fatwa, which amounted to a public declaration of war against the United States and any of its allies, and began to focus al-Qaeda's resources towards attacking the United States and its interests. Also occurring on June 25, 1996 was the bombing of the Khobar towers, located in Khobar, Saudi Arabia. On February 23, 1998, Osama bin Laden and Ayman al-Zawahiri, a leader of Egyptian Islamic Jihad, along with three other Islamist leaders, cosigned and issued a fatwa (binding religious edict) under the banner of the World Islamic Front for Combat Against the Jews and Crusaders (*al-Jabhah al-Islamiyya al-'Alamiyya li-Qital al-Yahud wal-Salibiyyin*) declaring:

[T]he ruling to kill the Americans and their allies-civilians and military — is an individual duty for every Muslim who can do it in any country in which it is possible to do it, in order to liberate the al-Aqsa Mosque (in Jerusalem) and the holy mosque (in Makka) from their grip, and in order for their armies to move out of all the lands of Islam, defeated and unable to threaten any Muslim. This is in accordance with the words of Almighty Allah, 'and fight the pagans all together as they fight you all together,' and 'fight them until there is no more tumult or oppression, and there prevail justice and faith in Allah'.

Neither bin Laden nor al-Zawahiri possessed the traditional Islamic scholarly qualifications to issue a fatwa of any kind; however, they rejected the authority of the contemporary ulema (seen as the paid servants of *jahiliyya* rulers) and took it upon themselves. Assassinated former FSB agent Alexander Litvinenko alleged that the Russian FSB trained al-Zawahiri in a camp in Dagestan eight months before the 1998 fatwa.

Expanding Operations

Toward the end of the Soviet military mission in Afghanistan, some mujahedeen wanted to expand their operations to include Islamist struggles in other parts of the world, such as Israel and Kashmir. A number of overlapping and interrelated organizations were formed to further those aspirations.

One of these was the organization that would eventually be called al-Qaeda, formed by Osama bin Laden with an initial meeting held on August 11, 1988. Bin Laden wished to establish nonmilitary operations in other parts of the world; Azzam, in contrast, wanted to remain focused on military campaigns. After Azzam was assassinated in 1989, the MAK split, with a significant number joining bin Laden's organization.

In November 1989, Ali Mohamed, a former special forces Sergeant stationed at Fort Bragg, North Carolina, left military service and moved to Santa Clara, California. He travelled to

Afghanistan and Pakistan and became "deeply involved with bin Laden's plans.". A year later, on November 8, 1990, the FBI raided the New Jersey home of Mohammed's associate El Sayyid Nosair, discovering a great deal of evidence of terrorist plots, including plans to blow up New York City skyscrapers. Nosair was eventually convicted in connection to the 1993 World Trade Centre bombing, and for the murder of Rabbi Meir Kahane on November 5, 1990. In 1991, Ali Mohammed is said to have helped orchestrate Osama bin Laden's relocation to Sudan.

Gulf War and the Start of U.S. Enmity

Following the Soviet Union's withdrawal from Afghanistan, Osama bin Laden returned to Saudi Arabia. The Iraqi invasion of Kuwait in 1990 had put the country of Saudi Arabia and its ruling House of Saud at risk as Saudi's most valuable oil fields (Hama) were within easy striking distance of Iraqi forces in Kuwait, and Saddam's call to pan-Arab/Islamism could potentially rally internal dissent. In the face of a seemingly massive Iraqi military presence, Saudi Arabia's own forces were well armed but far outnumbered. Bin Laden offered the services of his mujahedeen to King Fahd to protect Saudi Arabia from the Iraqi army. The Saudi monarch refused bin Laden's offer, opting instead to allow U.S. and allied forces to deploy on Saudi territory.

The deployment angered Bin Laden, as he believed the presence of foreign troops in the "land of the two mosques" (Mecca and Medina) profaned sacred soil. After speaking publicly against the Saudi government for harbouring American troops, he was quickly forced into exile to Sudan and on April 9, 1994 his Saudi citizenship was revoked. His family publicly disowned him. There is controversy over whether and to what extent he continued to garner support from members of his family and/or the Saudi government.

Sudan

From approximately 1992 to 1996, al-Qaeda and bin Laden were located in Sudan, coming at the invitation of Islamist theoretician Hassan al Turabi following an Islamist coup d'état, and leaving after being expelled by the Sudanese government. During this time bin Laden assisted the Sudanese government, bought or set up various business enterprises, and established training camps where insurgents trained. But in Sudan bin Laden lost his Saudi passport and source of income in response to his verbal attacks on the Saudi king. A key turning point for bin Laden occurred in 1993 when Saudi Arabia gave support for the Oslo Accords which set a path for peace between Israel and Palestine.

Zawahiri and the EIJ, who served as the core of al-Qaeda but also engaged in separate operations against the Egyptian government, had even worse luck in Sudan. In 1993, a young schoolgirl was killed in an unsuccessful EIJ attempt on the life of the Egyptian Interior Minister, Hasan al-Alfi. Egyptian public opinion turned against Islamist bombings and the police arrested 280 more of al-Jihad's members and executed six. In 1995 an even more ill-fated attempt to assassinate Egyptian president Mubarak led to the expulsion of EIJ and not long after of bin Laden by the Sudanese government.

ORGANIZATION STRUCTURE OF AL-QAEDA

Though the current structure of al-Qaeda is unknown, information mostly acquired from Jamal al-Fadl provided American authorities with a rough picture of how the group was organized. While the veracity of the information provided by al-Fadl and the motivation for his cooperation are both disputed, American authorities base much of their current knowledge of al-Qaeda on his testimony.

Osama bin Laden is the emir and Senior Operations Chief of al-Qaeda (although originally this role may have been filled by Abu Ayoub al-Iraqi), advised by a Shura Council, which consists of senior al-Qaeda members, estimated by Western officials at about twenty to thirty people.

Ayman al-Zawahiri is al-Qaeda's Deputy Operations Chief and Abu Ayyub al-Masri is possibly the senior leader of al-Qaeda in Iraq.

- The Military Committee is responsible for training operatives, acquiring weapons, and planning attacks.
- The Money/Business Committee runs business operations, provides air tickets and false passports, pays al-Qaeda members, and oversees profit-driven businesses. In the 9/

11 Commission Report, it is estimated that al-Qaeda requires $30,000,000 USD per year to conduct its operations.

- The Law Committee reviews Islamic law and decides if particular courses of action conform to the law.
- The Islamic Study/Fatwah Committee issues religious edicts, such as an edict in 1998 telling Muslims to kill Americans.
- In the late 1990s there was a publicly known Media Committee, which ran the now-defunct newspaper *Nashrat al Akhbar (Newscast)* and handled public relations.
- In 2005, al Qaeda formed As-Sahab, a media production house, to supply its video and audio materials.

The number of individuals belonging to the organization is also unknown. According to the controversial BBC documentary *The Power of Nightmares*, al-Qaeda is so weakly linked together that it is hard to say it exists apart from Osama bin Laden and a small clique of close associates. The lack of any significant numbers of convicted al-Qaeda members despite a large number of arrests on terrorism charges is cited by the documentary as a reason to doubt whether a widespread entity that meets the description of al-Qaeda exists at all. Therefore the extent and nature of al-Qaeda remains a topic of dispute.

Its rank and file has been described as changing from being "predominantly Arab," in its first years of operation, to "largely Pakistani," as of 2007. It has been estimated that 62% of al-Qaeda members have university education.

Organization v. Concept

When asked about the possibility of Al Qaeda's connection to the 7 July 2005 London bombings in 2005, Metropolitan Police Commissioner Sir Ian Blair said:

> *"Al Qaeda is not an organization. Al Qaeda is a way of working... but this has the hallmark of that approach.... Al Qaeda clearly has the ability to provide training... to provide expertise... and I think that is what has occurred here."*

What exactly al-Qaeda is, or was, remains in dispute. In the BBC documentary *The Power of Nightmares*, writer and journalist

Adam Curtis contends that the idea of al-Qaeda as a formal organization is primarily an American invention. Curtis contends the name "al-Qaeda" was first brought to the attention of the public in the 2001 trial of Osama bin Laden and the four men accused of the 1998 United States embassy bombings in East Africa.

As a matter of law, the U.S. Department of Justice needed to show that Osama bin Laden was the leader of a criminal organization in order to charge him *in absentia* under the Racketeer Influenced and Corrupt Organizations Act, also known as the RICO statutes.

The name of the organization and details of its structure were provided in the testimony of Jamal al-Fadl, who claimed to be a founding member of the organization and a former employee of Osama bin Laden. To quote the documentary directly:

The reality was that bin Laden and Ayman Zawahiri had become the focus of a loose association of disillusioned Islamist militants who were attracted by the new strategy. But there was no organization.

These were militants who mostly planned their own operations and looked to bin Laden for funding and assistance. He was not their commander. There is also no evidence that bin Laden used the term "al-Qaeda" to refer to the name of a group until after September the 11th, when he realized that this was the term the Americans had given it.

Questions about the reliability of al-Fadl's testimony have been raised by a number of sources because of his history of dishonesty and because he was delivering it as part of a plea bargain agreement after being convicted of conspiring to attack U.S. military establishments. Sam Schmidt, a defence lawyer from the trial, had the following to say about al-Fadl's testimony:

There were selective portions of al-Fadl's testimony that I believe was false, to help support the picture that he helped the Americans join together. I think he lied in a number of specific testimony about a unified image of what this organization was. It made al-Qaeda the new Mafia or the new Communists. It made them identifiable as a group and therefore made it easier to prosecute any person associated with al-Qaeda for any acts or statements made by bin Laden.

AL-QAEDA AND GLOBAL JIHAD ELEMENTS

The importance of the Arab Levant in Muslim history has given it a special status in the aspirations of al-Qaeda and its affliates to establish the Islamic caliphate in one of the countries in the region. Hence the supreme importance that al-Qaeda attaches to the fighting that developed in Iraq following the American occupation. The organization invested much effort and extensive resources to take advantage of the upheaval to reinvigorate global jihad. Bin Laden, and especially al-Zawahiri, who was already the organization's chief spokesman when Bin Laden was alive, encouraged the operatives in Iraq to continue the struggle to inflict severe damage on the US and its allies, and supported the establishment of the Islamic country in Iraq declared by al-Qaeda Iraq in 2006.

A concrete expression of the importance attributed to Iraq by the organization appeared in a letter from al-Zawahiri to al-Zarqawi, who was the organization's first "emir" in this country, and who was known for his murderous actions against his opponents, including Muslims, especially Shiites. The letter emphasizes the importance of preserving the gains already scored by al-Qaeda in Iraq, and requested that al-Zarqawi refrain from alienating the local population in order to avoid losing their support. Over the years al-Qaeda leaders have continued to support the struggle in Iraq, and they appointed figures they trusted to replace Zarqawi when he was killed in an American attack. Since he assumed his chief role, al-Zawahiri has also made statements in support of the local organization's activity and stressed its great importance. In a speech celebrating the eleventh anniversary of the terrorist attacks in the US, he claimed that the US had been defeated and in effect "was running away for its life, leaving behind a government of puppets to rule in Iraq, a government that was now feeling the might of the mujahidin...Allah gave them the honour of leading the local struggle and defeating the American ambition of controlling the Middle East."

Iraq is no longer the main theatre of jihad for al-Qaeda and its affliates that it was when foreign forces, headed by the US, occupied the country in 2003. Even after the last American soldier left Iraq on December 18, 2011, however, and despite President

Obama's statement that the purpose for which the US had entered Iraq had been achieved – the overthrow of Saddam Hussein and the establishment of a stable democracy in Iraq– terrorism was not eliminated from the country. In practice, al-Qaeda Iraq (operating under the title Islamic State of Iraq - ISI) and its affliates continue their activity. They focus their attacks primarily on targets identified with the current regime in Iraq, which is clearly under Shiite rule. Particularly in the second half of 2012, the organization carried out hundreds of attacks, principally in the cities of Baghdad, Nasiriyah, and Basra, where dozens of suicide bombings demonstrated the organization's ability to strike and disrupt the current regime's efforts to stabilize the country and control the level of inter-ethnic violence. The organization's attacks became even more frequent and daring in the final months of 2012. During several days of intense activity, simultaneous attacks were staged against army and police targets, combining multi-casualty suicide attacks with attacks aimed at freeing prisoners. For example, an armed squad broke into a prison in Tikrit on September 27, 2012 in a combined attack that included suicide terrorists and freed dozens of prisoners, some from al-Qaeda Iraq who had been sentenced to death. Furthermore, many of the organization's attacks were aimed directly at the Shiite civilian population – on Shiite holidays and against local Shiite leaders and institutions – heightening anxiety about a renewal of the sectarian civil war in Iraq.

In tandem with its local activity, al-Qaeda Iraq has devoted resources and manpower to supporting the opposition forces in Syria. This new policy was adopted as an answer to a public appeal by al-Zawahiri, who declared that Syria was a key theatre of jihad and urged Muslims from around the world to go to Syria and help the local mujahidin in their fight to oust the "murderer of all murderers," who will continue to slaughter Muslims until his regime is deposed. Al-Zawahiri called for the establishment of a regime that would free the Golan Heights and continue the jihad until the fag of victory files over the hills of conquered Jerusalem. Following al-Zawahiri's call, al-Qaeda Iraq operatives, under the name Jabhat al-Nusra – a name designed to prevent the group from accepting support from Western and leading Arab countries acting to overthrow the Assad regime – arrived in Syria. These operatives are conducting organized activity, based on their military ability and experience acquired during their years of fighting in Iraq. It appears that they were responsible for most of the especially daring and deadly attacks in Syria in recent months, particularly suicide attacks. Sporadic and less organized activity by global jihad elements from Yemen, Saudi Arabia, Libya, Jordan, and Gaza, who came to Syria without belonging to any group and joined the Free Syrian Army, is also underway.

Estimates of the number of fighters identified with global jihad vary from several hundred to several thousand.

The third key front emphasized in particular by al-Zawahiri, reflecting his new policy of exploiting the upheaval in the Arab world to escalate the struggle of global jihad parties in general and in the Levant in particular, is Egypt, particularly in Sinai. Al-Zawahiri hailed the fall of Mubarak's regime and its replacement by a religious Islamic regime as a supreme strategic target and a personal ideal for him and his Egyptian cohorts in the al-Qaeda leadership, who were part of the Egyptian jihadist organization that formally merged with al-Qaeda in 2001. Following Mubarak's fall from power and the subsequent governmental vacuum in Egypt, global jihad elements took advantage of the situation to promote their goals. The escape and release of their operatives from prison, where they were serving lengthy sentences for past activity, enabled these organizations to bolster their ranks with loyal foot soldiers with operational experience. Many of them found their way to Sinai and joined the local terrorist organizations, while taking advantage of the Egyptian government's lack of control in the area to solidify their religious Islamic autonomy there.

A number of groups identified with al-Qaeda and global jihad appeared in Sinai over the past year, the most prominent being Ansar Bayt al-Maqdis, al-Tawhid wal-Jihad, and Ansar al-Jihad. These organizations, and Ansar Bayt al-Maqdis in particular, operate in some measure against Egyptian targets but mostly against Israel. The terrorist attacks for which they took responsibility reflect al-Qaeda's ideology and operating strategy. For example, following the rocket attacks on Eilat and the strikes against the pipeline for transporting natural gas from Egypt to

Israel, Ansar Bayt al-Maqdis published a short film taking responsibility and listing the attacks designed to prevent the looting of the natural resources granted to Muslims by Allah through sale at a financial loss to the enemies of Islam, headed by Israel. This subject was frequently mentioned in the propaganda that described past activity by the central al-Qaeda organization that caused serious economic damage to the attacked countries. The organization also took care to include speeches by al-Zawahiri in which he praised the repeated strikes against the gas pipeline, and added a call to the new Egyptian government to cancel the peace agreement with Israel and institute Islamic religious law in Egypt.

Ansar Bayt al-Maqdis, considered the most active and dangerous of the Egyptian global jihad organizations in Sinai, was responsible for several of the deadliest attacks on the border between Egypt and Israel: the August 2011 attack on Highway 40 to Eilat, in which eight Israelis were murdered; the August 5, 2012 attack at the Egyptian-Israeli border, in which 16 Egyptian border guards were murdered; and the attack at Har Harif, on September 12, 2012, in which an IDF soldier was killed. In these attacks, the organization proved that it does not hesitate to kill Muslims serving regimes that oppose its views, and does not recognize borders between countries, as these were not determined by Allah. For its part, Ansar al-Jihad (which is probably identical to the Salaf Sinai Front), founded in December 2011, declared "that it would follow Bin Laden's example," and swore loyalty to Sheikh Ayman al-Zawahiri, the new al-Qaeda leader. Its members also swore to Allah "to do all they could to fight the corrupt government of the Jews, the Americans, and their allies," to fulfil Bin Laden's promise that "America, and those living in America, will never be secure as long as Palestine does not exist, and until the armies of the unbelievers leave the land of Muhammed," and swore to work for the vision they shared with al-Qaeda – the founding of an Islamic caliphate in Egypt.

In addition to the Egyptian organizations in Sinai, Salaf jihadist organizations from Gaza are also exploiting Sinai as a key region for terrorist activity against Israel, along with activity against Israel in Gaza. The use of Sinai as a theatre for activity is a result of pressure exerted on them by Hamas to restrict their activity against Israel from Gaza, owing to the fear of a harsh Israeli military strike against Hamas in Gaza in a way that would escalate to an all-out war. The most prominent of the Gaza organizations active in Sinai over the past year is the Mujahidin Shura Council in Greater Jerusalem, which serves as an umbrella organization for a number of Salaf Palestinian organizations, the most active and prominent of which is the Palestinian al-Tawhid wal-Jihad. The Mujahidin Shura Council in Greater Jerusalem claimed responsibility for the attack in the Be'er Milka area on June 18 that killed Said Fashfasha, an Israeli Arab who worked on the security fence on the border with Egypt. In a film about the attack, the organization noted that it had been prepared "as a gift to our brothers in al-Qaeda and Sheikh al-Zawahiri," and in response to the assassination of Bin Laden. In the film, the terrorists who took part in the operation, who were of Egyptian and Saudi Arabian origin, expressed their commitment to al-Zawahiri that the organization would uphold its commitment to "the way of jihad," and asserted that it "did not recognize the international border, but only the 'border of Allah.'"

Alongside this prominent organization, older Salaf organizations in Gaza operate directly against Israel, while using Sinai for their activity in order to evade restrictions enforced by Israel and to avoid inviting Israeli retaliation against Hamas in Gaza. Among these organizations, Jaish al-Islam (Army of Islam) is particularly noteworthy. Founded in 2006 by Mumtaz Dughmush, after he split off from the Popular Resistance Committees, the organization was very active in launching rockets and in attacks against Israel, and was involved in the Gilad Shalit kidnapping. Its activity extended beyond Sinai; it sent operatives to fight in Syria, a fact that became publicly known when one of its members was killed in battle. Another organization is the Popular Resistance Committees (PRC), which is active on both sides of the border, and enjoys close ties with global jihad groups in Sinai. The organization was linked directly to a number of attacks on the Egyptian border that were also attributed to Ansar Bayt al-Maqdis, which may indicate close cooperation between the Gaza organizations and their Egyptian counterparts. There are currently over ten groups belonging to the jihadist Salaf movement in Gaza, which presents a challenge to Hamas hegemony in Gaza. Their growing ability to conduct attacks from Gaza and from Sinai is liable to earn them support from al-Zawahiri, win his official recognition, and give them the title of al-Qaeda Gaza or part of a unified al-Qaeda Gaza force in Sinai.

AGENCY, IDEAS, AND AL-QAEDA'S POLITICAL THEORY

These structural changes are necessary but not sufficient to explain al-Qaeda's constructivist turn. Ideas matter, and al-Qaeda's political thought represented a uniquely constructivist understanding of political practice and possibility. Al-Qaeda embraces the artificiality and constructed nature of the sovereign state so central to much constructivist theory. Its conception of power is fundamentally nonmaterial, with ideas assumed to carry autonomous power and with great emphasis placed on the importance of personal conviction and faith. It places great importance on the definition and contestation of norms—both regulative and constitutive—and on the articulation of a distinctively normative mode of action. Its primary goal is the construction of a new, transnational and transstate identity based in Islam, to define the interests that follow from this identity, and to create transcendent norms that would establish a "logic of appropriateness" governing Muslim life. Its primary strategies in this are not only the use of sensational violence but also a sophisticated public and private outreach: from the global media, to innovative uses of the Internet, to intensely personal recruitment through religious and mosque networks that transform identity at the individual level. And although it rejects dialogue with the West, al-Qaeda is deeply enmeshed in ongoing intra-Islamist public arguments and understands their importance.

The field of contention: One of al-Qaeda's key conceptual innovations within Islamism was its reconceptualization of the field of contention from the local to the global. Through the mid-1990s, most Islamist action focused on particular states, with the secular autocratic existing regimes defined as the "Near Enemy" against which action should be directed. Moderate Islamists, such as the Muslim Brotherhood, attempted to work within the existing system, slowly cultivating an Islamic worldview among individuals and taking advantage of the political opportunities presented them (elections, newspapers, student elections). Radicals, such as the Egyptian Islamic Jihad led by Ayman al-Zawahiri, insisted on the need for violent, immediate change and launched local terrorist insurgencies. In both cases, despite ideological and even organizational linkages with their counterparts in other countries, the primary field of contention for these Islamists was the national state. Al-Qaeda challenged this national orientation by proposing a global field of contention, in which the only route to the hated "Near Enemy" was through its American patron. Although the structural changes noted here—along with the ever-growing involvement in Islamic politics of Muslim communities in Europe and elsewhere outside the Middle East—enabled this shift in conceptualization of the field of contention, it took the agency of al-Qaeda to globalize the field of jihadist contention in practice.

The international system: Taken to its fullest extension, al-Qaeda challenges not simply the United States, or local Arab regimes, but also the ontological status of the international system itself. Although bin Laden recognizes the power of states, he refuses to endow them with legitimacy as actors. In October 2001, bin Laden framed the struggle in religious, not nationalist, terms: "This battle is not between al-Qaeda and the US. This is a battle of Muslims against the global Crusaders." For Devji, "this initial statement is important because Bin Laden argues that the jihad must not be described in the ready-made terms of political life...[he is] setting the terms in which the struggle is to be seen." Evan as al-Qaeda seeks to transcend the state system from above, it also conceives of a central role for individuals working within transnational networks.

The Bush administration has argued that seizing a state such as Iraq is key to al-Qaeda's grand strategy: "Their stated objective is to drive the United States and coalition forces out of the Middle East so they can gain control of Iraq and use that country as a base from which to launch attacks against America, overthrow moderate governments in the Middle East, and establish a totalitarian Islamic empire that stretches from Spain to Indonesia." Daniel Benjamin and Steve Simon, former counterterrorism officials in the Clinton administration and otherwise fierce critics of Bush, offer a strikingly similar account: "a core tenet of al-Qaeda's strategy is that radical Islamists must gain control of a nation, from which they can expand the area controlled by believers. Holding a state, in their view, is the prelude to knocking over the dominoes of the world's secular Muslim regimes." Fred Halliday reminds us that "al-Qaida's current status as an apparently free floating and stateless group...is for Osama bin Laden and his cohorts very much a second best."

But Faisal Devji counters that holding territory has become peripheral and secondary to al-Qaeda's political agenda: "the jihad is not concerned with political parties, revolutions or the founding of ideological states...the particular sites of these struggles are themselves unimportant, their territories being subordinated to a larger and even metaphysical struggle for which they have become merely instrumental." Bin Laden himself, in his calls for a general withdrawal of real Muslims from the world of hypocrisy and their exertions on behalf of jihad, seems less concerned with seizing a state. Although controlling a state might be one objective for al-Qaeda, it is tangential to its ultimate goal of transforming the identity and interests of the world's Muslims, and setting them in existential conflict with the West. Or, in the words of Salema Nemaat: "Osama bin Laden would rather keep al Jazeera on his side than win Saudi Arabia." Iraq mattered for al-Qaeda primarily because America was there, offering it a potent focal point for the jihad and the chance to produce a seemingly endless parade of televised carnage.

Power: Al-Qaeda's theory of power is perhaps its most distinctively constructivist concept. In contrast to rationalists (whether Realist or liberals) who locate power within material capacities of various kinds, al-Qaeda's understanding of power highlights the autonomous role of identity, ideas, and rhetoric. Faith, not simply material capabilities, plays a decisive role in al-Qaeda's concept of political power. Like Emmaneul Adler, al-Qaeda understands that "the imposition of meanings on the material world is one of the ultimate forms of power." Like Christian Reus-Smit, al-Qaeda sees political power as "deeply embedded in webs of social exchange and mutual constitution." Like the constructivist authors in a recent special issue of

Millennium, al-Qaeda refuses a sharp distinction between "hard" and "soft" power with the latter in a supporting role; instead, it sees ideational and material power as intimately connected and mutually constitutive. Al-Qaeda's theorists cast faith both as the ultimate source of power and as a key battlefield between the West and Islam. Zawahiri has argued that "the strongest weapon which the mujahideen enjoy—after the help and granting of success by God—is popular support from the Muslim masses in Iraq, and the surrounding Muslim countries." This makes the battle for public opinion, and the battle over the definition of Islam, absolutely central to power relations: both an independent and a dependent variable, mutually constitutive in the truest constructivist sense. As Kepel put it, "bin Laden's counter-offensive recognized that, under the right circumstances, rhetoric and satellite propaganda can be on equal footing with unmanned bombers and cruise-missiles."

This is not to say that al-Qaeda scorns the conventional dimensions of power politics. Terrorism is seen as a way of evening the imbalance of power between Islam and the West. As bin Laden put it shortly after 9/11: "So as they kill us, without a doubt we have to kill them, until we obtain a balance of terror. This is the first time, in recent years, that the balance of terror evened out between the Muslims and the Americans; previously, the Americans did to us whatever they pleased, and the victim wasn't even allowed to complain." Al-Qaeda goes to great efforts to raise money, and invests heavily in the recruitment and training of personnel. Its training videos and the Encyclopedia of Jihad show a frank, clear eyed concern for military techniques, scientific knowledge, and the like. There is little reason to believe that al-Qaeda would forego the opportunity to acquire weapons of mass destruction, or a territorial base, or even conventional military forces should such an occasion arise.

But ultimately al-Qaeda's understandings of power focus more on the autonomous power of faith and identity than on strictly material concerns. Its political thought and practice has been shaped by the absence of such conventional material resources; and second, even it acquired such material resources, it would still have a distinctively Islamist understanding of the power of ideas and faith. Bin Laden put it like this: "God almighty said: 'The believers fight for God's cause, while those who reject faith fight for an unjust cause. Fight the allies of Satan: Satan's strategies are truly weak.' Second, we remind you that victory comes only with God. All we need to do is prepare and motivate for the jihad."

Bin Laden claims not only that power ultimately derives from closeness to God but also that the West is aware of this and is targeting true Islam in response. American-and European-led reform initiatives, whether in education curricula or in the fostering of civil society, are seen as attempts to sever Muslims from their true source of power—faith.

As bin Laden argued, "The West today is doing its utmost to tarnish jihad and kill anyone seeking jihad. The West is supported in this endeavor by hypocrites. This is because they all know that jihad is the effective power to foil all their conspiracies."

Western ideas such as democracy or nationalism aim at the "paralysis of the powers of our umma through other means, like the deceptive idea of democracy." Bin Laden cast Western policy as clearly aimed at eradicating Muslim identity, and therefore power: "The Americans' intentions have also become clear in their statements about the need to change the beliefs, curricula, and morals of Muslims in order to become more tolerant, as they put it. In clearer terms, it is a religious-economic war. They want the believers to desist from worshipping God so that they can enslave them, occupy their countries, and loot their wealth."

What the Muslim umma needed was not more material power, but rather the will to use it. If the Muslim world could unite, with its oil wealth and human resources, it would have all the material capabilities it needed: "Today, by the grace of God, our umma possesses enormous powers, sufficient to rescue Palestine and the rest of the Muslim lands. However these powers have been fettered and we must work to release them. For our umma has been promised victory. If it has been delayed, that is only because of our sins and our failure to help God." The real obstacle was ideational, not material: the failure of Muslims to realize their true identity and act upon it. Public support, and individual faith, is a key component of power: "in the absence of this popular support, the Islamic mujahed movement would be crushed in the shadows, far from the masses who are distracted and fearful, and the struggle between the jihadist elite and the arrogant authorities would be confined to prison dungeons far from the public and the light of day. This is precisely what the secular, apostate forces that are controlling our countries are striving for."

The jihad against the Soviet occupation of Afghanistan may have created a warped view of the importance of faith: according to Gerges, "the Afghan experience...went to bin Laden's head; he concluded that poorly armed but dedicated men can confront better-equipped adversaries."

Bin Laden himself has frequently claimed that the defeat of the Soviet Union made him believe in the possibility of confronting America. For example, in October 2001, he told Taysir Allouni: "So the One God, who sustained us with one of His helping hands and stabiliized us to defeat the Soviet empire, is capable of sustaining us again and of allowing us to defeat America on the same land, and with the same sayings. So we believe that the defeat of America is something achievable—with the permission of God—and it is easier for us...than the defeat of the Soviet Empire previously."

The same might follow from 9/11 itself, which to bin Laden offered "clear proof that this destructive usurious global economy that America uses, together with its military force, to impose unbelief and humiliation on poor peoples, can easily collapse." When looking at the United States, bin Laden was attentive to material reality but ultimately saw it as subordinate to the ideational as well: "We can conclude that America is a superpower, with enormous military strength and vast economic power, but that all of this is built on foundations of straw." Looking at the course of the jihad, bin Laden argued that "it has become clear to us during our defensive jihad against the American enemy and its enormous propaganda machine, that it depends for the most part on psychological warfare. It also depends on intense air strikes, which hide its most conspicuous weak points: fear, cowardice, and lack of fighting spirit among its troops."

In his October 29, 2004, address, he marveled at the Bush administration's self-defeating strategy: "It was easy for us to provoke this administration and lure it into perdition. All we had to do was send two mujahidin to the Far East to raise up a rag on which 'al-Qaeda' was written, and the generals came running. This inflicted human, financial, and political losses on America without them even achieving anything worth mentioning....We are continuing to make America bleed to the point of bankruptcy, by God's will....It seems as if we and the White House are on the same team shooting at the United States' own goal, despite our different intentions."

Identity: Al-Qaeda is trying to bring forward the Muslim component of identity in order to restructure political reality. Bin Laden and Zawahiri's rhetoric is replete with appeals to Muslims to awaken, to embrace their true identity and to act accordingly. Terrorism, and the ideational struggle that follows, is in large part aimed at awakening the Muslim identity of Arabs and Muslims. Zawahiri wrote that "the masses must become convinced that this battle, while it is taking place, involves every Muslim."

Bin Laden similarly framed the issue in terms of identities transcending the nation-state: "I say that the battle isn't between the al-Qaeda organization and the global crusaders. Rather, the battle is between Muslims—the people of Islam—and the global Crusaders."

There is nothing obvious or natural about the Islamist identity proclaimed by al-Qaeda. To take this as the evocation of a deep, essentialist identity is to grant bin Laden victory in the single most important stage of constructing social reality. In fact, this appeal to identity is a radical act, demanding that actors from an enormous range of social and cultural settings both renounce their current identities and embrace a new one. Muslims around the world have long juggled multiple claims on their identity. Al-Qaeda, like other Islamists, advances a claim on identity which is radically detached from the very concept of the state, one in which every individual is directly and personally linked to a global umma of believers. Just because Islamists declare the existence of a global Islamic umma—in which Islamic identity is the central and dominant aspect of every Muslim's identity—does not make it so. Al-Qaeda's rhetoric about a global Islamic identity aims at driving a self-fulfilling prophecy, constructing a collective identity rather than simply reflecting it.

This decades-long project to "Islamize" society from the bottom up is what gives resonance to al-Qaeda's discourse. Movements such as the Muslim Brotherhood differ profoundly with al-Qaeda on strategy, on doctrine, and on core normative beliefs. Moderates and radicals disagree intensely about political issues, about the value of democracy, about the legitimacy of violence, about the legitimacy of takfir, about the meaning of jihad, and so on. But where they agree is on the common project of constructing an Islamic identity that transcends all other aspects of personal and political identity.

Moderate and social Islamists have prepared the ground for al-Qaeda's invocation of Muslim identity through a long, patient project of reshaping personal identity. Arab and Muslim worldviews have been patiently reworked through persuasion, socialization, and internalization of ideas about the way the world works. Al-Qaeda is rather peripheral to this ongoing project of constructing a global Islamic identity. As Peter Mandaville describes it, "Al-Qaida is not the only game in town in terms of the transnational forces competing for Muslim hearts and minds." Al-Qaeda is trying to cash in on someone else's project—and, in the case of Zawahiri, a project he himself rejected.

This appropriation of a well-developed Islamist project creates vulnerabilities as well as strengths for al-Qaeda. Few constructivists would now argue that a particular set of political interests necessarily follows from a given political or civilizational identity. The contestation of the interests that follow from any collective identity is a key site of political struggle, as those within a collective identity fought over definitions of shared interests.

This means that al-Qaeda must engage in public arguments with other Islamists and other Arab political forces over the definition of interests, rather than simply presume its leadership. When moderate and radical views converge on the latter's narrative—as they did over Israel during the outbreak of the al-Aqsa Intifada in 2000, or over the American invasion of Iraq in 2003—al-Qaeda can command far greater power than it could hope to muster for its own project. But this leaves al-Qaeda particularly vulnerable to those moderate Islamist figures who challenge its positions.

2

9/11 Attack (WTC)

The worst attack ever in the world history. It is reported that 2.993 were dead and 8,900 were injured. It literally has some videos and pictures showing the fall of victims from the top most building (from burnt section) facing death very pathetically! 9/11 attack on World Trade Center is truly on top of the list as it is the worst terrorist attack so far that has been faced by humans living anywhere in any part of the world. As it is known to all, these attacks were planned, monitored and executed by the world's top most terrorist Osama Bin laden. He brought nightmares to all the US public.

Four planes were planned but only two were hit to the twin towers the others missed the target wherein one out of the other two hit the Washington pentagon and the last one was crashed into the field in Summer set County. It was a well planned tragic attack ever. It affected Nation's foreign and democratic rules and policies. It raised doubts against the nation's security and intelligence power.More importantly it affected all the IT countries which lead to a big set back called "recession"

SEPTEMBER 11 ATTACKS

The September 11 attacks (also referred to as September 11, September 11th, or9/11) were a series of four coordinated terrorist attacks by the Islamic terrorist group al-Qaeda on the United States in New York City and the Washington, D.C., metropolitan areaon Tuesday, September 11, 2001. The attacks killed 2,996 people and caused at least $10 billion in property and infrastructure damage.

Four passenger airliners were hijacked by 19 al-Qaeda terrorists to be flown into buildings insuicide attacks. Two of the planes, American Airlines Flight 11 and United Airlines Flight 175, were crashed into the North and South towers, respectively, of the World Trade Centercomplex in New York City. Within two hours, both 110-story towers collapsed with debris and the resulting fires causing partial or complete collapse of all other buildings in the WTC complex, including the 47-story 7 World Trade Center tower, as well as significant damage to ten other large surrounding structures. A third plane, American Airlines Flight 77, was crashed into the Pentagon (the headquarters of the United States Department of Defense), leading to a partial collapse in its western side. The fourth plane, United Airlines Flight 93, was targeted at Washington, D.C., but crashed into a field near Shanksville, Pennsylvaniaafter its passengers tried to overcome the hijackers. In total, 2,996 people died in the attacks, including the 227 civilians and 19 hijackers aboard the four planes. It was thedeadliest incident for firefighters and law enforcement officers in the history of the United States, with 343 and 72 killed respectively.

Suspicion quickly fell on al-Qaeda. Although the group's leader, Osama bin Laden, initially denied any involvement, in 2004, he claimed responsibility for the attacks. Al-Qaeda and bin Laden cited U.S. support of Israel, the presence of U.S. troops in Saudi Arabia, andsanctions against Iraq as motives. The United States responded by launching the War on Terror and invading Afghanistan to depose the Taliban, which had harbored al-Qaeda. Many countries strengthened their anti-terrorism legislation and expanded law enforcement powers. Having evaded capture for years, bin Laden was located and killed by U.S. forces in May 2011.

The destruction of the Twin Towers and other properties caused serious damage to the economy of Lower Manhattan and had a significant effect on global markets, closing Wall Street until September 17 and the civilian airspace in the U.S. and Canada until September 13. Many closings, evacuations, and cancellations followed, out of respect or fear of further attacks. Cleanup of the World Trade Center site was completed in May 2002, and the Pentagon was repaired within a year. Numerous memorials have been constructed, including the National September 11 Memorial

& Museum in New York, the Pentagon Memorial, and the Flight 93 National Memorial in Pennsylvania.

On November 18, 2006, construction of One World Trade Center began at the World Trade Center site. The building was officially opened on November 3, 2014.

BACKGROUND

al-Qaeda

The origins of al-Qaeda can be traced to 1979 when the Soviet Union invaded Afghanistan. Osama bin Laden traveled to Afghanistan and helped organize Arab mujahideen to resist the Soviets. Under the guidance ofAyman al-Zawahiri, bin Laden became more radical. In 1996, bin Laden issued his first *fatwâ*, calling for American soldiers to leave Saudi Arabia.

In a second *fatwâ* in 1998, bin Laden outlined his objections to American foreign policy with respect to Israel, as well as the continued presence of American troops in Saudi Arabia after the Gulf War. Bin Laden used Islamic texts to exhort Muslims to attack Americans until the stated grievances are reversed. According to bin Laden, Muslim legal scholars, "have throughout Islamic history unanimously agreed that the jihad is an individual duty if the enemy destroys the Muslim countries."

OSAMA BIN LADEN

Bin Laden, who orchestrated the attacks, initially denied but later admitted involvement. Al Jazeerabroadcast a statement by bin Laden on September 16, 2001, stating, "I stress that I have not carried out this act, which appears to have been carried out by individuals with their own motivation." In November 2001, U.S. forces recovered a videotape from a destroyed house in Jalalabad, Afghanistan. In the tape, bin Laden is seen talking to Khaled al-Harbi and admits foreknowledge of the attacks. On December 27, 2001, a second bin Laden video was released. In the video, he said, "It has become clear that the West in general and America in particular have an unspeakable hatred for Islam....It is the hatred of crusaders. Terrorism against America deserves to be praised because it was a response to injustice, aimed at forcing America to stop its support for Israel, which kills our people...We say that the end of the United States is imminent, whether Bin Laden or his followers are alive or dead, for the awakening of the Muslim umma (nation) has occurred", but he stopped short of admitting responsibility for the attacks. The transcript references several times to the United States specifically targeting Muslims.

Shortly before the U.S. presidential election in 2004, in a taped statement, bin Laden publicly acknowledged al-Qaeda's involvement in the attacks on the U.S. and admitted his direct link to the attacks. He said that the attacks were carried out because, "we are free... and want to regain freedom for our nation. As you undermine our security we undermine yours." Bin Laden said he had personally directed his followers to attack the World Trade Center. Another video obtained by Al Jazeera in September 2006 shows bin Laden with Ramzi bin al-Shibh, as well as two hijackers, Hamza al-Ghamdi and Wail al-Shehri, as they make preparations for the attacks. The U.S. never formally indicted bin Laden for the 9/11 attacks but he was on the FBI's Most Wanted List for the bombings of the U.S. Embassies in Dar es Salaam, Tanzania, and Nairobi, Kenya. After a nearly 10-year manhunt, bin Laden was killed by American special forces in acompound in Abbottabad, Pakistan on May 2, 2011.

Khalid Sheikh Mohammed

The journalist Yosri Fouda of the Arabic television channel Al Jazeera reported that, in April 2002, Khalid Sheikh Mohammed admitted his involvement, along with Ramzi bin al-Shibh. The9/11 Commission Report determined that the animosity towards the United States felt by Mohammed, the principal architect of the 9/11 attacks, stemmed from his "violent disagreement with U.S. foreign policy favoring Israel".

Mohammed was also an adviser and financier of the 1993 World Trade Center bombing and the uncle of Ramzi Yousef, the lead bomber in that attack.

Mohammed was arrested on March 1, 2003, in Rawalpindi, Pakistan, by Pakistani security officials working with the CIA, then transported to Guantanamo Bay and interrogated using methods including waterboarding. During U.S. hearings at Guantanamo Bay in March 2007, Mohammed again confessed his responsibility for the attacks, stating he "was responsible for the 9/11 operation from A to Z" and that his statement was not made under duress.

Other al-Qaeda members

In "Substitution for Testimony of Khalid Sheikh Mohammed" from the trial of Zacarias Moussaoui, five people are identified as having been completely aware of the operation's details. They are bin Laden, Khalid Sheikh Mohammed, Ramzi bin al-Shibh, Abu Turab al-Urduni, and Mohammed Atef. To date, only peripheral figures have been tried or convicted for the attacks.

On September 26, 2005, the Spanish high court sentenced Abu Dahdah to 27 years in prison for conspiracy on the 9/11 attacks and being a member of the terrorist organization al-Qaeda. At the same time, another 17 al-Qaeda members were sentenced to penalties of between six and eleven years. On February 16, 2006, the Spanish Supreme Court reduced the Abu Dahdah penalty to 12 years because it considered that his participation in the conspiracy was not proven.

Also, in 2006, Moussaoui, who some originally suspected might have been the assigned 20th hijacker, was convicted for the lesser role of conspiracy to commit acts of terrorism and air piracy. He is serving a life sentence without parole in the United States. Mounir el-Motassadeq, an associate of the Hamburg-based hijackers, is serving 15 years in Germany for his role in helping the hijackers prepare for the attacks.

The Hamburg cell in Germany included radical Islamists who eventually came to be key operatives in the 9/11 attacks. Mohamed Atta,Marwan al-Shehhi, Ziad Jarrah, Ramzi bin al-Shibh, and Said Bahaji were all members of al-Qaeda's Hamburg cell.

Motives

Osama bin Laden's declaration of a holy war against the United States, and a 1998 *fatwâ* signed by bin Laden and others, calling for the killing of American civilians, are seen by investigators as evidence of his motivation. In bin Laden's November 2002 "Letter to America", he explicitly stated that al-Qaeda's motives for their attacks include

- U.S. support of Israel
- Support for the "attacks against Muslims" in Somalia
- Support of Russian "atrocities against Muslims" in Chechnya
- Support of authoritarian regimes in the Middle East such as Egypt, Saudi Arabia and Jordan
- Support of Indian "oppression against Muslims" in Kashmir
- The presence of U.S. troops in Saudi Arabia
- The sanctions against Iraq

After the attacks, bin Laden and al-Zawahiri released additional video tapes and audio tapes, some of which repeated those reasons for the attacks. Two particularly important publications were bin Laden's 2002 "Letter to America", and a 2004 video tape by bin Laden.

Bin Laden interpreted Muhammad as having banned the "permanent presence of infidels in Arabia". In 1996, bin Laden issued a *fatwâ*calling for American troops to leave Saudi Arabia. In 1998, al-Qaeda wrote, "for over seven years the United States has been occupying the lands of Islam in the holiest of places, the Arabian Peninsula, plundering its riches, dictating to its rulers, humiliating its people, terrorizing its neighbors, and turning its bases in THE PENINSULA into a spearhead through which to fight the neighboring Muslim peoples."

In a December 1999 interview, bin Laden said he felt that Americans were "too near to Mecca", and considered this a provocation to the entire Muslim world. One analysis of suicide terrorism suggested that without U.S. troops in Saudi Arabia, al-Qaeda likely would not have been able to get people to commit to suicide missions.

In the 1998 *fatwâ*, al-Qaeda identified the Iraq sanctions as a reason to kill Americans, condemning the "protracted blockade" among other actions that constitute a declaration of war against "Allah, his messenger, and Muslims." The *fatwâ* declared that "the ruling to kill the Americans and their allies – civilians and military – is an individual duty for every Muslim who can do it in any country in which it is possible to do it, in order to liberate the al-

Aqsa Mosque and the holy mosque of Mecca from their grip, and in order for their [the Americans'] armies to move out of all the lands of Islam, defeated and unable to threaten any Muslim."

Bin Laden claimed, in 2004, that the idea of destroying the towers had first occurred to him in 1982, when he witnessed Israel's bombardment of high-rise apartment buildings during the 1982 Lebanon War. Some analysts, including Mearsheimer and Walt, also claim that one motivation for the attacks was U.S. support of Israel. In 2004 and 2010, bin Laden again connected the September 11 attacks with U.S. support of Israel, although most of the letter expressed bin Laden's disdain with President Bush and bin Laden's hope to "destroy and bankrupt" the U.S.

In addition to those cited by bin Laden and al-Qaeda, analysts have suggested other motives, including western support of Islamist and non-Islamist authoritarian regimes in Saudi Arabia, Iran, Egypt, Iraq, Pakistan and northern Africa, and the presence of western troops in some of these countries. Other authors suggest the "humiliation" resulting from the Islamic world falling behind the Western world – this discrepancy rendered especially visible by the globalization trend and a desire to provoke the U.S. into a broader war against the Islamic world in the hope of motivating more allies to support al-Qaeda.

Others have argued that 9/11 was a strategic move with the objective of provoking America into a war that would incite a pan-Islamicrevolution.

Planning of the attacks

The idea for the attacks came from Khalid Sheikh Mohammed, who first presented it to Osama bin Laden in 1996. At that time, bin Laden and al-Qaeda were in a period of transition, having just relocated back to Afghanistan from Sudan. The 1998 African Embassy bombings and bin Laden's 1998 fatwâ marked a turning point, as bin Laden became intent on attacking the United States.

In late 1998 or early 1999, bin Laden gave approval for Mohammed to go forward with organizing the plot. A series of meetings occurred in early 1999, involving Mohammed, bin Laden, and his deputyMohammed Atef. Atef provided operational support for the plot, including target selections and helping arrange travel for the hijackers. Bin Laden overruled Mohammed, rejecting some potential targets such as the U.S. Bank Tower in Los Angeles because, "there was not enough time to prepare for such an operation".

Bin Laden provided leadership and financial support for the plot, and was involved in selecting participants. Bin Laden initially selected Nawaf al-Hazmi and Khalid al-Mihdhar, both experienced jihadists who had fought in Bosnia. Hazmi and Mihdhar arrived in the United States in mid-January 2000. In spring 2000, Hazmi and Mihdhar took flying lessons in San Diego, California, but both spoke little English, did poorly with flying lessons, and eventually served as secondary – or "muscle" – hijackers.

In late 1999, a group of men from Hamburg, Germany arrived in Afghanistan, including Mohamed Atta,Marwan al-Shehhi, Ziad Jarrah, and Ramzi bin al-Shibh. Bin Laden selected these men because they were educated, could speak English, and had experience living in the West. New recruits were routinely screened for special skills and al-Qaeda leaders consequently discovered that Hani Hanjour already had a commercial pilot's license.

Hanjour arrived in San Diego on December 8, 2000, joining Hazmi. They soon left for Arizona, where Hanjour took refresher training. Marwan al-Shehhi arrived at the end of May 2000, while Atta arrived on June 3, 2000, and Jarrah arrived on June 27, 2000. Bin al-Shibh applied several times for a visa to the United States, but as a Yemeni, he was rejected out of concerns he would overstay his visa and remain as an illegal immigrant. Bin al-Shibh stayed in Hamburg, providing coordination between Atta and Mohammed. The three Hamburg cell members all took pilot training in South Florida.

In spring 2001, the secondary hijackers began arriving in the United States. In July 2001, Atta met with bin al-Shibh in Spain, where they coordinated details of the plot, including final target selection. Bin al-Shibh also passed along bin Laden's wish for the attacks to be carried out as soon as possible.

ATTACKS

Early on the morning of September 11, 2001, 19 hijackers took control of four commercial airliners (two Boeing 757 and two

Boeing 767) en route to California (three headed to LAXin Los Angeles, and one to San Francisco) after takeoffs from Boston, Massachusetts;Newark, New Jersey; and Washington, D.C. Large planes with long flights were selected for hijacking because they would be heavily fueled.

The four flights were:

- American Airlines Flight 11: Left Boston's Logan Airport at 7:59 a.m. en route to Los Angeles with a crew of 11 and 76 passengers, not including five hijackers. The hijackers flew the plane into the North Tower of the World Trade Center at 8:46 a.m.
- United Airlines Flight 175: Left Logan Airport at 8:14 a.m. en route to Los Angeles with a crew of nine and 51 passengers, not including five hijackers. The hijackers flew the plane into the South Tower of the World Trade Center at 9:03 a.m.
- American Airlines Flight 77: Left Washington Dulles International Airport in Virginia at 8:20 a.m. en route to Los Angeles with a crew of six and 53 passengers, not including five hijackers. The hijackers flew the plane into the Pentagon at 9:37 a.m.
- United Airlines Flight 93: Left Newark International Airport at 8:42 a.m. en route to San Francisco, with a crew of seven and 33 passengers, not including four hijackers. As passengers attempted to subdue the hijackers, the aircraft crashed into the ground nearShanksville, Pennsylvania, at 10:03 a.m.

Media coverage was intense during the attacks and aftermath, beginning moments after the first crash into the World Trade Center.

Events

At 8:46 a.m., five hijackers crashed American Airlines Flight 11 into the northern facade of the World Trade Center's North Tower (1 WTC), and at 9:03 a.m., another five hijackers crashed United Airlines Flight 175 into the southern facade of the South Tower (2 WTC). Five hijackers flew American Airlines Flight 77 into the Pentagon at 9:37 a.m.

A fourth flight, United Airlines Flight 93, under the control of four hijackers, crashed near Shanksville, Pennsylvania, southeast of Pittsburgh, at 10:03 a.m. after the passengers fought the hijackers. Flight 93's target is believed to have been either the Capitol or the White House. Flight 93's cockpit voice recorder revealed crew and passengers tried to seize control of the plane from the hijackers after learning through phone calls that Flights 11, 77, and 175 had been crashed into buildings that morning. Once it became evident to the hijackers that the passengers might regain control of the plane, the hijackers rolled the plane and intentionally crashed it.

Some passengers and crew members who called from the aircraft using the cabin airphone service and mobile phones provided details: several hijackers were aboard each plane; they used mace, tear gas, or pepper spray to overcome attendants; and some people aboard had been stabbed. Reports indicated hijackers stabbed and killed pilots, flight attendants, and one or more passengers. In their final report, the 9/11 Commission found the hijackers had recently purchased multi-function hand tools and assorted knives and blades. A flight attendant on Flight 11, a passenger on Flight 175, and passengers on Flight 93 said the hijackers had bombs, but one of the passengers said he thought the bombs were fake. The FBI found no traces of explosives at the crash sites, and the 9/11 Commission concluded that the bombs were probably fake.

Three buildings in the World Trade Center complex collapsed due to fire-induced structural failure. The South Tower collapsed at 9:59 a.m. after burning for 56 minutes in a fire caused by the impact of United Airlines Flight 175 and the explosion of its fuel. The North Tower collapsed at 10:28 a.m. after burning for 102 minutes. When the North Tower collapsed, debris fell on the nearby 7 World Trade Center building (7 WTC), damaging it and starting fires. These fires burned for hours, compromising the building's structural integrity, and 7 WTC collapsed at 5:21 p.m. The Pentagon sustained major damage.

At 9:40 a.m., the FAA grounded all aircraft within the continental U.S., and aircraft already in flight were told to land immediately. All international civilian aircraft were either turned back or redirected to airports in Canada or Mexico, and all international flights were banned from landing on U.S. soil for three days. The attacks created widespread confusion among news organizations and air traffic controllers. Among the unconfirmed and often contradictory news reports aired throughout the day, one of the most prevalent said a car bomb had been detonated at the U.S. State Department's headquarters in Washington, D.C. Another jet—Delta Air Lines Flight 1989—was suspected of having been hijacked, but the aircraft responded to controllers and landed safely in Cleveland, Ohio.

In a September 2002 interview, Khalid Sheikh Mohammed and Ramzi bin al-Shibh, who are believed to have organized the attacks, said Flight 93's intended target was the United States Capitol, not the White House. During the planning stage of the attacks, Mohamed Atta, the hijacker and pilot of Flight 11, thought the White House might be too tough a target and sought an assessment from Hani Hanjour, who would later hijack and pilot Flight 77. Mohammed said al-Qaeda initially planned to target nuclear installations rather than the World Trade Center and the Pentagon, but decided against it, fearing things could "get out of control". Final decisions on targets, according to Mohammed, were left in the hands of the pilots.

Casualties

The attacks resulted in the deaths of 2,996 people, including the 19 hijackers and 2,977 victims. The victims included 246 on the four planes (from which there were no survivors), 2,606 in New York City in the towers and on the ground, and 125 at the Pentagon. Nearly all of the victims were civilians; 55 military personnel were among those killed at the Pentagon.

More than 90% of the workers and visitors who died in the towers had been at or above the points of impact. In the North Tower, 1,355 people at or above the point of impact were trapped and died of smoke inhalation, fell or jumped from the tower to escape the smoke and flames, or were killed in the building's eventual collapse. The destruction of all three staircases in the tower when Flight 11 hit made it impossible for anyone above the impact zone to escape. 107 people below the point of impact died as well.

In the South Tower, one stairwell (A), was left intact after Flight 175 hit, allowing 14 people located on the floors of impact (including one man who saw the plane coming at him) and four more from the floors above to escape. 911 operators who received calls from individuals inside the tower were not well informed of the situation as it rapidly unfolded and as a result, told callers not to descend the tower on their own. 630 people died in that tower, fewer than half the number killed in the North Tower. Casualties in the South Tower were significantly reduced by some occupants deciding to start evacuating as soon as the North Tower was struck.

At least 200 people fell or jumped to their deaths from the burning towers (as exemplified in the photograph *The Falling Man*), landing on the streets and rooftops of adjacent buildings hundreds of feet below. Some occupants of each tower above the point of impact made their way toward the roof in hope of helicopter rescue, but the roof access doors were locked. No plan existed for helicopter rescues, and the combination of roof equipment and thick smoke and intense heat prevented helicopters from approaching.

A total of 411 emergency workers died as they tried to rescue people and fight fires. The New York City Fire Department (FDNY) lost 340 firefighters, a chaplain, and two paramedics. The New York City Police Department (NYPD) lost 23 officers. The Port Authority Police Department lost 37 officers. Eight emergency medical technicians (EMTs) and paramedics from private emergency medical services units were killed.

Cantor Fitzgerald L.P., an INVESTMENT bank on the 101st–105th floors of the North Tower, lost 658 employees, considerably more than any other employer. Marsh Inc., located immediately below Cantor Fitzgerald on floors 93–100, lost 358 employees, and 175 employees of Aon Corporation were also killed. The National Institute of Standards and Technology (NIST) estimated that about 17,400 civilians were in the World Trade Center complex at the time of the attacks. Turnstile counts from the Port Authority suggest 14,154 people were typically in the Twin Towers by 8:45 a.m. The vast majority of people below the impact zone safely evacuated the buildings.

After New York, New Jersey lost the most state citizens, with the city of Hoboken sustaining the most deaths. More than 90 countries lost citizens in the attacks on the World Trade Center. Two people were added to the official death toll after dying from health conditions linked to exposure to dust from the collapse of the World Trade Center.

Deaths (victims + hijackers)

New York City	World Trade Center	2,606
	American 11	87 + 5
	United 175	60 + 5
Arlington	Pentagon	125
	American 77	59 + 5
Near Shanksville	United 93	40 + 4
Total		2,977 + 19

Weeks after the attack, the death toll was estimated to be over 6,000, more than twice the number of deaths eventually confirmed. The city was only able to identify remains for about 1,600 of the World Trade Center victims.

The medical examiner's office collected "about 10,000 unidentified bone and tissue fragments that cannot be matched to the list of the dead". Bone fragments were still being found in 2006 by workers who were preparing to demolish the damaged Deutsche Bank Building.

In 2010, a team of anthropologists and archaeologists searched for human remains and personal items at theFresh Kills Landfill, where seventy-two more human remains were recovered, bringing the total found to 1,845. DNA profiling continues in an attempt to identify additional victims. The remains are being held in storage in Memorial Park, outside the New York City Medical Examiner's facilities. It was expected that the remains would be moved in 2013 to a repository behind a wall at the 9/11 museum. In July 2011, a team of scientists at the Office of Chief Medical Examiner was still trying to identify remains, in the hope that improved technology will allow them to identify other victims. On September 16, 2013, the 1,638th victim was identified. There are still 1,115 victims that have not been identified.

Damage

Along with the 110-floor Twin Towers, numerous other buildings at the World Trade Center site were destroyed or badly damaged, including WTC buildings 3 through 7 and St. Nicholas Greek Orthodox Church. The North Tower, South Tower, the Marriott Hotel (3 WTC), and 7 WTC were completely destroyed. The U.S. Customs House (6 World Trade Center), 4 World Trade Center, 5 World Trade Center, and both pedestrian bridges connecting buildings were severely damaged. The Deutsche Bank Building on 130 Liberty Street was partially damaged and demolished some years later, starting in 2007. The two buildings of the World Financial Center also suffered damage.

The Deutsche Bank Building across Liberty Street from the World Trade Center complex was later condemned as being uninhabitable because of toxic conditions inside the office tower, and wasdeconstructed.

The Borough of Manhattan Community College's Fiterman Hall at 30 West Broadway was condemned due to extensive damage in the attacks, and is being rebuilt. Other neighboring buildings including 90 West Street and the Verizon Building suffered major damage but have been restored. World Financial Center buildings, One Liberty Plaza, the Millenium Hilton, and 90 Church Street had moderate damage and have since been restored. Communications equipment on top of the North Tower was also destroyed, but media stations were quickly able to reroute signals and resume broadcasts.

The Pentagon was severely damaged by the impact of American Airlines Flight 77 and ensuing fires, causing one section of the building to collapse. As it approached the Pentagon, the airplane's wings knocked over light poles and its right engine smashed into a power generator before crashing into the western side of the building, killing all 53 passengers, 5 hijackers, and 6 crew. The plane hit the Pentagon at the first-floor level. The front part of the fuselage disintegrated on impact, while the mid and tail sections kept moving for another fraction of a second. Debris from the tail section penetrated furthest into the building, breaking through 310 feet (94 m) of the three outermost of the building's five rings.

Rescue efforts

The New York City Fire Department deployed 200 units (half of the department) to the site. Their efforts were supplemented by numerous off-duty firefighters and emergency medical technicians. The New York City Police Department sent Emergency Service Units and other police personnel, and deployed its aviation unit.

Once on the scene, the FDNY, NYPD, andPort Authority police did not coordinate efforts and performed redundant searches for civilians. As conditions deteriorated, the NYPD aviation unit relayed information to police commanders, who issued orders for its personnel to evacuate the towers; most NYPD officers were able to safely evacuate before the buildings collapsed. With separate command posts set up and incompatible radio communications between the agencies, warnings were not passed along to FDNY commanders.

After the first tower collapsed, FDNY commanders issued evacuation warnings; however, due totechnical difficulties with malfunctioning radio repeater systems, many firefighters never heard the evacuation orders. 9-1-1 dispatchers also received information from callers that was not passed along to commanders on the scene. Within hours of the attack, a substantial search and rescue operation was launched. After months of around-the-clock operations, the World Trade Center site was cleared by the end of May 2002.

AFTERMATH

Immediate response

At 8:32 a.m., Federal Aviation Administration (FAA) officials were notified Flight 11 had been hijacked and they in turn notified the North American Aerospace Defense Command (NORAD). NORAD scrambled two F-15s from Otis Air National Guard Base in Massachusetts and they were airborne by 8:53 a.m. Because of slow and confused communication from FAA officials, NORAD had 9 minutes' notice that Flight 11 had been hijacked, and no notice about any of the other flights before they crashed. After both of the Twin Towers had already been hit, more fighters were scrambled from Langley Air Force Base in Virginia at 9:30 a.m. At 10:20 a.m. Vice PresidentDick Cheney issued orders to shoot down any commercial aircraft that could be positively identified as being hijacked. However, these instructions were not relayed in time for the fighters to take action. Some fighters took to the air without live ammunition, knowing that to prevent the hijackers from striking their intended targets, the pilots might have to intercept and crash their fighters into the hijacked planes, possibly ejecting at the last moment.

For the first time in U.S. history, SCATANA was invoked, closing all airspace and immediately grounding all non-emergency civilian aircraft in the United States, Canada, and several other countries, thus stranding tens of thousands of passengers across the world. TheFederal Aviation Administration closed American airspace to all international flights, causing about five hundred flights to be turned back or redirected to other countries. Canada received 226 of the diverted flights and launched Operation Yellow Ribbon to deal with the large numbers of grounded planes and stranded passengers.

The 9/11 attacks had immediate effects upon the American people. Police and rescue workers from around the country took leaves of absence, traveling to New York City to help recover bodies from the twisted remnants of the Twin Towers. Blood donations across the U.S. surged in the weeks after 9/11.

The deaths of adults who were killed in the attacks or died in rescue operations resulted in over 3,000 children losing a parent. Subsequent studies documented children's reactions to these actual losses and to feared losses of life, the protective environment in the aftermath of the attacks, and effects on surviving caregivers.

Domestic reactions

Following the attacks, President Bush's approval rating soared to 90%. On September 20, 2001, he addressed the nation and a joint session of the United States Congress regarding the events of September 11 and the subsequent nine days of rescue and recovery efforts, and described his intended response to the attacks. New York City mayor Rudy Giuliani's highly visible role won him high praise in New York and nationally.

Many relief funds were immediately set up to assist victims of the attacks, with the task of providingfinancial assistance to the survivors of the attacks and to the families of victims. By the deadline for victim's compensation on September 11, 2003, 2,833 applications had been received from the families of those who were killed. Contingency plans for the continuity of government and the evacuation of leaders were implemented soon after the attacks. However, Congress was not told that the United States had been under a continuity of government status until February 2002.

In the largest restructuring of the U.S. government in contemporary history, the United States enacted the Homeland Security Act of 2002, creating the Department of Homeland Security. Congress also passed the USA PATRIOT Act, saying it would help detect and prosecute terrorism and other crimes. Civil liberties groups have criticized the PATRIOT Act, saying it allows law enforcement to invade the privacy of citizens and that it eliminates judicial oversight of law enforcement and domestic intelligence. In an effort to effectively combat future acts of terrorism, the National Security Agency (NSA) was given broad powers. NSA commenced warrantless surveillance of telecommunications which was sometimes criticized since it permitted the agency "to eavesdrop on telephone and e-mail communications between the United States and people overseas without a warrant". In response to requests by various intelligence agencies, the United States Foreign Intelligence Surveillance Court permitted an expansion of powers by the US Government in seeking, obtaining, and sharing information on US citizens as well as non-US people from around the world.

Hate crimes

Numerous incidents of harassment and hate crimes against Muslims and South Asians were reported in the days following the 9/11 attacks. Sikhs were also targeted because Sikh males usually wear turbans, which are stereotypically associated with Muslims. There were reports of attacks on mosques and other religious buildings (including the firebombing of a Hindu temple), and assaults on people, including one murder: Balbir Singh Sodhi, a Sikh mistaken for a Muslim, was fatally shot on September 15, 2001, inMesa, Arizona.

According to an academic study, people perceived to be Middle Eastern were as likely to be victims of hate crimes as followers of Islam during this time. The study also found a similar increase in hate crimes against people who may have been perceived as Muslims, Arabs, and others thought to be of Middle Eastern origin. A report by the South Asian American advocacy group known as South Asian Americans Leading Together, documented media coverage of 645 bias incidents against Americans of South Asian or Middle Eastern descent between September 11 and 17. Various crimes such as vandalism, arson, assault, shootings, harassment, and threats in numerous places were documented.

Muslim American response

Muslim organizations in the United States were swift to condemn the attacks and called "upon Muslim Americans to come forward with their skills and resources to help alleviate the sufferings of the affected people and their families". These organizations included theIslamic Society of North America, American Muslim Alliance, American Muslim Council, Council on American-Islamic Relations, Islamic Circle of North America, and the Shari'a Scholars Association of North America. Along with monetary donations, many Islamic organizations launched blood drives and provided medical assistance, food, and shelter for victims.

International reactions

The attacks were denounced by mass media and governments worldwide. Across the globe, nations offered pro-American support and solidarity. Leaders in most Middle Eastern countries, and Afghanistan, condemned the attacks. Iraq was a notable exception, with an immediate official statement that, "the American cowboys are reaping the fruit of their crimes against humanity". While the government of Saudi Arabia officially condemned the attacks, privately many Saudis favored bin Laden's cause. As in the United States, the aftermath of the attacks saw tensions increase in other countries between Muslims and non-Muslims.

United Nations Security Council Resolution 1368 condemned the attacks, and expressed readiness to take all necessary steps to respond and combat all forms of terrorism in accordance with theirCharter. Numerous countries introduced anti-terrorism legislation and froze bank accounts they suspected of al-Qaeda ties. Law enforcement and intelligence agencies in a number of countries arrested alleged terrorists.

British Prime Minister Tony Blair said Britain stood "shoulder to shoulder" with the United States. A few days later, Blair flew to Washington to affirm British solidarity with the United States. In a speech to Congress, nine days after the attacks, which Blair attended as a guest, President Bush declared "America has no truer friend than Great Britain." Subsequently, Prime Minister Blair embarked on two months of diplomacy to rally international support for military action; he held 54 meetings with world leaders and travelled more than 40,000 miles (60,000 km).

Tens of thousands of people attempted to flee Afghanistan following the attacks, fearing a response by the United States. Pakistan, alreadyhome to many Afghan refugees from previous conflicts, closed its border with Afghanistan on September 17, 2001. Approximately one month after the attacks, the United States led a broad coalition of international forces to overthrow the Taliban regime from Afghanistan for their harboring of al-Qaeda. Though Pakistani authorities were initially reluctant to align themselves with the United States against the Taliban, they permitted the coalition access to their military bases, and arrested and handed over to the U.S. over 600 suspected al-Qaeda members.

The U.S. set up the Guantanamo Bay detention camp to hold inmates they defined as "illegal enemy combatants". The legitimacy of these detentions has been questioned by the European Union and human rights organizations.

Military operations

At 2:40 p.m. in the afternoon of September 11, Secretary of Defense Donald Rumsfeld was issuing rapid orders to his aides to look for evidence of Iraqi involvement. According to notes taken by senior policy official Stephen Cambone, Rumsfeld asked for, "Best info fast. Judge whether good enough hit S.H." (Saddam

Hussein) "at same time. Not only UBL" (Osama bin Laden). Cambone's notes quoted Rumsfeld as saying, "Need to move swiftly – Near term target needs – go massive – sweep it all up. Things related and not."

The NATO council declared the attacks on the United States were an attack on all NATO nations which satisfied Article 5 of the NATO charter. This marked the first invocation of Article 5, which had been written during the Cold War with an attack by the Soviet Union in mind. Australian Prime Minister John Howard who was in Washington D.C. during the attacks invoked Article IV of theANZUS treaty. The Bush administration announced a War on Terror, with the stated goals of bringing bin Laden and al-Qaeda to justice and preventing the emergence of other terrorist networks. These goals would be accomplished by imposing economic and military sanctions against states harboring terrorists, and increasing global surveillance and intelligence sharing.

On September 14, 2001, the U.S. Congress passed the Authorization for Use of Military Force Against Terrorists. Still in effect, it grants the President the authority to use all "necessary and appropriate force" against those whom he determined "planned, authorized, committed or aided" the September 11th attacks, or who harbored said persons or groups.

On October 7, 2001, the War in Afghanistan began when U.S. and British forces initiated aerial bombing campaigns targeting Taliban and al-Qaeda camps, then later invaded Afghanistan with ground troops of the Special Forces. The overthrow of the Taliban rule of Afghanistan by a U.S.-led coalition was the second-biggest operation of the U.S. Global War on Terrorism outside the United States, and the largest directly connected to terrorism. Conflict in Afghanistan between the Taliban insurgency and the International Security Assistance Force is ongoing. The Philippines and Indonesia, among other nations with their own internal conflicts with Islamic terrorism, also increased their military readiness.

MEMORIALS

In the days immediately following the attacks, many memorials and vigils were held around the world, and photographs of the dead and missing were posted around Ground Zero. A witness described being unable to "get away from faces of innocent victims who were killed. Their pictures are everywhere, on phone booths, street lights, walls of subway stations. Everything reminded me of a huge funeral, people quiet and sad, but also very nice. Before, New York gave me a cold feeling; now people were reaching out to help each other."

One of the first memorials was the Tribute in Light, an installation of 88 searchlights at the footprints of the World Trade Center towers. In New York, the World Trade Center Site Memorial Competition was held to design an appropriate memorial on the site. The winning design, *Reflecting Absence*, was selected in August 2006, and consists of a pair of reflecting pools in the footprints of the towers, surrounded by a list of the victims' names in an underground memorial space.

The Pentagon Memorial was completed and opened to the public on the seventh anniversary of the attacks in 2008. It consists of a landscaped park with 184 benches facing the Pentagon. When the Pentagon was repaired in 2001–2002, a private chapel and indoor memorial were included, located at the spot where Flight 77 crashed into the building.

In Shanksville, a permanent Flight 93 National Memorial is planned to include a sculpted grove of trees forming a circle around the crash site, bisected by the plane's path, while wind chimes will bear the names of the victims. A temporary memorial is located 500 yards (457 m) from the crash site. New York City firefighters donated a cross made of steel from the World Trade Center and mounted on top of a platform shaped like the Pentagon. It was installed outside the firehouse on August 25, 2008. Many other permanent memorials are elsewhere. Scholarships and charities have been established by the victims' families, and by many other organizations and private figures.

On every anniversary, in New York City, the names of the victims who died there are read out against a background of somber music. The President of the United States attends a memorial service at the Pentagon, and asks Americans to observe Patriot Day with a moment of silence. Smaller services are held in Shanksville, Pennsylvania, which are usually attended by the President's spouse.

3

Indian Mujahideen

Unknown before 2008, the Indian Mujahedeen (IM) has emerged as a well-organized jihadi terrorist group in India, claiming responsibility for a number of terror attacks perpetrated in various urban centers of India during 2007-2008. Even though the exact moment of IM's formation is not known, the recent arrest of a number of IM operatives has revealed its possible existence and involvement in terror strikes in India as far back as late October 2005. The name "Indian Mujahideen" was reportedly conceived at a terrorist conclave attended by top leaders of the Lashkar-e-Taiba (LeT) and Harkat-ul-Jehadi Islami (HuJI) in Pakistani-administered Kashmir in early May 2008 (Rediff.com, July 29, 2008).

The well-concealed rise of the Indian Mujahedeen as a home grown jihadi organization is not a good omen for India's security. IM came into the open for the first time in November 2007, when simultaneous bomb blasts targeted lawyers in court premises in three Uttar Pradesh cities—Varanasi, Faizabad (Ayodhya), and Lucknow (NDTV, November 23, 2007). IM described the attacks as "Islamic raids" and justified them as revenge against lawyers who had allegedly assaulted a couple of Jaish-e-Muhammad terrorist suspects. IM also alleged that the lawyers had refused to take cases involving other alleged terrorists, including suspected HuJI leader and Phulpur-based Islamic cleric Muhammad Waliullah, the alleged mastermind of the March 2006 Sankatmochan temple blasts in Varanasi. In IM terror strikes, email messages have typically been sent out to the media prior to the attacks, describing IM viewpoints on issues such as the Babri mosque demolition, the Mumbai riots, the communal violence in Gujarat that followed the 2002 torching of a train carrying Hindus, and various atrocities against the Muslim community in Gujarat and beyond. IM cites these incidents as reasons for their Islamic Jihad. IM's email manifestos shed some light on its objectives. The group calls for spreading Islam in India and waging Jihad against the "infidels" (non-Muslims, i.e. Hindus) and establishing "God's government" according to Quranic tenets.

After prolonged investigations, Indian intelligence agencies have corroborated that members of IM are mainly drawn from proscribed outfits such as the Students Islamic Movement of India (SIMI), the Pakistan-based LeT and the Bangladesh-based HuJI. IM's email statements indicate their ties with SIMI when they put forward demands for the release of SIMI cadres under detention or serving jail terms. However, the newly emerged IM continues to deny any connection with Pakistan, Bangladesh, or any of their agencies (e.g. Pakistan's Inter-Services Intelligence [ISI] and Bangladesh's Directorate General of Forces Intelligence [DGFI]). It also denies any links with terrorist groups such as LeT and HuJI.

The Indian Mujahideen has been trying to garner support from India's teeming Muslim population, often by raising indigenous issues in its manifestos. Since the Uttar Pradesh Court attacks, IM, as a home-grown jihadi outfit, has claimed responsibility for at least four major terror strikes in 2008 that targeted civilians. Each attack came with prior emails to media citing a list of anti-Muslim atrocities in the country. The group justifies the violence by tagging the terror campaign as the "rise of Jihad" and the "revenge of Gujarat."

BACKGROUND

Factionalism

Even though IM came to light in 2008, in the same year it was already seen to have a faction. The 30 October 2008 Assam bombingswere claimed by alleged offspring of the IM, Islamic Security Force-Indian Mujahideen, though police were still investigating this link.

Members

It is suspected that these are the major leaders of the Indian group.

- Abdul Subhan Qureshi alias Tauqeer, 36, sought: A software engineer from Mumbai. An expert In bomb-making and is an expert bomber.
- Safdar Nagori, 38, under arrest: Architect the transformation from SIMI to Indian Mujahideen.
- Mufti Abu Bashir, 28, under arrest: A preacher from Azamgarh In Uttar Pradesh.
- Qayamuddin Kapadia, 28, under arrest: A trader of Vadodara, He started the first-ever mosque of the Ahle Hadis Tanzeem In Vadodara a few years ago.
- Sajid Mansuri, 35, under arrest: A graduate In psychology and formerly a marketing executive.
- Usman Agarbattiwala, sought, 25: A PG diploma holder from Vadodara In human rights
- Alamzeb Afridi, 24, sought: A jobless youth from Ahmedabad. He purchased bicycles and then planted them In Ahmedabad after tying bombs.
- Abdul Razik Mansuri, 27, sought: An embroidery unit owner.
- Mujib Shaikh, 25, sought: A stone polishing artisan.
- Zahid Shaikh, 27, sought: A mobile phone repair shop owner from Ahmedabad.
- Amil Parwaz, sought: A native of Ujjain. Believed to Be involved In the court bomb blasts In Uttar Pradesh In November 2007.
- Yasin Bhatkal, 30, under arrest: Native of Bhatkal in North Karnataka.

Delhi group

The local group at Delhi is thought to include the following, most of them from Azamgarh:

- Mohammad Atif (24) aka Bashir: alleged planner and recruiter, killed In Batla House, Jamia Nagar encounter on

19September. Alleged to have planted a bomb at M-block market in Greater Kailash-I, and Varanasi bombs.

- Mohammad Saif arrested from Batla House in Jamia Nagar after 19September encounter. Alleged to have planted a bomb at Regal Cinema in Connaught Place.
- Zeeshan: arrested after the Jamia Nagar encounter. Alleged to have planted a bomb At Barakhamba Road In Connaught Place.
- Mohammed Sajid (16) aka Pankaj, killed during the Batla House encounter. Alleged to have planted a bomb at Barakhamba Road in Connaught Place.
- Junaid: Escaped during the Batla House encounter. Alleged to have planted a bomb at M-block market in Greater Kailash-I, and Varanasi bombs.
- Mohammad Shakeel (24): arrested him on 21September from Jamia Nagar. Alleged to have planted a bomb at Nehru Place in south Delhi
- Zia-ur-Rehman (22): arrested on 21September from Jamia Nagar. Alleged to have planted a bomb at Connaught Place and on a cycle in Ahmedabad.
- Saqib Nisar (23): arrested him on 21September from Jamia Nagar.
- Shahzad alias Pappu: Arrested from Azamgarh by UP STF, He was escaped during the Jamia Nagar encounter. Alleged to have planted a bomb At in Central Park, Connaught Place.
- Alihas Malik: sought. Alleged to have planted a bomb At Central Park, Connaught Place.
- Mohammad Khalif: sought.
- Arif: sought.
- Salman: Arrested by Special Cell.

ATTACKS CLAIMED BY INDIAN MUJAHIDEEN

The emails sent by Indian Mujahideen claimed that they were responsible for the following terror incidents. One warning email was received 5 minutes before the first blast in Ahmedabad. Another was received soon after the first blast of Delhi bombings. The timing makes it impossible for any other groups to have sent the two emails.

- 2007 Uttar Pradesh bombings
- 13 May 2008 Jaipur bombings
- 2008 Bangalore serial blasts
- 2008 Ahmedabad serial blasts
- 13 September 2008 Delhi bombings
- 2010 Pune bombing
- 2010 Jama Masjid attack
- 2010 Varanasi bombing
- 2011 Mumbai serial blasts
- 2013 Bodh Gaya blasts

Suspects and arrests

On 28 August 2013, in a major breakthrough Yasin Bhatkal, co-founder of IM and another IM terrorist have been arrested by Indian Police and NIA near Indo-Nepal border. According to Gujarat police, the breakthrough in 2008 Ahmedabad serial blasts case came from five 'switched-off' mobile phone numbers. Joint Commissioner of Police (crime) Ashish Bhatia said that the terrorists had procured five SIM cards of phones that were switched off on the day of the blasts — 26 July. The analysis of the phone calls made to those SIM cards from PCOs provided them the key leads.

The arrest of ten suspects included the leader, Mufti Abu Bashir Ishlahi alias Abdul Wasir, who was arrested the help of Uttar Pradesh police At his father's home At Sarai Mir In Azamgarh UP on 14August 2008. Bashir studied in the local Madarsatul Islah and later in Deoband in Saharanpur. According to the reports Bashir claimed that the bombings cost Rs 75,000 a SIMI activist sold his house in Kutch to get the amount.

Bashir, who had stayed in Ahmedabad along with Abdul Subhan Qureshi alias Tauqeer, a Co-conspirator, had bought five SIM cards using local names and addresses. He had used these cellphone numbers to remain in touch with the other members of the module at the planning stage of the conspiracy. Bashir had given the SIM cards to the bomb planters on 26 July, who had used them carefully. Each member had contacted the others through

STD-PCO booths after successfully planting the bombs. These numbers were used only for receiving calls. Many of the calls were from Juhapura, where Zahid Shaikh, one of the key members of the group, lived at Sandhi Avenue near the Sarkhej highway. These numbers had become inactive immediately after the blasts.

Also, the Government suspects Indian mujahideen for the two blasts in Hyderabad, on 21 February 2013 at 7:01 pm.

Key members of the Indian Mujahideen in Mumbai police custody want to turn approver. In March 2014, a special cell of police in India arrested four members of IM, out of which one was Waqas alias Javed a bomb making expert in this group. They were arrested in Jaipur and Jodhpur in Rajasthan.

Jamia Nagar encounter

On 19 September 2008, the police raided an apartment in Jamia Nagar, near Jamia Millia Islamia In Delhi. There is speculation that the prime suspect in the Ahmedabad blasts, Mufti Abu Bashir, a madrasa teacher from Azamgarh, may have pointed out the apartment.

The raid resulted in the death of terrorists Bashir alias Mohammed Atif Amin (son of Mohammed Amin, cloth merchant in Bhiwandi, Mumbai), Mohammad Sajid and a decorated police officer Mohan Chand Sharma In the gunfight. Mohammad Saif (the son of Samajwadi Party leader Shadab Ahmed) was arrested while two hostiles managed to flee by possibly jumping the rooftops. All of the suspects were from Azamgarh district'S Sarai Mir town. They claimed to be students, but that was denied by Jamia Millia

The five were responsible for manufacturing bombs used in Ahmedabad, Jaipur and Delhi blasts.

Atif claimed to have been studying for a diploma in Human Resources Development from Jamia Milia Islamia University. However Jamia Milia denied having him As a student. Some residents of Sarai Mir thought He was pursuing his bachelors In technology from Jamia Hamdard.

Atif was said to have been the leader of a group of 14 young men belong to Azamgarh in Uttar Pradesh, all claiming to have been studying in Delhi: Atif (24), Sajid alias Pankaj (19), (both now dead), Shehzad alias Pappu (22), Junaid (27), Shahdab Bhai alias Mallick (27), Sajid (24), Mohammad Khalid (25), Arif (22), Shakil (26), Zia Khan (24) and Salman (25), Zeeshan (24) and Mohammad Saif (23).

Zeeshan Jawed was arrested from the offices of a private TV station, He worked for a private company, Monarch International on Vikas Marg, and is also said to be studying management. Both him and Saif claim to have been recruited by Atif.

It is reported that Mohammad Saif has said that the plans to carry out several blasts across the country were mooted about three years ago when the Indian Mujahideen (IM) was formed. Although the blasts spanned over a period of 10 months (the first blasts took place in August 2007 in Hyderabad), the planning was made far back in 2005. After that series of explosions occurred Uttar Pradesh, Jaipur, Ahmedabad and Delhi.

There is considerable resentment In Sarai Mir over the death of the local boys. Villagers have blamed the media for giving a bad name to Azamgarh by calling it a "nursery of terror". Mafia don Abu Salem hails from here. Azamgarh used to export its famous country-made pistols, known as kattas, whose factories dot the region. The district was also known for young sharpshooters who joined Mumbai gangs. Individuals from the area have been accused of the murders of Bollywood producer Gulshan Kumar in Mumbai and Left leaderShankar Guha Niyogi in Chhattisgarh.

THE INDIAN MUJAHIDEEN: A RESURGENCE OF TERROR

The blood that flowed through Varanasi on the evening of December 7, 2010, marked yet another appalling episode in the history of India's prolonged combat with the various subversive elements spread throughout the length and breadth of the country. Soon after the devastating attack that rocked the portals of the temple town, an e-mail was sent to various prominent media houses by the Indian Mujahideen claiming responsibility for the attack. The e-mail claimed that the blast was in retaliation to the verdict in the Babri Masjid-Ram Janambhoomi title suit case. Security agencies traced the Internet Protocol address of the five-page e-mail signed by 'Al-Arbi' to the suburbs of Mumbai.i Police teams were immediately despatched to the area for further investigation, the results of which are awaited.

At this juncture, it would be prudent to look into the inception as well the activities of the Indian Mujahideen (IM) in order to understand their composition, terror tactics, modus operandi, as well as the issues that inflame their operations. Thus, this chapter focuses on the inception of the IM, their links with the Students Islamic Movement of India (SIMI), the ideology that they profess, and the various attacks that have been attributed to the same. Since the subject requires an in-depth research into the intricacies of the terror group as well as its links with other groups, this chapter deals with certain aspects of the same. It is the initial part of a series of papers based on a study of the Indian Mujahideen.

TERROR AND THE INDIAN MUJAHIDEEN

There is something disquieting in what Ashish Khetan has written and said recently on terror in India (in The Hindu and on Tehelka.tv), and centrally within it, the Indian Mujahideen. More so, because it comes from one of the most credible journalist's today, who has done some commendable work over the years. A journalist I personally respect. But there are several reasons which compel this response. And yet, this is not just a response, but also an attempt to elucidate the many complex processes within which 'terror' is located today, and the way the discourse has transformed, and has implications for a people's negotiated relationship with their state.

Over the last one year, through Gulail.com, Ashish Khetan has exposed several cases which have been fabricated against individuals and groups, all of them Muslims. This expose, through the revelation of classified Interrogation Reports in the public realm-using the police's own documents to challenge their own story-has been, till now, the most brilliant and effective way to challenge the cases, which many, suspected to be fabricated from the very start. And this expose was, and remains, a brave and mammoth task requiring extensive contacts, sources, and credibility, as anyone working in the fiercely guarded territories of national security and 'terror' would know.

It is this body of work that constitutes the historical background and legitimating authority of his recent op-ed in The Hindu on terror in India, and forms its silent and silencing basis. And yet, the work itself is neither the point of the article, nor forms the basis of what Mr. Khetan is trying to say, while the article exists primarily in the realm of speculation and an authoritative *khutba* meant for the country's muslims. The larger argument in the opinion piece-the first one in which Mr. Khetan has made sense of his one year long research on terror cases in India-is not based on facts, beyond the jurisdiction of journalistic inquiry, unwarranted, un-necessary, laced with presumptions, and even possibly incorrect. But what makes it dangerous, so much so that the article seemingly overturns the very idea that Mr. Khetan has been challenging in the past, is the way it is implicated, and plays to, an extremely communal politics and narrative within which terror today has been a central rallying point. The ideological framework within which the fabricated terror cases have been expounded-neither supported by facts, nor seeking in any way to serve the struggle for human rights of the citizen-, sits comfortably with particular political agendas today. Let's take it piece by piece.

I am compelled to state that I do not write here as a Muslim. I am neither trying to contest a narrative of terror that has been associated with Muslims, nor am I speaking from the location of a Muslim in whatever else I am trying to say. I write here, today, as a citizen contesting and challenging the infringement of human rights of its citizens by the state-whether minorities or tribals, or any of those peoples, communities, religious groups who have been expendable in the state's slow and gradual weakening of democratic institutions. All in a political game of power and control over peoples and dissent.

Mr. Khetan's central argument is this: the Indian Mujahideen is a reality, a terrible spectre responsible for many of the blasts that have taken place in the last decade, and that Muslims should come to terms with it, develop a political understanding, move out of narrow narratives of victimization, stop defending all and any who have been accused of terrorism, and demand that all should be brought to justice-including the IM who are Muslims. Tactfully arranged within it is a secondary argument: that before the IM was busted in 2008, many innocent Muslims were wrongly prosecuted-as he has shown-and that the police and the judiciary has been complicit in producing and convicting them, making a mockery of the criminal justice system.

The stakes are high. To claim that the IM exists and that it is responsible for the many bomb blasts has huge implications, something that will be discussed later. But it is a claim that cannot be lightly made. What proof is offered behind the claim? None. Only Mr. Khetan's own reading and privileged access to Interrogation Reports(IR), none of which he deigns to share with his readers. Ironically, the only Interrogation Reports that have been revealed are those which have helped prove that the cases against some have been fabricated. It is based on this credibility that Mr Khetan argues that the Interrogation reports reveal a sinister reality of the IM that we as a people, or rather, muslims, have to come to terms with. But there appears to be a misplaced sense of value put on the Interrogation Reports', as well as limited understanding of how they can help prove that the accused in the 7/11 blast, or the others that Mr Khetan has revealed, were innocent.

There are three questions that need to be asked here:

1. Whether such a claim can be made based on IRs
2. Mr Khetan's authority or legitimacy to make such a claim
3. The possible, factual incorrectness of the claim.

The IRs are classified documents and are not meant to be shared publicly. They are prepared by the police for their own use. Though, that in no way raises its credibility, it does make them crucial if these internal reports stand in stark contradiction to another official case made by the same agency on the same matter. At the same time, IRs in themselves are of no evidentiary value in any court of law, nor do they have any inherent truth value as they could be lacking in any material basis as the information obtained by the police could be through the use of third degree and the person may be compelled to state what the agency *wants* to hear rather than the truth. Even in the realm of the commonsensical, the IRs are just that-reports prepared by the police of a suspect's interrogation, with no value whatsoever but as investigative leads. Since Mr. Khetan does not reveal the source and content of these IRs, one has to largely and only accept his word about there being anything in the IR's about the IM, if at all.

However, it is inconsequetial if there is anything in the IR's about the IM or not. The credibility of the previous work by Mr. Khetan, stems not from any inherent truth value of the IR's, but from something entirely different-the fact that these reports, prepared by the police themselves, *were contradictory* to the official case. And hence, a crucial part of the defence case against the official prosecution.

The plea for the innocence of those prosecuted by the revelation of the IRs, has nothing to do with whether the IRs are true or not, but rests on contradictory evidence being available and the conscious and deliberate suppression of the same by the police. To put it simply while it is the job of the court to weigh the evidence and make a value judgment as to the truth or otherwise of the prosecution's case, the prosecution itself cannot act knowing that its case is false.

In these cases, the IRs revealed that not only did the prosecution itself not believe in its own case, it infact had reason to believe that it was false. The good faith of the prosecution was hence absent and the prosecution was proved to have acted in bad faith. The IRs, in themselves are in no way any proof of the guilt of Sadiq sheikh or any others who have been clubbed together with the overarching term of the Indian Mujahideen. It would be enlightening to look at what Justice A.M Thipsey of the Bombay High Court who dealt with this issue in the 7/11 case had to say regarding this very point.

Much before the revelation by Mr. Khetan, the defence council of the 13 accused in the 7/11 train blast case wanted to tender as part of the evidence the confession of Sadiq Sheikh who claimed to have done the blast. The prosecution objected to the confession being tendered as evidence in this case by arguing, among other things, that the confession if admitted here would be:

"inconsistent with the guilt of the accused in this case...[and that]it would prejudice the accused in that case(Crime Branch IM case-MCOCA Special case no.4 of 2009) and would not afford them the chance." (Pg 37.)

The trial Court accepted the prosecution's argument. When the defense took it to the High court, Justice A.M. Thipsey setting aside the order explicitly pointed out:

"It is not possible to accept the view of the learned judge. In the first place, the appellants had not claimed-and could not have claimed that the confessions of those accused 'were true'. They were not expecting to 'prove' those confessions against those accused. What they were saying is that someone else has confessed of having committed the offense with which they are charged...and it is the court that decides whether the fact of a confession having been made is true and also whether the facts stated in the confession are true. Confessions are treated as circumstantial evidence of the truth of the facts stated therein and it is the court that decides whether the facts stated in a confession are to be believed or not in a given case. It is a matter of evaluation of evidence to be done by the court after it is tendered."(Pg 26,29)

It is important to note that a confession is immeasurably more valuable when compared to an Interrogation report. It can be tendered as evidence in court. Despite this, as the High court points out and rightly so, that even then there is no presumption to their inherent truth value, and, it is the job of the court of law to evaluate if they do and can be believed and relief upon. For, the court remains the final arbitrator of guilt or innocence.

How is it possible, then, to proclaim the guilt of the IM based on Interrogation reports, even when the cases of Sadiq Sheikh and the rest, under the rubric of the IM, are still sub-judice? Can a claim be made even on the basis of certain facts which journalistic research might have brought to light, when those facts are yet to be tested in court?

Mr Khetan offers us neither proofs nor explanations. What is offered instead is a narrative of how 5 people-Sadiq Sheikh, Mujahid Saleem, Asif and Amir Reza Khan, and Riaz Bhatkal-fired by ideas of Jihad and retributive justice, bankrolled by forces across the border, went about bombing places one after the other.

The preposterousness of the claim, in the sheer absence of any proof offered, even when all these cases are sub-judice, do not warrant a rebuttal. If anything, it warrants the forceful disciplining of the clause of 'contempt of court'-for the sheer damage that the claim could possible wreck for all the cases that are presently under trial at a time when the 'collective conscience of the people' has assumed legal weight.

And yet, as the narrative has been expounded by Mr. Khetan, I shall take it seriously within the bounds of this chapter, as, unfortunately the entire fabric of the discourse of terror has been created by such unsubstantiated and baseless allegations. Allegations which have assumed the status of commonsense-and through repetition-gained legitimacy and have become the "truth". And it needs to be said that this narrative is thoroughly contested-factually.

For the last one year, as a Research Fellow at the Tata Institute of Social Sciences, I have been researching on terror cases across the 4 cities-Hyderabad, Mumbai, Bangalore and Kolkata. Over this period, I have gone through all relevant documents-legal and otherwise-, met lawyers (both prosecution and defense) as well as accused and their families, of almost all the cases of bomb blasts and attacks in these four cities. This research has encompassed the criminal and social history of two of the 5 people that Mr. Khetan authoritatively mentions as the original member who started the Indian Mujahideen-Mujahid Saleem, and Asif Reza Khan. And the picture that emerges is completely different from what Mr Khetan has attributed to them without proofs or explanations.

Mujahid Saleem: A study of the 4 bomb blast cases of Hyderabad (*forthcoming in EPW*), as well as my meeting with the lawyer associated with his encounter case, his friends, as well as his father Aleem Islahi (whose provocative writing on Jihad and Babri Masjid is the sudden and only explanation offered by Mr. Khetan of Mujahid's crime) makes a story worth telling.

But, it is Maulana Naseeruddin, a cleric who has been a friend of Aleem Islahi as well as his son, whose story of prosecution is directly linked to that of Mujahid. The families of both Maulana Naseeruddin and Aleem Islahi live next to each other in Saidabad-a densely populated Muslim pocket of Hyderabad. Maulana Naseeruddin was first arrested in 1992 when he organized public prayer for the 'martyrship' of the Babri Masjid. He was arrested along with 62 other young men under TADA. Since then Maulana Naseeruddin has been accused in several cases of terror in Hyderabad, including the famous case of the murder of the Haren

Pandya. Last year Maulana Naseeruddin, after spending almost 2 decades in prison, was acquitted of *all* charges in*all* the cases. A minor case is still pending against him. In 2004, when Naseerudin was first accused in the Haren Pandya murder case, there were protests and people had gathered when the Gujarat contingent came to arrest him. The Gujarat contingent was led by IPS officer Narendra Amin who is presently an accused in the Ishrat Jahan fake encounter case. Mujahid Saleem, then a 20 year old boy, was standing the closest to Naseeruddin, protesting with the others. He was shot at point blank range by Narendra Amin. At the time of his death, there was not a single case against him.

Md Rayeesuddin, a friend of Mujahid, was also there that day. He is the prime witness in the case of encounter against Narendra Amin. The case is presently lying dormant. Since the time time Md Rayeesuddin listed as a witness, he has been arrested and interrogated, in every single case of bomb blast in Hyderabad. He was Accused no 16 in the case no 198/2007, one of the 4 Mecca Masjid Blast cases. In that case, his name was included in the chargesheet after he refused to step down as a witness. Even after receiving compensation for the false framing, he has been picked up and tortured after the recent 2013 Dilsukhnagar blast. Ironically, previously listed in the chargesheet as a member of Huji, Rayeesuddin was picked up and interrogated even as the police claimed that it was the Indian Mujahideen. He still refuses to step down as a witness in the day-light encounter of his friend Mujahid Saleem.

Aleem Islahi: The mere holding of an opinion, irrespective of its nature, does not constitute crime, unless an overtly violent act has been done. Though it is difficult to understand the link with the opinions of Aleem Islahi with the guilt of his son Mujahid, it remains a fact that Aleem Islahi has not been accused in a single case of crime or terror in Hyderabad. His name was in the FIR in case no 198/2007, it was however not included in the chargesheet.

Asif Reza Khan: Asif Reza Khan, a resident of Kolkata, was 22 years old when he was first arrested in 1994 under TADA. A student at Aligarh Muslim University then, Asif had just finished his graduation from the well known Maulana Azad College in Calcutta. At AMU, Asif had Kashmiri friends with whom he lived in the hostel. The arrest was among the hundreds of arrests of Muslims across the country for alleged 'Jihadi' links and disruptive activities pertaining to Kashmir. Also arrested under TADA at the same time was ShahidAzmi-the lawyer who was later killed defending those who were falsely accused in terror cases.

Asif Reza and Shahid Azmi spent 5 years in Delhi's Tihar Jail. Released in 1999, after the Supreme Court acquitted them of all charges, both Asif and Shahid, like most others who were released, were re-arrested in several cases, especially in the many hi-profile cases of kidnapping of businessman in the country. After their release, all three of them-Shahid and Asif and Aftab-were accused in the kidnapping of Partha Roy Burman, the 'Khadim's' shoe baron from Kolkata. Shahid and Asif were taken in custody and interrogated. Asif was also accused in the kidnapping of a Gujarat diamond merchant, Bhaskar Parekh. *(Gathered from my conversation with Abdul Azeez, JamiluddinNasir, Aftab Ansari. Abdul Azeez is friend of the Asif Reza family and knew Asif well. The facts are corroborated in the deposition of Ali Reza Khan, the brother of Asif.)*

In 2001, immidietly after SIMI was banned, the Gujarat police took Asif into police custody, and took him to Rajkot where they shot him on December 7 -one and half months before the American Centre attack. The police said, officially, that Asif, a member of SIMI, in a bid to escape, fired upon them by snatching the AK-47 of one of the policemen. They shot him in retaliation. None of the policemen were hurt.

The entire case of the Calcutta attack is built on the assumption that Asif Reza Khan was a terrorist with links with 'Jihadi organisations'. An assumption which is not substantiated by any proof or corroboration.

According to the official case, the American Centre attack which was a ride by shooting of the guards stationed outside the United States Information Service which lasted 40s, was carried out by friends of Asif (one of the two shooters was Sadiq Sheikh according to the police) who wanted to avenge his death. Strangely, the attack took place in Kolkata, even though Asif was killed in Gujarat, as Asif was initially in custody of the Kolkata police according to a confession in the case. Out of the total of 9 accused, 7 were sentence to death by the trial court. The High court acquitted two of them and reduced the punishment of 3 others to 5 years of imprisonment. Two of the accused who presently stand between the complete collapse of the case, face the death penalty in a case which is laced with irregularities, and where the possibility of fabricated evidence cannot be ruled out, as I have concluded after studying the records of the case and speaking to people concerned.. The appeal by the two accused against their convictions is up for hearing in the Supreme Court the next month, where the entire narrative of Asif as well as the attacks by his friends, including Sadiq Sheikh, will be put to test. Strangely, in this case where the accused have veered between two judicial extremes-from death penalty to acquittal-Sadiq Sheikh, the prime accused who was shown as absconding till 2008, is yet to be tried even though the final appeal of the other two who only have minor conspiratorial roles is being heard.

The reality of the IM is sub-judice in many courts of the country with the allegations against them yet to be evaluated and appraised by examination to the level of evidence. For, along with allegations, are also irregularities, severe contestations and allegation of possible fabrication as well as violence-as the legal and extra legal stories of two out of the five named by Mr. Khetan reveal. And this, here, is the crucial point: this is not a contestation of facts. The above facts about the individuals who have been condemned unheard by Mr. Khetan, have not been narrated here to proclaim the innocence of Asif Reza Khan or Mujahid Saleem, but rather, to reveal the falsity of the innuendos which form the basis of Mr. Khetan's proclamation of their guilt.

This chapter is also not a proclamation of the innocence of the Indian Mujahideen. What is intended here is to raise a crucial question: On what basis can the Indian Mujahideen be declared as a reality responsible for many blasts across the country – without evidence-when the matter is sub-judice and also deeply riven with contestation and stories of state violence?

Purely on the basis of a personal, closeted reading of Interrogation reports whose validity is less reliable than the facts pointed out above or the testimonies of all those who are willing to testify in court against it?

4

26/11 Mumbai Attacks

This is the most fiery and weird attack that took place in the Indian History. The spot was India's most famous and royal Hotel group Hotel Taj Mahal which is in the premises of Gate way of India. There was a 64 hours long battle between the Military / police forces and the terrorists. There were shooting and bombing continuously from both the sides. It was like a hotel arrest by terrorist. The date 26 November 2008 will remain in the forever as a black day in the Indian history. There were 10 attacks on the same registered in several places of Mumbai on the same day; however Hotel Taj was the main target which witnessed the death of 100 innocent people who stayed in Taj.

2008 MUMBAI ATTACKS

A series of twelve coordinated shooting and bombing attacks lasting four days occurred acrossMumbai, carried out by Pakistani members of Lashkar-e-Taiba. Ajmal Kasab, the only attacker who was captured alive, later confessed upon interrogation that the attacks were conducted with the support of Pakistan Government's intelligence agency ISI. The involvement of Pakistan's ISI was also supported by statements made by David Headley, a U.S. citizen of Pakistani origin, though an ISI spokesman denied any involvement in the attacks. The attacks, which drew widespread global condemnation, began on Wednesday, 26 November and lasted until Saturday, 29 November 2008, killing 164 people and wounding at least 308.

Eight of the attacks occurred in South Mumbai: at Chhatrapati Shivaji Terminus, the Oberoi Trident, the Taj Mahal Palace & Tower,

Leopold Cafe, Cama Hospital, the Nariman House Jewish community centre, the Metro Cinema, and in a lane behind the *Times of India* building and St. Xavier's College. There was also an explosion at Mazagaon, in Mumbai's port area, and in a taxi at Vile Parle. By the early morning of 28 November, all sites except for the Taj hotel had been secured by Mumbai Police and security forces. On 29 November, India's National Security Guards (NSG) conducted 'Operation Black Tornado' to flush out the remaining attackers; it resulted in the deaths of the last remaining attackers at the Taj hotel and ending all fighting in the attacks.

Ajmal Kasab disclosed that the attackers were members of Lashkar-e-Taiba, among others. The Government of India said that the attackers came from Pakistan, and theircontrollers were in Pakistan. On 7 January 2009, Pakistan's Information Minister Sherry Rehman officially accepted Ajmal Kasab's nationality as Pakistani. On 12 February 2009, Pakistan's Interior Minister Rehman Malik asserted that parts of the attack had been planned in Pakistan. A trial court on 6 May 2010 sentenced Ajmal Kasab to death on all the 86 charges for which he was convicted. On his appeal against this verdict, Bombay High Courton 21 February 2011 and Supreme Court of India on 29 August 2012 upheld his death sentence. Kasab was executed by hanging at Yerwada Jail in Pune on 21 November 2012. On 9 January, 2015; the foremost mastermind of the attacks Zaki ur Rehman Lakhvi was granted bail against surety bonds of 200,000 (US$3,100) though he may still remain in jail for a month.

BACKGROUND

There have been many bombings in Mumbai since the 13 coordinated bomb explosions that killed 257 people and injured 700 on 12 March 1993. The 1993 attacks are believed to have been in retaliation for the Babri Mosque demolition.

On 6 December 2002, a blast in a BEST bus near Ghatkopar station killed two people and injured 28. The bombing occurred on the 10th anniversary of the demolition of the Babri Mosque inAyodhya. A bicycle bomb exploded near the Vile Parle station in Mumbai, killing one person and injuring 25 on 27 January 2003, a day before the visit of the Prime Minister of India Atal Bihari

Vajpayee to the city. On 13 March 2003, a day after the 10th anniversary of the 1993 Bombay bombings, a bomb exploded in a train compartment near the Mulund station, killing 10 people and injuring 70. On 28 July 2003, a blast in a BEST bus in Ghatkopar killed 4 people and injured 32. On 25 August 2003, two bombs exploded in South Mumbai, one near the Gateway of Indiaand the other at Zaveri Bazaar in Kalbadevi. At least 44 people were killed and 150 injured. On 11 July 2006, seven bombs exploded within 11 minutes on the Suburban Railway in Mumbai. 209 people were killed, including 22 foreigners and over 700 injured. According to the Mumbai Police, the bombings were carried out by Lashkar-e-Taiba and Students Islamic Movement of India (SIMI).

Training

A group of men, sometimes stated as 24, at other times 26 received training in marine warfare at a remote camp in mountainousMuzaffarabad, occupied Kashmir. Part of the training was reported to have taken place on the Mangla Dam reservoir.

The recruits went through the following stages of training, according to the Indian and U.S. media:

- Psychological: Indoctrination to Islamist ideas, including imagery of atrocities suffered by Muslims in India, Chechnya, Palestine and across the globe.
- Basic Combat: Lashkar's basic combat training and methodology course, the *Daura Aam*.
- Advanced Training: Selected to undergo advanced combat training at a camp near Mansehra, a course the organisation calls the *Daura Khaas*. According to an unnamed source at the US Defense Department this includes advanced weapons and explosives training supervised by retired personnel of the Pakistan Army, along with survival training and further indoctrination.
- Commando Training: Finally, an even smaller group selected for specialised commando tactics training and marine navigation training given to the Fedayeen unit selected in order to target Mumbai.

From the students, 10 were handpicked for the Mumbai mission. They also received training in swimming and sailing, besides the use of high-end weapons and explosives under the supervision of LeT commanders. According to a media report citing an unnamed former Defence Department Official of the US, the intelligence agencies of the US had determined that former officers from Pakistan's Army andInter-Services Intelligence agency assisted actively and continuously in training. They were given blueprints of all the four targets – Taj Mahal Palace & Tower, Oberoi Trident, Nariman House and Chhatrapati Shivaji Terminus.

ATTACKS

The first events were detailed around 20:00 Indian Standard Time (IST) on 26 November, when 10 men in inflatable speedboats came ashore at two locations in Colaba. They reportedly told local Marathi-speaking fishermen who asked them who they were to "mind their own business" before they split up and headed two different ways. The fishermen's subsequent report to police received little response.

Chhatrapati Shivaji Terminus

The Chhatrapati Shivaji Terminus (CST) was attacked by two gunmen, one of whom, Ajmal Kasab, was later caught alive by the police and identified by eyewitnesses. The attacks began around 21:30 when the two men entered the passenger hall and opened fire, using AK-47 rifles. The attackers killed 58 people and injured 104 others, their assault ending at about 22:45. Security forces and emergency services arrived shortly afterwards. The two gunmen fled the scene and fired at pedestrians and police officers in the streets, killing eight police officers. The attackers passed a police station. Many of the outgunned police officers were afraid to confront the attackers, and instead switched off the lights and secured the gates. The attackers then headed towards Cama Hospital with an intention to kill patients, but the hospital staff locked all of the patient wards. A team of the Mumbai Anti-Terrorist Squad led by police chief Hemant Karkare searched the Chhatrapati Shivaji Terminus and then left in pursuit of Kasab and Khan. Kasab and Khan opened fire on the vehicle in a lane next to the hospital and the police returned fire. Karkare, Vijay Salaskar, Ashok Kamte and one of their officers were killed, though the only survivor, Constable Arun Jadhav, was wounded. Kasab and Khan seized the police vehicle but later abandoned it and seized a passenger car instead. They then ran into a police roadblock, which had been set up after Jadhav radioed for help. A gun battle then ensued in which Khan was killed and Kasab was wounded. After a physical struggle, Kasab was arrested. A police officer, Tukaram Omble was also killed when he ran in front of Kasab to shoot him.

Leopold Cafe

The Leopold Cafe, a popular restaurant and bar on Colaba Causeway in South Mumbai, was one of the first sites to be attacked. Two attackers opened fire on the cafe on the evening of 26 November, killing at least 10 people, (including some foreigners), and injuring many more.

Bomb blasts in taxis

There were two explosions in taxis caused by timer bombs. The first one occurred at 22:40 at Vile Parle, killing the driver and a passenger. The second explosion took place at Wadi Bunder between 22:20 and 22:25. Three people, including the driver of the taxi were killed, and about 15 others were injured.

Taj Mahal Hotel and Oberoi Trident

Two hotels, the Taj Mahal Palace & Tower and the Oberoi Trident, were among the four locations targeted. Six explosions were reported at the Taj hotel – one in the lobby, two in the elevators, three in the restaurant – and one at the Oberoi Trident. At the Taj Mahal, firefighters rescued 200 hostages from windows using ladders during the first night.

CNN initially reported on the morning of 27 November 2008 that the hostage situation at the Taj had been resolved and quoted the police chief of Maharashtra stating that all hostages were freed; however, it was learned later that day that there were still two attackers holding hostages, including foreigners, in the Taj Mahal hotel.

A number of European Parliament Committee on International Trade delegates were staying in the Taj Mahal hotel when it was attacked, but none of them were injured. British Conservative

Member of the European Parliament (MEP) Sajjad Karim (who was in the lobby when attackers initially opened fire there) and German Social Democrat MEP Erika Mann were hiding in different parts of the building.

Also reported present was Spanish MEP Ignasi Guardans, who was barricaded in a hotel room. Another British Conservative MEP, Syed Kamall, reported that he along with several other MEPs left the hotel and went to a nearby restaurant shortly before the attack. Kamall also reported that Polish MEP Jan Masielwas thought to have been sleeping in his hotel room when the attacks started, but eventually left the hotel safely. Kamall and Guardans reported that a Hungarian MEP's assistant was shot. Also caught up in the shooting were the President of Madrid, Esperanza Aguirre, while checking in at the Oberoi Trident, and Indian MP N. N. Krishnadas of Kerala and Gulam Noon while having dinner at a restaurant in the Taj hotel.

Nariman House

Nariman House, a Chabad Lubavitch Jewish center in Colaba known as the Mumbai Chabad House, was taken over by two attackers and several residents were held hostage. Police evacuated adjacent buildings and exchanged fire with the attackers, wounding one. Local residents were told to stay inside. The attackers threw a grenade into a nearby lane, causing no casualties. NSG commandos arrived from Delhi, and a Naval helicopter took an aerial survey. During the first day, 9 hostages were rescued from the first floor. The following day, the house was stormed by NSG commandos fast-roping from helicopters onto the roof, covered by snipers positioned in nearby buildings. After a long battle, one NSG commando Havaldar Gajender Singh Bisht and both perpetrators were killed. Rabbi Gavriel Holtzberg and his wife Rivka Holtzberg, who was six months pregnant, were murdered with four other hostages inside the house by the attackers.

According to radio transmissions picked up by Indian intelligence, the attackers "would be told by their handlers in Pakistan that the lives of Jews were worth 50 times those of non-Jews." Injuries on some of the bodies indicated that they may have been tortured.

NSG raid

During the attacks, both hotels were surrounded by Rapid Action Force personnel and Marine Commandos (MARCOS) and National Security Guards (NSG) commandos. When reports emerged that attackers were receiving television broadcasts, feeds to the hotels were blocked. Security forces stormed both hotels, and all nine attackers were killed by the morning of 29 November. Major Sandeep Unnikrishnan of the NSG was killed during the rescue of Commando Sunil Yadav, who was hit in the leg by a bullet during the rescue operations at Taj. 32 hostages were killed at the Oberoi Trident.

NSG commandos then took on the Nariman house, and a Naval helicopter took an aerial survey. During the first day, 9 hostages were rescued from the first floor. The following day, the house was stormed by NSG commandos fast-roping from helicopters onto the roof, covered by snipers positioned in nearby buildings. NSG Commando Havaldar Gajender Singh Bisht, who was part of the team that fast-roped onto Nariman House, died after a long battle in which both perpetrors were also killed. Rabbi Gavriel Holtzberg and his wife Rivka Holtzberg, who was six months pregnant, were murdered with four other hostages inside the house by the attackers. By the morning of 27 November, the NSG had secured the Jewish outreach center at Nariman House as well as the Oberoi Trident hotel. They also incorrectly believed that the Taj Mahal Palace and Towers had been cleared of attackers, and soldiers were leading hostages and holed-up guests to safety, and removing bodies of those killed in the attacks. However, later news reports indicated that there were still two or three attackers in the Taj, with explosions heard and gunfire exchanged. Fires were also reported at the ground floor of the Taj with plumes of smoke arising from the first floor. The final operation at the Taj Mahal Palace hotel was completed by the NSG commandos at 08:00 on 29 November, killing three attackers and resulting in the conclusion of the attacks. TheNSG rescued 250 people from the Oberoi, 300 from the Taj and 60 people (members of 12 different families) from Nariman House. In addition, police seized a boat filled with arms and explosives anchored at Mazgaon dock off Mumbai harbour.

ATTRIBUTION

The Mumbai attacks were planned and directed by Lashkar-e-Taiba militants inside Pakistan, and carried out by ten young armed men trained and sent to Mumbai and directed from inside Pakistan via mobile phones and VoIP.

In July 2009 Pakistani authorities confirmed that LeT plotted and financed the attacks from LeT camps in Karachi and Thatta. In November 2009, Pakistani authorities charged seven men they had arrested earlier, of planning and executing the assault.

Mumbai police originally identified 37 suspects—including two army officers—for their alleged involvement in the plot. All but two of the suspects, many of whom are identified only through aliases, are Pakistani. Two more suspects arrested in the United States in October 2009 for other attacks were also found to have been involved in planning the Mumbai attacks. One of these men, Pakistani American David Headley, was found to have made several trips to India before the attacks and gathered video and GPS information on behalf of the plotters.

In April 2011, the United States issued arrest warrants for four Pakistani men as suspects in the attack. The men, Sajid Mir, Abu Qahafa, Mazhar Iqbal alias "Major Iqbal", are believed to be members of Lashkar-e-Taiba and helped plan and train the attackers.

Negotiations with Pakistan

Pakistan initially denied that Pakistanis were responsible for the attacks, blaming plotters in Bangladesh and Indian criminals, a claim refuted by India, and saying they needed information from India on other bombings first.

Pakistani authorities finally agreed that Ajmal Kasab was a Pakistani on 7 January 2009, and registered a case against three other Pakistani nationals.

The Indian government supplied evidence to Pakistan and other governments, in the form of interrogations, weapons, and call records of conversations during the attacks. In addition, Indian government officials said that the attacks were so sophisticated that they must have had official backing from Pakistani "agencies", an accusation denied by Pakistan. Under US and UN pressure,

Pakistan arrested a few members of Jamaat ud-Dawa and briefly put its founder under house arrest, but he was found to be free a few days later. A year after the attacks, Mumbai police continued to complain that Pakistani authorities were not cooperating by providing information for their investigation. Meanwhile, journalists in Pakistan said security agencies were preventing them from interviewing people from Kasab's village. Home Minister P. Chidambaram said the Pakistani authorities had not shared any information about American suspects Headley and Rana, but that the FBI had been more forthcoming.

An Indian report, summarising intelligence gained from India's interrogation of David Headley, was released in October 2010. It alleged that Pakistan's intelligence agency (ISI) had provided support for the attacks by providing funding for reconnaissance missions in Mumbai. The report included Headley's claim that Lashkar-e-Taiba's chief military commander, Zaki-ur-Rahman Lakhvi, had close ties to the ISI. He alleged that "every big action of LeT is done in close coordination with [the] ISI."

Investigation

According to investigations, the attackers travelled by sea from Karachi, Pakistan, across theArabian Sea, hijacked the Indian fishing trawler 'Kuber', killed the crew of four, then forced the captain to sail to Mumbai. After murdering the captain, the attackers entered Mumbai on arubber dinghy. The captain of 'Kuber', Amar Singh Solanki, had earlier been imprisoned for six months in a Pakistani jail for illegally fishing in Pakistani waters. The attackers stayed and were trained by the Lashkar-e-Taiba in a safehouse at Azizabad near Karachi before boarding a small boat for Mumbai.

David Headley was a member of Lashkar-e-Taiba, and between 2002 and 2009 Headley travelled extensively as part of his work for LeT. Headley received training in small arms and countersurveillance from LeT, built a network of connections for the group, and was chief scout in scoping out targets for Mumbai attack having allegedly been given $25,000 in cash in 2006 by an ISI officer known as Major Iqbal, The officer also helped him arrange a communications system for the attack, and oversaw a model of the Taj Mahal Hotel so that gunmen could know their way inside the target, according to Headley's testimony to Indian authorities. Headley also helped ISI recruit Indian agents to monitor Indian troop levels and movements, according to a US official. At the same time, Headley was also an informant for the U.S. Drug Enforcement Administration, and Headley's wives warned American officials of Headley's involvement with LeT and his plotting attacks, warning specifically that the Taj Mahal Hotel may be their target.

US officials believed that the Inter-Services Intelligence (I.S.I.) officers provided support to Lashkar-e-Taiba militants who carried out the attacks.

The arrest of Zabiuddin Ansari alias Abu Hamza in June 2012 provided further clarity on how the plot was hatched. According to Abu Hamza, the attacks were previously scheduled for 2006, using Indian youth for the job. However, a huge cache of AK-47's and RDX, which were to be used for the attacks, was recovered from Aurangabad in 2006, thus leading to the dismantling of the original plot. Subsequently, Abu Hamza fled to Pakistan and along with Lashkar commanders, scouted for Pakistani youth to be used for the attacks. In September 2007, ten people were selected for the mission. In September 2008, these people tried sailing to Mumbai from Karachi, but couldn't complete their mission due to choppy waters. These men made a second attempt in November 2008, and successfully managed to execute the final attacks. David Headley's disclosures, that three Pakistani army officers were associated with the planning and execution of the attack were substantiated by Ansari's revelations during his interrogation. After Ansari's arrest, Pakistan's Foreign Office claimed they had received information that up to 40 Indian nationals were involved in the attacks.

Method

The attackers had planned the attack several months ahead of time and knew some areas well enough to vanish and reappear after security forces had left. Several sources have quoted Kasab telling the police that the group received help from Mumbai residents. The attackers used at least three SIM cards purchased on the Indian side of the border with Bangladesh. There were also reports of a SIM card purchased in the US state New Jersey. Police had also mentioned that Faheem Ansari, an Indian Lashkar operative who had been arrested in February 2008, had scouted the Mumbai targets for the November attacks. Later, the police arrested two Indian suspects, Mikhtar Ahmad, who is from Srinagar in Kashmir, and Tausif Rehman, a resident of Kolkata. They supplied the SIM cards, one in Calcutta, and the other in New Delhi.

Type 86 Grenades made by China's state-owned Norinco were used in the attacks.

Blood tests on the attackers indicate that they had taken cocaine and LSD during the attacks, to sustain their energy and stay awake for 50 hours. Police say that they found syringes on the scenes of the attacks. There were also indications that they had been taking steroids. The gunman who survived said that the attackers had used Google Earth to familiarise themselves with the locations of buildings used in the attacks.

There were ten gunmen, nine of whom were subsequently shot dead and one captured by security forces. Witnesses reported that they seemed to be in their early twenties, wore black T-shirts and jeans, and that they smiled and looked happy as they shot their victims.

It was initially reported that some of the attackers were British citizens, but the Indian government later stated that there was no evidence to confirm this. Similarly, early reports of twelve gunmen were also later shown to be incorrect.

On 9 December, the ten attackers were identified by Mumbai police, along with their home towns in Pakistan: Ajmal Amir from Faridkot,Abu Ismail Dera Ismail Khan from Dera Ismail Khan, Hafiz Arshad and Babr Imran from Multan, Javed from Okara, Shoaib from Narowal, Nazih and Nasr from Faisalabad, Abdul Rahman from Arifwalla, and Fahad Ullah from Dipalpur Taluka. Dera Ismail Khan is in the North-West Frontier Province; the rest of the towns are in Pakistani Punjab.

On 6 April 2010, the Home Minister of Maharashtra State, which includes Mumbai, informed the Assembly that the bodies of the nine killed Pakistani gunmen from the 2008 attack on Mumbai were buried in a secret location in January 2010. The bodies had been in the mortuary of a Mumbai hospital after Muslim clerics in the city refused to let them be buried on their grounds.

Attackers

Only one of the 10 attackers, Ajmal Kasab, survived the attack. He was hanged in Yerwada jail. Killed during the onslaught were:

1. Abdul Rehman
2. Abdul Rahman Chhota
3. Abu Ali
4. Fahad Ullah
5. Ismail Khan
6. Babar Imran
7. Abu Umar
8. Abu Sohrab
9. Shoaib alias Soheb.

Arrests

Ajmal Kasab was the only attacker arrested alive by police. Much of the information about the attackers' preparation, travel, and movements comes from his confessions to the Mumbai police.

On 12 February 2009 Pakistan's Interior Minister Rehman Malik said that Pakistani national Javed Iqbal, who acquired VoIP phones in Spain for the Mumbai attackers, and Hamad Ameen Sadiq, who had facilitated money transfer for the attack, had been arrested. Two other men known as Khan and Riaz, but whose full names were not given, were also arrested. Two Pakistanis were arrested in Brescia, Italy (East of Milan), on 21 November 2009, after being accused of providing logistical support to the attacks and transferring over US$200 to internet accounts using a false ID. They had Red Corner Notices issued against them by Interpol for their suspected involvement and it was issued after the last year's strikes.

In October 2009, two Chicago men were arrested and charged by the FBI for involvement in "terrorism" abroad, David Coleman Headley andTahawwur Hussain Rana. Headley, a Pakistani-American, was charged in November 2009 with scouting locations for the 2008 Mumbai attacks. Headley is reported to have posed as an American Jew and is believed to have links with militant Islamist groups based in Bangladesh. On 18 March 2010, Headley pled guilty to a dozen charges against him thereby avoiding going to trial.

In December 2009, the FBI charged Abdur Rehman Hashim Syed, a retired major in the Pakistani army, for planning the attacks in association with Headley.

On 15 January 2010, in a successful snatch operation R&AW agents nabbed Sheikh Abdul Khwaja, one of the handlers of the 26/11 attacks, chief of HuJI India operations and a most wanted suspect in India, from Colombo, Sri Lanka, and brought him over to Hyderabad, India for formal arrest.

On 25 June 2012, the Delhi Police arrested Zabiuddin Ansari alias Abu Hamza, one of the key suspects in the attack at the Indira Gandhi International Airport in New Delhi. His arrest was touted as the most significant development in the case since Kasab's arrest. Security agencies had been chasing him for three years in Delhi. Ansari is a Lashker-e-Taiba ultra and the Hindi tutor of the 10 attackers who were responsible for the Mumbai attacks in 2008. He was apprehended, after he was arrested and deported to India by Saudi Intelligence officials as per official request by Indian authorities. After Ansari's arrest, investigations revealed that in 2009 he allegedly stayed for a day in a room in Old Legislators's Hostel, belonging to Fauzia Khan, a former MLA and minister in Maharashtra Government. The minister, however, denied having any links with him. Home Minister P. Chidambaram, asserted that Ansari was provided a safe place in Pakistan and was present in the control room, which could not have been established without active State support. Ansari's interrogation further revealed that Sajid Mir and a Pakistani Army major visited India under fake names as cricket spectators to survey targets in Delhi and Mumbai for about a fortnight.

5

Lashkar-e-Taiba

Lashkar-e-Taiba also transliterated as Lashkar-i-Tayyaba, Lashkar-e-Tayyaba, Lashkar-e-Tayyiba, Lashkar-i-Taiba, Lashkar Taiba or LeT – is one of the largest and most active terrorist organizations in South Asia, operating mainly from Pakistan.

It was founded in 1990 by Hafez Saeed, Abdullah Azzam and Zafar Iqbal in Afghanistan. With its headquarters based in Muridke, near Lahore in Punjab province of Pakistan, the group operates several training camps in Pakistan-administered Kashmir.

Lashkar-e-Taiba has been accused by India of attacking military and civilian targets in India, most notably the 2001 Indian Parliament attack and the 2008 Mumbai attacks. Its stated objective is to introduce an Islamic state in South Asia and to "liberate" Muslims residing in Indian Kashmir. The organization is banned as a terrorist organization by India, Pakistan, the United States, the United Kingdom, the European Union, Russia and Australia. Some experts such as former French investigating magistrate Jean-Louis Bruguière and New America Foundation president Steve Coll believe that Pakistan's main intelligence agency, the Inter-Services Intelligence (ISI), continues to give LeT intelligence help and protection.

While the primary area of operations of LeT's militant activities is the Kashmir Valley, their professed goal is not limited to challenging India's sovereignty over Jammu and Kashmir.

LeT sees the issue of Kashmir as part of a wider global struggle. The group has repeatedly claimed through its journals and web sites that its main aim is to destroy the Indian republic and to annihilate Hinduism and Judaism. LeT has declared Hindus and Jews to be the "enemies of Islam", as well as India and Israel to be the "enemies of Pakistan". In a pamphlet entitled "Why Are We Waging Jihad?" the group defined its agenda as the restoration of Islamic rule over all parts of India and declared India, Israel and the United States as existential enemies of Islam. The LeT believes that violent jihad is the duty of all Muslims and must be waged until eight objectives are met: ending persecution against Muslims, establishing Islam as the dominant way of life in the world, forcing infidels to pay jizya, fighting for the weak and feeble against oppressors, exacting revenge for killed Muslims, punishing enemies for violating oaths and treaties, defending all Muslim states, and recapturing occupied Muslim territory.

In the wake of the November 2008 Mumbai attacks, investigations of computer and e-mail accounts revealed a list of 320 locations worldwide deemed as possible targets for attack. 20 of the targets were locations within India. Analysts believed that the list was a statement of intent rather than a list of locations where LeT cells had been established and were ready to strike.

In January 2009, LeT publicly declared that it would pursue a peaceful resolution in the Kashmir issue and that it did not have global jihadist aims, but the group is still believed to be active in several other spheres of anti-Indian terrorism. The disclosures of Abu Jundal, who was extradited to India by the Saudi Arabian government, however, revealed that LeT is planning to revive militancy in Jammu and Kashmir and conduct major terror strikes in India.

Goals

Saeed has stated that Kashmir is the "gateway to capture India" and that LeT would begin to push for independence of majority-Muslim areas in India such as Gujurat and Hyderabad (Andhra Pradesh). Further, some claim that LeT aims not only to eject India from Kashmir, but also seeks to re-establish Islamic rule over the entire Indian Union. However, others disagree and assert that despite the fact that LeT has advocated extending its "Jihad" from IHK to the rest of India, its goal is to establish two independent homelands for Muslims in southern and northern India.

Nonetheless, LeT has forged relationships with militant movements (though the strength of these ties is the source of much debate) in Afghanistan, Bosnia, the Palestinian territories, and Kashmir in order to pool resources, share experience, and to improve the effectiveness of their operations. However, these partnerships are a reflection of shared tactical interests rather than a by-product of a larger strategic alignment. Although its infrastructure spans the globe, LeT prioritizes the South Asian theater regarding its operations and propaganda efforts. Much of this cooperation is simply information exchange and the sharing of best practices and tactics. Affiliation with iconic struggles such as the Palestinian issue also helps to boost legitimacy amongst potential as well as current donors and aids recruitment efforts within Pakistan.

Many analysts point to the joint attack by LeT and Jaish-e-Mohammed (JeM) on the Indian Parliament in December 2001 that brought India and Pakistan to the brink of war as proof positive that there were not massive differences between the Kashmir-centered terrorist groups in terms of their strategic thinking and use of tactics, and that many of the differentiations between the groups were artificial. However, such analyses fail to realize that LeT does not view itself as one among equals but rather as the premier terrorist group in South Asia. Though it recognizes and likely respects the capabilities of JeM and others, the joint attack on Parliament was the result of a desire by LeT (and possibly JeM) to share risk in what was likely somewhat of an experiment in the use of *fidayeen* attacks in a major urban environment and possibly a precursor for the November 2008 Mumbai attacks. Unlike suicide bombing, even though the death of a *fidayeen* attacker is likely, it is not guaranteed and interrogations of too many LeT cadre could severely damage the group's operational security and its networks in India. The lesson to take away from this episode is that while LeT will partner with like-minded groups to obtain short-term benefits and to enhance its organizational learning, LeT still charts its own path and views such partnerships as a component of its strategy to become the most effective terrorist organization in the Subcontinent.

Although there is considerable disagreement regarding LeT's motives aside from ridding Kashmir of Indian rule, two statements from Saeed in 1996 and 1997 provide substantial insight. Speaking to journalists, Saeed said:

The Jihad in Kashmir would soon spread to entire India. Our Mujahideen would create three Pakistans in India.

We feel that Kashmir should be liberated at the earliest. Thereafter, Indian Muslims should be aroused to rise in revolt against the Indian Union so that India gets disintegrated.

These direct quotes clearly illustrate that even though LeT's initial focus was on Kashmir, the organization has developed a more radical regional agenda and is willing to use the Kashmir conflict as a beacon to carry out attacks throughout India. Further, evidence suggests that LeT seeks to establish an Islamic Caliphate of all Muslim-majority states surrounding Pakistan, is believed to have become involved in Chechnya and other parts of Central Asia, and has trained other Pan-Islamist militant groups such as JI in Pakistan-held Kashmir and Afghanistan.

In addition to India, Saeed considers Israel and the United States as LeT's primary enemies. The controversial B. Raman even alleges that on behalf of the bin Laden-founded International Islamic Front for Jihad Against the Crusaders and the Jewish People (IIF), LeT issued a *fatwa* claiming that it was the duty of all Muslims to kill the Pope.

It is also noteworthy that LeT has links to al-Qaeda, as was demonstrated by the March 2002 arrest of senior al-Qaeda lieutenant Abu Zubaydah in a LeT safe house in Faisalabad, Pakistan. This arrest gave rise to the belief that LeT assists in the movements of al-Qaeda fighters within Pakistan. All of this demonstrates that Pakistan's initial belief that it could use proxies to wage an asymmetric conflict with limited objectives against an adversary (India) was clearly misguided.

More than 2 decades later, as opposed to remaining deeply committed to Pakistan and even more obedient to its limited objectives, as Islamabad undoubtedly intended, LeT now threatens Pakistan's own security with its activities throughout South Asia and runs counter to Pakistan's own declared policies thus jeopardizing its already-tenuous relationship with India as well as the United States, United Kingdom (UK), other Western powers, and even its long-time ally, China. In regards to the latter, Beijing interprets the rising unrest in its Muslim-majority Xinjiang province as a result of happenings in South and Central Asia.

LeT's recent involvement in the November 2008 attacks in Mumbai possibly represents a considerable shift in the organization's strategic thought. Although some of the gunmen were undoubtedly Pakistani, sustained attacks on such symbolic targets could not have occurred without Indian assets. Further, although the majority of victims were Indians, the militants also deliberately targeted foreigners, namely British and American citizens as well as Israelis.

These practices are new to LeT and suggest an increasing ideological overlap with more prominent transnational terrorist groups such as al-Qeda.

The timing of the attacks also cannot be ignored as they occurred during the first sustained Pakistani offensive against al-Qaeda and both the Afghan and Pakistani Taliban in the tribal areas. It can be reasonably argued that the primary intention of this attack was to reignite hostilities between India and Pakistan, thus forcing Pakistan to redeploy a large portion of its troops from the tribal areas to its eastern border with India. As such, the possibility of tactical cooperation between LeT and other regional antagonists, such as Afghan/Pakistani Taliban as well as al-Qaeda, cannot be ruled out.

Leadership

- Hafiz Muhammad Saeed – Living in Pakistan – Founder of Lashkar-e-Taiba and *aamir* of its political arm, Jamaat-ud-Dawa (JuD). Shortly after the November 2008 Mumbai attacks Saeed denied any links between the two groups: "No Lashkar-e-Taiba man is in Jamaat-ud-Dawa and I have never been a chief of Lashkar-e-Taiba." On 25 June 2014, United States of America declared Jamaat-ud-Dawa an affiliate of Lashkar-e-Taiba.
- Abdul Rehman Makki– Living in Pakistan – second in command of Lashkar-e-Taiba. He is the brother in law of Hafiz Muhammad Saeed. US has announced a reward of $2 million for information leading to the location of Makki.

- Zaki-ur-Rehman Lakhvi – In custody of Pakistan military – Senior member of LeT. Named as being one of the masterminds of the Mumbai attack.
- Yusuf Muzammil – Senior member of LeT. Named as a mastermind of the November 2008 Mumbai attacks by surviving gunman Ajmal Kasab.
- Zarrar Shah – in Pakistani custody – one of Lashkar-e-Taiba's primary liaisons to the ISI. An American official said that he was a "central character" in the planning behind the Mumbai attacks in 2008. Zarrar Shah has boasted to Pakistani investigators about his role in the attacks.
- Muhammad Ashraf – LeT's top financial officer. Although not directly connected to the 2008 Mumbai plot, he was added to the U.N. list of people that sponsor terrorism after the attacks. However, Geo TV reported that six years earlier Ashraf became seriously ill while in custody and died at Civil Hospital on 11 June 2002.
- Mahmoud Mohamed Ahmed Bahaziq – The leader of LeT in Saudi Arabia and one of its financiers. Although not directly connected to the Mumbai plot, the U.N. added him to its list of individuals that sponsor terrorism after the 2008 Mumbai attacks.
- Nasr Javed – A Kashmiri senior operative, is on the list of individuals banned from entering the United Kingdom for "engaging in unacceptable behaviour by seeking to foment, justify or glorify terrorist violence in furtherance of particular beliefs."

History

Formation

In 1985, Hafiz Mohammed Saeed and Zafar Iqbal formed the *Jamaat-ud-Dawa* (Organization for Preaching, or JuD) as a small missionary group dedicated to promoting an Ahl-e-Hadith version of Islam. In the next year, Zaki-ur Rehman Lakvi merged his group of anti-Soviet jihadists with the JuD to form the *Markaz-ud Dawa-wal-Irshad* (Center for Preaching and Guidance, or MDI). The MDI had 17 founders originally, and notable among them was Abdullah

Azzam. The LeT was formed in Afghanistan's Kunar province in 1990 and gained prominence in the early 1990s as a military offshoot of MDI. MDI's primary concerns were dawah and the LeT focused on jihad although the members did not distinguish between the two groups' functions. According to Hafiz Saeed, "Islam propounds both dawa and jihad. Both are equally important and inseparable. Since our life revolves around Islam, therefore both dawa and jihad are essential; we cannot prefer one over the other."

Most of these training camps were located in North-West Frontier Province (NWFP) and many were shifted to Azad Kashmir for the sole purpose of training volunteers for the Kashmir Jihad. From 1991 onwards, militancy surged in Indian Kashmir, as many Lashkar-e-Taiba volunteers were infiltrated into Indian Kashmir from Azad Kashmir with the help of the Pakistan Army and ISI. As of 2010, the degree of control that Pakistani intelligence retains over LeT's operations is not known.

Designation as terrorist group

Lashkar-e-Taiba had links to Jama'at-ud-Da'wah, however Jama'at-ud-Da'wah publicly retracted any association with them after the United States Department of State declared Lashkar-e-Taiba to be a terrorist organization.

- On 28 March 2001, in Statutory Instrument 2001 No. 1261, British Home Secretary Jack Straw designated the group a Proscribed Terrorist Organization under the Terrorism Act 2000.
- On 5 December 2001, the group was added to the Terrorist Exclusion List. In a notification dated 26 December 2001, United States Secretary of State Colin Powell, designated Lashkar-e-Taiba a Foreign Terrorist Organisation.
- Lashkar-e-Taiba was banned in Pakistan on 12 January 2002.
- It is banned in India as a designated terrorist group under the Unlawful Activities (Prevention) Act.
- It was listed as a terrorist organisation in Australia under the Security Legislation Amendment (Terrorism) Act 2002 on 11 April 2003 and was re-listed 11 April 2005 and 31 March 2007.

- On 2 May 2008 it was placed on the Consolidated List established and maintained by the Committee established by the United Nations Security Council Resolution 1267 as an entity associated with al-Qaeda. The report also proscribed Jamaat-ud-Dawa as a front group of the LeT. Bruce Riedel, an expert on terrorism, believes that LeT with the support of its Pakistani backers is more dangerous than al-Qaeda.

Aftermath of Mumbai attacks

According to a media report, the U.S. accused JuD of being the front group for the prime suspects of the November 2008 Mumbai attacks, the Lashkar-e-Taiba, the organization that trained the 10 gunmen involved in these attacks.

On 7 December 2008, under pressure from USA and India, Pakistani army launched an operation against LeT and raided a *markaz* (centre) of the LeT at Shawai Nullah, 5 km from Muzaffarabad in Pakistan-controlled Azad Kashmir. The army arrested more than twenty members of the Lashkar-e-Taiba and Zaki-ur-Rehman Lakhvi, the alleged mastermind of the November 2008 Mumbai attacks. They are said to have sealed off the centre, which included a madrasah and a mosque alongside offices of the LeT according to the government of Pakistan.

On 10 December 2008 India formally requested the United Nations Security Council to designate JuD as a terrorist organization. Subsequently, Pakistan's ambassador to the United Nations Abdullah Hussain gave an undertaking, saying,

- After the designation of Jamaat-ud-Dawah (JUD) under (resolution) 1267, the government on receiving communication from the Security Council shall proscribe the JUD and take other consequential actions, as required, including the freezing of assets.

A similar assurance was given by Pakistan in 2002 when it clamped down on the LeT; however, the LeT was covertly allowed to function under the guide of the JuD. While arrests have been made, the Pakistani Government has categorically refused to allow any foreign investigators access to Hafiz Saeed.

On 11 December 2008 the United Nations Security Council imposed sanctions on JuD, declaring it a global terrorist group. Hafiz Muhammad Saeed, the chief of JuD declared that his group will challenge the sanctions imposed on it in all forums. Pakistan's government also banned the JuD on the same day and issued an order to seal the JuD in all four provinces, as well as Pakistan-controlled Kashmir. Before the ban JuD ran a weekly newspaper named *Ghazwah,* two monthly magazines called *Majalla Tud Dawaa* and *Zarb e Taiba,* and a fortnightly magazine for children, *Nanhe Mujahid.* The publications have since been banned by the Pakistani government. In addition to the prohibition of JuD's print publications, the organisation's web sites were also shut down by the Pakistani government.

After the ban imposed by UNSC, Hindu minority groups in Pakistan came out in support of JuD. At protest marches in Hyderabad, Hindu groups said that JuD does charity work such as setting up water wells in desert regions and providing food to the poor. However, the credibility of the level of support during the protest is questionable.

Several protesters claim to have been under the impression they were protesting price rises. The BBC reported that protesters on their way to what they believed was a rally against price rises were handed signs in support of JuD. The organizations' banning has been met with heavy criticism in many Pakistani circles, as JuD was the first to react to the Kashmir earthquake and the Ziarat Earthquake. It also ran over 160 schools with thousands of students and provided aid in hospitals as well.

In January 2009 the JuD spokesperson, Abdullah Muntazir, stressed that the group did not have global jihadist aspirations and would welcome a peaceful resolution of the Kashmir issue. He also publicly disowned LeT commanders Zaki-ur-Rehman Lakhvi and Zarrar Shah, who have both been accused of being the masterminds behind the November 2008 Mumbai attacks.

In response to the UN resolution and the government ban, the JuD reorganized itself under the name of Tehreek-e-Tahafuz Qibla Awal (TTQA).

On 25 June 2014, United States added several of LeT affiliates including Jamaat-ud-Dawa, Al-Anfal Trust, Tehrik-e-Hurmat-e-

Rasool, and Tehrik-e-Tahafuz Qibla Awwal to the list of foreign terrorist organisations.

Activities

The group conducts training camps and humanitarian work. Across Pakistan, the organization runs 16 Islamic institutions, 135 secondary schools, an ambulance service, mobile clinics, blood banks and seminaries according to the South Asia Terrorism Portal. The group actively carried out attacks on Indian Armed Forces in Kashmir and Jammu. Some breakaway Lashkar members have been accused of carrying out attacks in Pakistan, particularly in Karachi, to mark its opposition to the policies of former president Pervez Musharraf.

Training camps

The Lashkar-e-Taiba training camps are presently located at a number of locations in Pakistan. These camps, which include its base camp, Markaz-e-Taiba in Muridke near Lahore and the one near Manshera, are used to impart training to militants.

In these camps, the following trainings are imparted:

- The 21-day sectarian religious course (*Daura-e-Sufa*)
- The 21-day basic combat course (*Daura-e-Aam*)
- The three-months advanced combat course (*Daura-e-Khaas*)

26/11 mastermind, Zabiuddin Ansari alias, Abu Jundal arrested recently by Indian intelligence agencies is reported to have disclosed that paragliding training was also included in the training curriculum of LeT cadres at is camps in Muzaffarabad. These camps have long been tolerated by the Pakistan's powerful Inter-Services Intelligence (ISI) agency because of their usefulness against India and in Afghanistan although they have been instructed not to mount any operations for now.

A French anti-terrorism expert, Jean-Louis Bruguière, in his *Some Things that I Wasn't Able to Say* has stated that the regular Pakistani army officers trained the militants in the LeT training camps until recently. He reached this conclusion after interrogating a French militant, Willy Brigitte, who had been trained by the LeT and arrested in Australia in 2003.

Markaz-e-Taiba

The LeT base camp Markaz-e-Taiba is in Nangal Saday, about 5 km North of Muridke, on East side of G.T. road; about 30 km from Lahore, was established in 1988. It is spread over 200 acres (0.81 km) of land and contains a madrassa, hospital, market, residences, a fish farm and agricultural tracts. The initial sectarian religious training, *Daura-e-Sufa* is imparted here to the militants.

Other training camps

In 1987, LeT established two training camps in Afghanistan. The first one was the Muaskar-e-Taiba at Jaji in Paktia Province and the second one was the Muaskar-e-Aqsa in Kunar Province. American intelligence analysts justify the extrajudicial detention of at least one Guantanamo detainees because they allege he attended a Lashkar-e-Taiba training camp in Afghanistan. A memorandum summarizing the factors for and against the continued detention of Bader Al Bakri Al Samiri asserts that he attended a Lashkar-e-Taiba training camp.

Mariam Abou Zahab and Olivier Roy in their *Islamist Networks: The Afghan-Pakistan Connection* mentioned about three training camps in Pakistan-administered Kashmir, the principal one is the Umm-al-Qura training camp at Muzaffarabad. Every month five hundred militants are trained in these camps. Muhammad Amir Rana in his *A to Z of Jehadi Organizations in Pakistan* listed five training camps. Four of them, the Muaskar-e-Taiba, the Muaskar-e-Aqsa, the Muaskar Umm-al-Qura and the Muaskar Abdullah bin Masood are in Pakistan-administered Kashmir and the Markaz Mohammed bin Qasim training camp is in Sanghar District of Sindh. Ten thousand militants had been trained in these camps till 2004.

Funding

Pakistan began to fund the LeT during the early 1990s and by around 1995 the funding had grown considerably. During this time the army and the ISI helped establish the LeT's military structure with the specific intent to use the militant group against India. The LeT also obtained funds through efforts of the MDI's Department of Finance.

Until 2002 the group collected funds through public fundraising events usually using charity boxes in shops and mosques. The group also received money through donations at MDI offices, through personal donations collected at public celebrations of an operative's martyrdom, and through its web site. The outfit also collected donations from the Pakistani immigrant community in the Persian Gulf and United Kingdom, Islamic Non-Governmental Organisations, and Pakistani and Kashmiri businessmen. Lashkar-e-Taiba operatives have also been apprehended in India, where they had been obtaining funds from sections of the Muslim Community.

Although many of the funds collected went towards legitimate uses, *e.g.* factories and other businesses, a significant portion was dedicated to military activities. According to U.S. intelligence, the LeT had a military budget of more than $5 million by 2009.

Use of charity aid to fund operations

LeT assisted victims after the 2005 Kashmir earthquake. In many instances, they were the first on the scene, arriving before the army or other civilians.

A large amount of funds collected among the Pakistani expatriate community in Britain to aid victims of the earthquake were funneled for the activities of Lashkar-e-Taiba although the donors were unaware. About £5 million were collected, but more than half of the funds were directed towards LeT rather than towards relief efforts. Intelligence officials stated that some of the funds were used to prepare for an attack that would have detonated explosives on board transatlantic airflights. Other investigations also indicated the aid given for earthquake victims was directly involved to expand Lashkar-e-Taiba's activities within India.

Use of teenagers

On 2 August 2012 Lashkar-e-Taiba hired two teenage boys aged 12 and 13 years to lob grenades at a police post in Sopore town in return of ₹1000 (US$17). The two children were caught on the CC camera pushing a handcart. They took cover while throwing the grenade and then melted away into a narrow lane. This was reported as the first incidence of Lashkar-e-Taiba using poor children from weaker section of the society for terror acts.

Notable incidents

- *1998 Wandhama massacre:* 23 Kashmiri pandits were murdered on 25 January 1998.
- In March 2000, Lashkar-e-Taiba militants are claimed to have been involved in the Chittisinghpura massacre, where 35 Sikhs in the town of Chittisinghpura in Kashmir were killed. An 18-year-old male, who was arrested in December of that year, admitted in an interview with a *New York Times* correspondent to the involvement of the group and expressed no regret in perpetrating the anti-Sikh massacre. In a separate interview with the same correspondent, Hafiz Muhammad Saeed denied knowing the young man and dismissed any possible involvement of LeT. In 2010, the Lashkar-e-Taiba (LeT) associate David Headley, who was arrested in connection with the 2008 Mumbai attacks, reportedly confessed to the National Investigation Agency that the LeT carried out the Chittisinghpura massacre. He is said to have identified an LeT militant named Muzzamil as part of the group which carried out the killings apparently to create communal tension just before Clinton's visit.
- The LeT was also held responsible by the government for the 2000 terrorist attack on Red Fort, New Delhi. LeT confirmed its participation in the Red Fort attack.
- LeT claimed responsibility for an attack on the Srinagar Airport that left five Indians and six militants dead.
- The group claimed responsibility for an attack on Indian security forces along the border.
- The Indian government blamed LeT, in coordination with Jaish-e-Mohammed, for a 13 December 2001 assault on parliament in Delhi.
- 2002 Kaluchak massacre 31 killed 14 May 2002. Australian government attributed this massacre to Lashkar-e-Taiba when it designated it as a terrorist organization.
- 2003 Nadimarg Massacre 24 Kashmiri pandits gunned down on the night of 23 March 2003.
- *2005 Delhi bombings:* During Diwali, Lashkar-e-Taiba

bombed crowded festive Delhi markets killing 60 civilians and maiming 527.

- *2006 Varanasi bombings:* Lashkar-e-Taiba was involved in serial blasts in Varanasi in the state of Uttar Pradesh. 37 people died and 89 were seriously injured.
- 2006 Doda massacre 34 Hindus were killed in Kashmir on 30 April 2006.
- *2006 Mumbai train bombings:* The investigation launched by Indian forces and US officials have pointed to the involvement of Lashkar-e-Taiba in Mumbai serial blasts on 11 July 2006. The Mumbai serial blasts on 11 July claimed 211 lives and maimed about 407 people and seriously injured another 768.
- On 12 September 2006 the propaganda arm of the Lashkar-e-Taiba issued a fatwa against Pope Benedict XVI demanding that Muslims assassinate him for his controversial statements about the prophet Muhammad.
- On 16 September 2006, a top Lashkar-e-Taiba militant, Abu Saad, was killed by the troops of 9-Rashtriya Rifles in Nandi Marg forest in Kulgam. Saad belongs to Lahore in Pakistan and also oversaw LeT operations for the past three years in Gul Gulabhgash as the outfit's area commander. Apart from a large quantity of arms and ammunition, high denomination Indian and Pakistani currencies were also recovered from the slain militant.
- 2008 Mumbai attacks In November 2008, Lashkar-e-Taiba was the primary suspect behind the Mumbai attacks but denied any part. The lone surviving gunman, Ajmal Amir Kasab, captured by Indian authorities admitted the attacks were planned and executed by the organization. United States intelligence sources confirmed that their evidence suggested Lashkar-e-Taiba is behind the attacks. A July 2009 report from Pakistani investigators confirmed that LeT was behind the attack.
- On 7 December 2008, under pressure from USA and India, the Pakistan Army launched an operation against LeT and Jamat-ud-Dawa to arrest people suspected of 26/11 Mumbai attacks.

- In August 2009, LeT issued an ultimatum to impose Islamic dress code in all colleges in Jammu and Kashmir, sparking fresh fears in the tense region.
- In September and October 2009, Israeli and Indian intelligence agencies issued alerts warning that LeT is planning to attack Jewish religious places in Pune, India and other locations visited by Western and Israeli tourists in India. The gunmen who attacked the Mumbai headquarters of the Chabad Lubavitch movement during the November 2008 attacks were reportedly instructed that "Every person you kill where you are is worth 50 of the ones killed elsewhere."
- News sources have reported that members of LeT were planning to attack the U.S. and Indian embassies in Dhaka, Bangladesh, on 26 November 2009, to coincide with the one-year anniversary of the November 2008 Mumbai attacks. At least seven men have been arrested in connection to the plot, including a senior member of LeT.
- Two Chicago residents, David Coleman Headley and Tahawwur Hussain Rana, were allegedly working with LeT in planning an attack against the offices and employees of Jyllands-Posten, a Danish newspaper that published controversial cartoons of the Prophet Muhammad. Indian news sources have also implicated the men in the November 2008 Mumbai attacks and in LeT's Fall 2009 plans to attack the U.S. and Indian embassies in Bangladesh.

6

Taliban

The Taliban, alternative spelling Taleban, is an Islamic fundamentalist political movement in Afghanistan. It spread throughout Afghanistan and formed a government, ruling as the Islamic Emirate of Afghanistan from September 1996 until December 2001, with Kandahar as the capital. However, it gained diplomatic recognition from only three states: Pakistan, Saudi Arabia, and the United Arab Emirates. Mohammed Omar has been serving as the spiritual leader of the Taliban since 1994.

While in power, it enforced its strict interpretation of Sharia law, and leading Muslims have been highly critical of the Taliban's interpretations of Islamic law. The Taliban were condemned internationally for their brutal treatment of women. The majority of the Taliban are made up of Afghan Pashtun tribesmen. The Taliban's leaders were influenced by Deobandi fundamentalism, and many also strictly follow the social and cultural norm called Pashtunwali.

From 1995 to 2001, the Pakistani Inter-Services Intelligence and military are widely alleged by the international community to have provided support to the Taliban. Their connections are possibly through Harkat-ul-Mujahideen, a terrorist group founded by Sami ul Haq. Pakistan is accused by many international officials of continuing to support the Taliban; Pakistan states that it dropped all support for the group after 9/11. Al-Qaeda also supported the Taliban with regiments of imported fighters from Arab countries and Central Asia. Saudi Arabia provided financial support. The Taliban and their allies committed massacres against Afghan civilians, denied UN food supplies to 160,000 starving civilians and conducted a policy of scorched earth, burning vast areas of fertile land and destroying tens of thousands of homes during their rule from 1996 to 2001. Hundreds of thousands of people were forced to flee to United Front-controlled territory, Pakistan, and Iran.

After the attacks of September 11, 2001, the Taliban were overthrown by the American-led invasion of Afghanistan. Later it regrouped as an insurgency movement to fight the American-backed Karzai administration and the NATO-led International Security Assistance Force (ISAF). The Taliban have been accused of using terrorism as a specific tactic to further their ideological and political goals. According to the United Nations, the Taliban and their allies were responsible for 75 per cent of Afghan civilian casualties in 2010, 80 per cent in 2011, and 80 per cent in 2012.

RISE OF THE TALIBAN

The Taliban was formed in the early 1990s by an Afghan faction of mujahideen, Islamic fighters who had resisted the Soviet occupation of Afghanistan (1979–89) with the covert backing of the U.S. Central Intelligence Agency and its Pakistani counterpart, the Inter-Services Intelligence directorate (ISI). They were joined by younger Pashtun tribesmen who studied in Pakistani madrassas, or seminaries; *taliban* is Pashto for "students." Pashtuns comprise a plurality in Afghanistan and are the predominant ethnic group in much of the country's south and east.

The movement attracted popular support in the initial post-Soviet era by promising to impose stability and rule of law after four years of conflict (1992–1996) among rival mujahideen groups. Talibs entered Kandahar in November 1994 to pacify the crime-ridden southern city, and by September 1996 seized the capital, Kabul, from President Burhanuddin Rabbani, an ethnic Tajik whom they viewed as anti-Pashtun and corrupt. The Taliban regime controlled some 90 percent of the country before its 2001 overthrow, analysts say.

The Taliban imposed its brand of justice as it consolidated territorial control. Taliban jurisprudence was drawn from the Pashtuns' pre-Islamic tribal code and interpretations of sharia colored by the austere Wahhabi doctrines of the madrassas' Saudi benefactors. The regime neglected social services and other basic state functions even as its Ministry for the Promotion of Virtue and Prevention of Vice enforced prohibitions on behavior the Taliban deemed un-Islamic, requiring women to wear the head-to-toe *burqa,* or *chadri;* banning music and television; and jailing men whose beards it deemed too short.

The regime was internationally isolated from its inception. Two UN Security Council resolutions passed in 1998 urged the Taliban to end its abusive treatment of women. The following year the council imposed sanctions on the regime for harboring al-Qaeda. Only Saudi Arabia, the United Arab Emirates, and Pakistan recognized the government. Many analysts say Islamabad supported the Taliban as a force that could unify and stabilize Afghanistan while staving off Indian, Iranian, and Russian influence.

LEADERSHIP AND SUPPORT

Mullah Omar, a cleric and veteran of the anti-Soviet resistance, led Taliban-ruled Afghanistan from 1996 to 2001 as *amir al-mu'minin,* or "commander of the faithful." He granted al-Qaeda sanctuary on the condition that it not antagonize the United States, but bin Laden reneged on their agreement in 1998 when he orchestrated bombings of U.S. embassies in East Africa. The episode was indicative of tensions that emerged between the two groups, analysts say. The Taliban was fundamentally parochial while al-Qaeda had its sights set on global jihad—yet after 9/11, Omar rejected U.S. demands that he give up bin Laden. Ethnic minority Tajiks, Uzbeks, and Hazaras in northern Afghanistan opposed to Taliban rule formed the Northern Alliance, which assisted U.S.-led forces in routing the Taliban after 9/11. Though the regime was dismantled during the occupation, Mullah Omar and many of his top aides escaped to the frontier territories of Pakistan, where they reconstituted the Taliban's central leadership.

Dubbed the "Quetta Shura" for the capital of Balochistan province, where they are believed to have taken refuge, they maintain a degree of operational authority over Afghan Taliban fighters, but appear "unwilling or unable to monopolize anti-state violence," a UN Security Council monitoring team foundin September 2013.

Many experts suspect the Pakistani security establishment continues to provide Taliban militants sanctuary in the country's western tribal areas in an effort to counter India's influence in Afghanistan. Islamabad dismisses these charges. (Tehrik-i-Taliban Pakistan, commonly known as the Pakistani Taliban, is an insurgent group distinct from its Afghan namesake; it coalesced in response to the Pakistani military's incursions into that country's tribal areas. The Afghan Taliban, by contrast, views Pakistan as a benefactor.)

The Taliban's post-2001 resurgence has partially been financed by narcotics production and trafficking, though Mullah Omar issued injunctions against opium production, and the Taliban eradicated much of the poppy crop during its rule. Insurgents and other strongmen extort *ushr*, an agricultural tithe, from farmers and levies at roadside checkpoints. Revenues from illicit mining also contribute to Taliban coffers, whichnet some $400 million a year, the UN estimated in 2012.

Public Opinion of the Taliban

More than a decade since its fall from power, the Taliban enjoys continued, if declining, support. The Asia Foundation found that in 2013, a third of Afghans—mostly Pashtuns and rural Afghans—had sympathy for armed opposition groups (AOGs), primarily the Taliban. Nearly two-thirds of Afghans, the survey found, believed that reconciliation between the government and AOGs would stabilize the country.

Afghan support for the Taliban and allied groups stems in part from grievances directed at public institutions. While the Asia Foundation survey found the Afghan National Army and Afghan National Police garner high public confidence, many civilians see government institutions such as the militia-like Afghan Local Police as predatory. Likewise, international forces' support for warlords and strongmen, an expedient in securing territory, likely also alienated many rural Afghans from Kabul, analysts say.

Many rural Afghans have come to trust the Taliban's extensive judicial network over government courts to "solve disputes in a fair war, without tribal or ethnic bias, or more commonly, without having to pay bribes," says Graeme Smith, a Kabul-based senior analyst at the International Crisis Group.

A Resilient Insurgency

As the Obama administration wound down the war in Iraq, it recommitted the United States to counterinsurgency operations against the Taliban and allied groups in Afghanistan, authorizing a surge that brought peak troop levels to about one hundred thousand in June 2011 and redoubled civilian efforts. Pakistani safe havens stymied U.S. counterinsurgency efforts, though the CIA's targeted-killing program there has sought, in part, to fulfill a "force protection" mission where the U.S. military cannot operate.

But as the Pentagon withdrew the surge troops in 2012, further drew down its military footprint in 2013, and handed lead security authority over to Afghan forces in June of that year, the Taliban-led insurgency escalated.

The United Nations Assistance Mission in Afghanistan (UNAMA) documented 8,615 civilian deaths and injuries in 2013, a 14 percent increase over the previous year and the highest toll since it began keeping these records in 2009. UNAMA attributed the vast majority of these casualties to insurgents who deliberately targeted civilians or used such indiscriminate tactics as improvised explosive devices; other civilians were caught in the crossfire between insurgents and government forces.

In some outlying districts, Afghan forces and local insurgents have reached informal ceasefires that effectively cede a degree of authority to the Taliban. The UN reported in 2014 that the Taliban maintained outright control of four districts, out of 373 nationwide, but the insurgency's reach extends much further: Afghan security forces judged in late 2013 that some 40 percent of districts had a "raised" or "high" threat level.

IDEOLOGY

The Taliban initially enjoyed goodwill from Afghans weary of the warlords' corruption, brutality, and incessant fighting. However, this popularity was not universal, particularly among non-Pashtuns. The Taliban's extremely strict and anti-modern ideology has been described as an "innovative form of *sharia* combining Pashtun tribal codes," or Pashtunwali, with radical Deobandi interpretations of Islam favored by JUI and its splinter groups. Also contributing to the mix was the jihadism and pan-Islamism of Osama bin Laden. Their ideology was a departure from the Islamism of the anti-Soviet mujahideen rulers they replaced who tended to be mystical Sufis, traditionalists, or radical Islamicists inspired by the Muslim Brotherhood (Ikhwan).

Under the Taliban regime, Sharia law was interpreted to forbid a wide variety of previously lawful activities in Afghanistan. One Taliban list of prohibitions included: pork, pig, pig oil, anything made from human hair, satellite dishes, cinematography, musical equipment, pool tables, chess, masks, alcohol, tapes, computers, VCRs, television, anything that propagates sex and is full of music, wine, lobster, nail polish, firecrackers, statues, sewing catalogs, pictures, Christmas cards. They also got rid of employment, education, sports for all women, dancing, clapping during sports events, kite flying, and characterizations of living things, including drawings, paintings, photographs, stuffed animals, and dolls. Men had to have a fist size beard at the bottom of their chin. Conversely, they had to wear their head hair short. They had to wear a head covering.

Many of these activities were hitherto lawful in Afghanistan. Critics complained that most Afghans followed a different, less strict, and less intrusive interpretation of Islam. The Taliban did not eschew all traditional popular practices. For example, they did not destroy the graves of Sufi pirs (holy men), and emphasized dreams as a means of revelation.

Taliban have been described as both anti-nationalist and Pushtun nationalist. According to journalist Ahmed Rashid, at least in the first years of their rule, they adopted Deobandi and Islamist anti-nationalist beliefs, and opposed "tribal and feudal structures," eliminating traditional tribal or feudal leaders from leadership roles. According to Ali A. Jalali and Lester Grau, the Taliban "received extensive support from Pashtuns across the country who thought that the movement might restore their national dominance. Even Pashtun intellectuals in the West, who differed with the Taliban on many issues, expressed support for the movement on purely ethnic grounds." Like *Wahhabi* and other Deobandis, the Taliban do not consider Shi@i to be Muslims. The Shia in Afghanistan consist mostly of the Hazara ethnic group which totaled almost 10 per cent of Afghanistan's population.

The Taliban were averse to debating doctrine with other Muslims. "The Taliban did not allow even Muslim reporters to question [their] edicts or to discuss interpretations of the Qur'an."

The Taliban mainly strictly enforced its ideologies in major cities like Herat, Kabul, and Kandahar. In rural areas the Taliban had little direct control, and the Taliban had promoted village jirgas, so it did not as stringently enforce its ideology in rural areas.

Bamyan Buddhas

In 1999, Mullah Omar issued a decree protecting the Buddha statues at Bamyan, two 6th-century monumental statues of standing buddhas carved into the side of a cliff in the Bamyan valley in the Hazarajat region of central Afghanistan. He did this because Afghanistan had no Buddhists, so idolatry would not be a problem.

But in March 2001 the statues were destroyed by the Taliban of Mullah Omar following a decree stating: "all the statues around Afghanistan must be destroyed."

- Yahya Massoud, brother of the anti-Taliban and resistance leader Ahmad Shah Massoud, recalls the following incident after the destruction of the Buddha statues at Bamyan:
- It was the spring of 2001. I was in Afghanistan's Panjshir Valley, together with my brother Ahmad Shah Massoud, the leader of the Afghan resistance against the Taliban, and Bismillah Khan, who currently serves as Afghanistan's interior minister. One of our commanders, Commandant Momin, wanted us to see 30 Taliban fighters who had been taken hostage after a gun battle. My brother agreed to meet them.
- I remember that his first question concerned the centuries-old Buddha statues that were dynamited by the Taliban in March of that year, shortly before our encounter. Two Taliban combatants from Kandahar confidently responded that worshiping anything outside of Islam was unacceptable

and that therefore these statues had to be destroyed. My brother looked at them and said, this time in Pashto, 'There are still many sun- worshippers in this country. Will you also try to get rid of the sun and drop darkness over the Earth?'"'

Explanation of ideology

The author Ahmed Rashid suggests that the devastation and hardship of the Soviet invasion and the following period influenced Taliban ideology.

It is said the Taliban did not include scholars learned in Islamic law and history. The refugee students, brought up in a totally male society, not only had no education in mathematics, science, history or geography, but also had no traditional skills of farming, herding, or handicraft-making, nor even knowledge of their tribal and clan lineages.

In such an environment, war meant employment, peace meant unemployment. Dominating women simply affirmed manhood. For their leadership, rigid fundamentalism was a matter not only of principle, but also of political survival. Taliban leaders "repeatedly told" Rashid that "if they gave women greater freedom or a chance to go to school, they would lose the support of their rank and file."

Criticisms

The Taliban were criticized for their strictness towards those who disobeyed their imposed rules. Many Muslims complained that most Taliban rules had no basis in the Qur'an or sharia. Mullah Omar's title as Amir al-Mu'minin was criticized on the grounds that he lacked scholarly learning, tribal pedigree, or connections to the Prophet's family. Sanction for the title traditionally required the support of all of the country's ulema, whereas only some 1,200 Pashtun Taliban-supporting Mullahs had declared Omar the Amir. "No Afghan had adopted the title since 1834, when King Dost Mohammed Khan assumed the title before he declared jihad against the Sikh kingdom in Peshawar. But Dost Mohammed was fighting foreigners, while Omar had declared jihad against other Afghans."

Another criticism was that the Taliban called their 20 per cent tax on truckloads of opium "zakat", which is traditionally limited to 2.5 per cent of the zakat-payers' disposable income (or wealth).

Governance

The Taliban, *de jure*, controlled 85 per cent of Afghanistan. *De facto* the areas under its direct control were mainly Afghanistan's major cities and highways. Tribal khans and warlords had *de facto* direct control over various small towns, villages, and rural areas.

Rashid described the Taliban government as "a secret society run by Kandaharis... mysterious, secretive, and dictatorial." They did not hold elections, as their spokesman explained:

The *Sharia* does not allow politics or political parties. That is why we give no salaries to officials or soldiers, just food, clothes, shoes, and weapons. We want to live a life like the Prophet lived 1400 years ago, and *jihad* is our right. We want to recreate the time of the Prophet, and we are only carrying out what the Afghan people have wanted for the past 14 years.

They modeled their decision-making process on the Pashtun tribal council (*jirga*), together with what they believed to be the early Islamic model. Discussion was followed by a building of a consensus by the "believers". Before capturing Kabul, there was talk of stepping aside once a government of "good Muslims" took power, and law and order were restored.

As the Taliban's power grew, decisions were made by Mullah Omar without consulting the *jirga* and without consulting other parts of the country. He visited the capital, Kabul, only twice while in power. Instead of an election, their leader's legitimacy came from an oath of allegiance ("Bay'ah"), in imitation of the Prophet and the first four Caliphs. On April 4, 1996, Mullah Omar had "the Cloak of the Prophet Mohammed" taken from its shrine for the first time in 60 years. Wrapping himself in the relic, he appeared on the roof of a building in the center of Kandahar while hundreds of Pashtun mullahs below shouted "Amir al-Mu'minin!" (Commander of the Faithful), in a pledge of support.

Taliban spokesman Mullah Wakil explained:

- Decisions are based on the advice of the Amir-ul Momineen. For us consultation is not necessary. We believe that this

> is in line with the *Sharia*. We abide by the Amir's view even if he alone takes this view. There will not be a head of state. Instead there will be an Amir al-Mu'minin. Mullah Omar will be the highest authority, and the government will not be able to implement any decision to which he does not agree. General elections are incompatible with *Sharia* and therefore we reject them.

The Taliban were very reluctant to share power, and since their ranks were overwhelmingly Pashtun they ruled as overlords over the 60 per cent of Afghans from other ethnic groups. In local government, such as Kabul city council or Herat, Taliban loyalists, not locals, dominated, even when the Pashto-speaking Taliban could not communicate with the roughly half of the population who spoke Dari or other non-Pashtun tongues. Critics complained that this "lack of local representation in urban administration made the Taliban appear as an occupying force."

Organization

Consistent with the governance of early Muslims was the absence of state institutions or "a methodology for command and control" that is standard today even among non-Westernized states. The Taliban did not issue press releases, policy statements, or hold regular press conferences. The outside world and most Afghans did not even know what their leaders looked like, since photography was banned. The "regular army" resembled a lashkar or traditional tribal militia force with only 25,000 men (of whom 11,000 were non-Afghans). Cabinet ministers and deputies were mullahs with a "madrasah education." Several of them, such as the Minister of Health and Governor of the State bank, were primarily military commanders who left their administrative posts to fight when needed. Military reverses that trapped them behind lines or led to their deaths increased the chaos in the national administration. At the national level, "all senior Tajik, Uzbek and Hazara bureaucrats" were replaced "with Pashtuns, whether qualified or not." Consequently, the ministries "by and large ceased to function."

The Ministry of Finance had neither a budget nor "qualified economist or banker." Mullah Omar collected and dispersed cash without bookkeeping.

U.S. STRATEGY TOWARD THE TALIBAN DURING ITS RULE

The Clinton Administration opened talks with the Taliban after it captured Qandahar in 1994, and engaged the movement after it took power. However, the Administration was unable to moderate its policies and relations worsened throughout the Taliban period of rule. The United States withheld recognition of Taliban as the legitimate government of Afghanistan, formally recognizing no faction as the government. The United Nations continued to seat representatives of the Rabbani government, not the Taliban. The State Department ordered the Afghan embassy in Washington, DC, closed in August 1997. U.N. Security Council Resolution 1193 (August 28, 1998) and 1214 (December 8, 1998) urged the Taliban to end discrimination against women.

Women's rights groups urged the Clinton Administration not to recognize the Taliban government. In May 1999, the Senate-passed S.Res. 68 called on the President not to recognize an Afghan government that oppresses women.

The Taliban's hosting of Al Qaeda's leadership gradually became the Clinton Administration's overriding agenda item with Afghanistan. In April 1998, then-U.S. Ambassador to the United Nations Bill Richardson (along with Assistant Secretary of State Karl Inderfurth and NSC senior official Bruce Riedel) visited Afghanistan, but the Taliban refused to hand over Bin Laden. They did not meet Mullah Umar. After the August 7, 1998, Al Qaeda bombings of U.S. embassies in Kenya and Tanzania, the Clinton Administration began to strongly pressure the Taliban to extradite him, imposing U.S. sanctions on Taliban-controlled Afghanistan and achieving adoption of some U.N. sanctions as well. On August 20, 1998, as a response to the Africa embassy bombings, the United States fired cruise missiles at alleged Al Qaeda training camps in eastern Afghanistan, but Bin Laden was not hit. Some observers assert that the Administration missed several other opportunities to strike him, including a purported sighting of him by an unarmed Predator drone at the Tarnak Farm camp in Afghanistan in the fall of 2000. Clinton Administration officials said that domestic and international support for ousting the Taliban militarily was lacking.

The "Northern Alliance" Congeals

The Taliban's policies caused different Afghan factions to ally with the Tajik core of the anti-Taliban opposition—the ousted President Rabbani, Ahmad Shah Masud, and their ally in the Herat area, Ismail Khan. Joining the Tajik factions in the broader "Northern Alliance" were Uzbek, Hazara Shiite, and even some Pashtun Islamist factions. Virtually all the figures mentioned remain key players in politics in Afghanistan, sometimes allied with and at other times adversaries of President Hamid Karzai.

- Uzbeks/General Dostam. One major faction was the Uzbek militia (the Junbush-Melli, or National Islamic Movement of Afghanistan) of General Abdul Rashid Dostam. Frequently referred to by some Afghans as one of the "warlords" who gained power during the anti-Soviet war, Dostam first joined those seeking to oust Rabbani during his 1992-1996 presidency, but later joined him and the other Northern Alliance factions opposed to the Taliban.
- Hazara Shiites. Members of Hazara tribes, mostly Shiite Muslims, are prominent in Bamiyan, Dai Kundi, and Ghazni provinces (central Afghanistan) and are always fearful of, and subject to some extent to, repression by Pashtuns and other larger ethnic factions. The Hazaras have tended to serve in working class and domestic household jobs, although more recently they have been prominent in technology jobs in Kabul, raising their economic status. They are also increasingly cohesive politically, leading to gains in the September 2010 parliamentary elections. During the various Afghan wars, the main Hazara Shiite militia was Hizb-e-Wahdat (Unity Party, composed of eight different groups). Hizb-e-Wahdat suffered a major setback in 1995 when the Taliban captured and killed its leader Abdul Ali Mazari. One of Karzai's vice president's Karim Khalili, is a Hazara. Another prominent Hazara faction leader, Mohammad Mohaqeq, is a Karzai critic.
- Pashtun Islamists/Sayyaf. Abd-i-Rab Rasul Sayyaf, now a leading Islamic conservative in parliament, headed a Pashtun-dominated hardline Islamist *mujahedin* faction (Islamic Union for the Liberation of Afghanistan, *Ittihad*

Islami) during the anti-Soviet war. Even though he is an Islamist conservative, Sayyaf viewed the Taliban as selling out Afghanistan to Al Qaeda and he joined the Northern Alliance.

Strategy Pre-September 11, 2001

Throughout 2001, but prior to the September 11 attacks, Bush Administration policy differed little from Clinton Administration policy—applying economic and political pressure on the Taliban while retaining some dialogue with it, and refraining from militarily assisting the Northern Alliance. The September 11 Commission report said that, in the months prior to the September 11 attacks, Administration officials leaned toward such a step. The report added that some officials wanted, in addition, to assist ethnic Pashtuns who were opposed to the Taliban. Other covert options were reportedly under consideration as well. In accordance with U.N. Security Council Resolution 1333, in February 2001 the State Department ordered the Taliban representative office in New York closed, although Taliban representative Abdul Hakim Mujahid continued to operate informally. In March 2001, Administration officials received a Taliban envoy to discuss bilateral issues. In one significant departure from Clinton Administration policy, the Bush Administration stepped up engagement with Pakistan to try to reduce its support for the Taliban. At that time, there were widespread but unconfirmed allegations by U.S. experts that Pakistani advisers were helping the Taliban in their fight against the Northern Alliance.

Even though the Northern Alliance was supplied with Iranian, Russian, and Indian financial and military support—all of whom had different motives for that support—the Northern Alliance nonetheless continued to lose ground to the Taliban after it lost Kabul in 1996. By the time of the September 11 attacks, the Taliban controlled at least 75% of the country, including almost all provincial capitals. The Alliance suffered a major setback on September 9, 2001 (two days before, and possibly an integral part of, the September 11 attacks), when Ahmad Shah Masud was assassinated by Al Qaeda operatives posing as journalists. He was succeeded by his intelligence chief, Muhammad Fahim, a veteran figure but one who lacked Masud's undisputed authority.

THE TALIBAN STAKES OF PAKISTAN

As Ahmad Rashid has described so well, the Taliban (Islamic student) movement sprang from Pushtun refugees in Pakistan, concentrated in temporary camps in western Pakistan. Pushtun young men who had grown up in these camps were drawn back to the Afghan homeland after the Soviet exit, but under civil war conditions in their country. These youths had been trained in the use of small arms (carrying weapons was a natural legacy of their culture) and taught to believe they could impose a peaceful, Islamic moral order on their country. Most had no deep memory of traditional social life in Afghanistan itself, many had lost their parents and, being displaced, few were accustomed to the valued roles women played in Afghan society. The Taliban religious outlook was a product of the free, but largely Quranic, obscurantist education available to boys in the austere camp environments. Their teachers themselves typically were religious leaders (*maulvis* or *mullahs*) from Deobandi or Wahabi brands of fundamentalist Islam who ran traditional religious schools (*madrassas*) with hostels, frequently using them as recruiting grounds for political ends.

When the Soviet forces withdrew from Afghanistan in 1989, the United States essentially washed its hands of responsibility for the future of that debilitated country. Having defeated Soviet power and installed a weak Islamic republic under Tajik cleric Burhanuddin Rabbani in Kabul, Afghan mujahideen groups increasingly quarreled among themselves on ethnic and tribal lines and most of Afghanistan succumbed to internal warfare. Pakistan's elected, bureaucratic and armed leaders could not so easily ignore this turbulence and groped for a strategy that would restore civil order beyond Pakistan's borders in Afghanistan.

Under liberal Prime Minister and Interior Minister in 1993, the government of Pakistan worked out a two-fold strategy toward Afghanistan: (a) to support the revival of traditional Pushtun rule in the hope of extinguishing inter-tribal war, suppressing banditry, reopening roads, reviving trade with Iran and Central Asia, and securing Afghanistan for Western-financed pipeline projects that could provide Afghanistan revenue while transporting natural gas from Turkmenistan to Pakistan and on to India; and (b) to preempt Pushtun revival of the demand for a separate Pushtun state (Pakhtunistan) that had threatened Pakistan's integrity in the northwest tribal belt for many years after Independence, by ensuring the primacy of Pushtun stakes in Afghanistan's future.

The Taliban association emerging from the refugee settlements provided a natural political vehicle for this Pakistani strategy. It depended on the cooperation of the Islamist political parties that sponsored the Taliban in the camps. The task merely involved lightly arming and training Taliban cadres, and negotiating their entry through Quetta to join those Pushtun militia leaders inside Afghanistan who deplored the country's internal disintegration and aspired, however crudely, to pacify, reunify and rebuild Afghanistan. The Pakistani armed intelligence arm, the Inter-Services Intelligence agency (ISI)—which had served as the main American and Saudi conduit for training, financial support, and transferring arms to the Afghan mujahideen—became the overseers and managers of Pakistan's assistance to the Taliban. This ISI role was secretive, but it was no rogue operation—as some in Pakistan and the United States may now wish to believe. Rather, it was the policy of Pakistan's elected governments from 1993, including that of the Harvard- and Oxford-educated Benazir Bhutto, Pakistan's first female prime minister.

The Taliban gained a local foothold around Kandahar in 1994 and then rapidly spread within southern and eastern Afghanistan, seizing Kabul and asserting a claim to govern Afghanistan in 1996, with all but a northeastern tenth of the country falling under their sway by 1998. Some financial support for the Taliban came from Saudi Arabia and other Gulf states. The Taliban regime was formally recognized by Saudi Arabia, Pakistan, and United Arab Emirates as the government of Afghanistan. Other governments and the United Nations either continued to recognize the first mujahideen (Rabbani) government even after it fled Kabul, or declined to recognize the Taliban regime, hoping that diplomacy and United Nations relief could patch together a workable, coalition government more representative of the country as a whole.

Almost imperceptible to Westerners at the start, the Taliban project at first was not considered objectionable in Washington. The Taliban became anathema only later, after word of its brutality spread. Having seized power in Kabul, the Taliban's inhumane governing practices undercut its once positive reputation for disarming warlord factions and bringing peace in one locality after another. From Kabul, the new regime imposed uniquely harsh judicial procedures and tried to force the surviving remnants of Afghanistan's battered urban society to give up music and entertainment. On pain of beating or even execution, men were forced to grow beards and wear traditional clothes, and women to leave jobs and whenever outdoors to wear the head-to-toe covering known as *burqas*. Western revulsion was aroused by media reports of the Taliban's draconian interpretation of Islamic law, confinement of women, suppression of female education, arbitrary arrests, mutilation or execution as punishments, and intolerance of non-Muslim religious minorities.

However a great deal the Taliban was eventually despised in the West, it was not the offspring of, nor originally associated with, al-Qaeda. Osama bin Laden apparently left Sudan in 1996 and moved back to Afghanistan some time in 1997. Thereafter, al-Qaeda gradually extended influence over the Taliban by spending its own resources to win the favour of senior Taliban leaders. Al-Qaeda also provided armed support and guidance to Taliban fighters who were fighting the Northern Alliance forces and other autonomous factions elsewhere in the country. The United States focused only on the significance of the Taliban's grant of sanctuary to al-Qaeda after its bombing of U.S. Embassies in East Africa in 1998.

Toward the end of its tenure, the Clinton administration put considerable pressure on Pakistan to arrange communication with Taliban officials, hoping to persuade them to expel Osama bin Laden and his associates. But the Taliban's counter demand was that it be recognized as Afghanistan's de jure government. This price the United States was unwilling to pay. How deeply the Taliban depended on al-Qaeda for armed operations against the Northern Alliance was not apparent to ordinary observers until after 9/11. What was clear, however, was that Pakistan had a major stake in the Taliban's claim to govern Afghanistan, was opposed to the Northern Alliance, and could not disengage from those positions in Afghanistan, short of a world-shaking crisis. September 11 brought just that crisis.

This analysis indicates that Pakistan's stakes in the Taliban were not based on a ordinary religion or on matters or Islamic principle, per se. Pakistan was interested in geopolitical objectives, not in the religious aims of the Taliban or its parochial justification of a strict Islamic discipline. Pakistan hoped to foster order through a client regime in a war-torn country on its borders. In doing so, it aimed to promote the revival of trade, to link Central Asian energy resources with the subcontinent, and to extinguish any Pushtun impulse to tear part of Pakistan away as a separate Pushtun state.

Exploiting reservoirs of Afghan Islamic fervor was useful to Pakistan (as well as to the United States) against the Soviet forces in Afghanistan, and useful again to Pakistan in helping the Taliban come to power, but the Taliban movement's Islamic fundamentalist orientation was never for Pakistan's government an end in itself. Only a smattering of individual Pakistanis and fundamentalist groups—mainly Pushtun tribes and Islamic political parties with roots in the Pushtun tribal regions—identified with the Taliban cause emotionally or ideologically. For the Pakistani authorities, the Taliban's religious appeal was only a tool.

Far more basic for Pakistan's government, and painful to abandon, was the aim of Pushtun dominance within Afghanistan as a means of resolving the civil war and opening the way to the trans-Afghanistan energy project. In achieving this aim, to cut off the Taliban even after George W. Bush threw down the gauntlet was tantamount to sacrificing Pushtun interests in Afghan politics and undermining Pakistan's interests in Afghanistan's stability and its own security. Pakistan's view of the power of the Northern Alliance, perhaps mistakenly, was that it jeopardized stability in Afghanistan. Thus, when Pakistani chief Pervez Musharraf turned against the Taliban under U.S. pressure, the decision was acutely difficult. Because Pakistan's strategy toward Afghanistan—and its own security on its western borders—was based on a successful Taliban campaign for power, it required accepting a fundamentally different calculation of Pakistan's national interests.

The new calculation was that Pakistan could not afford to be stigmatized by the West as a terrorist state. Once the Taliban refused to dissociate itself from al-Qaeda, Islamabad recognized that the United States would regard the Taliban as a de facto "terrorist" regime, and a legitimate object of armed attack. For Pakistan to be associated with the Taliban political cause after that would not only put Pakistan on a slippery slope toward international ostracism but could be used, potentially, to justify armed attack on Pakistan itself. Indeed, it was exactly this sensitivity that India latched onto when it initiated a armed confrontation with Pakistan after the attack on parliament in December 2001. But before we examine that crisis, the dramatic progress of the U.S. war in Afghanistan and the potential effects on the Kashmir side of Pakistan's Afghanistan-related entanglement need separate discussion.

ARMED MOVEMENT AGAINST THE TALIBAN AND AL-QAEDA

Pakistan had to make a decision very quickly whether it would support the U.S. armed effort in Afghanistan. Senior Pakistani officials announced on September 15, *within four days* of the 9/11 terrorist attacks on the United States, that they had agreed to give "full support" to U.S. efforts to combat international terrorism. President Musharraf 's address in Urdu to the nation three days later informed his people that the United States had demanded armed overflight rights, logistical support, and intelligence cooperation against three targets—Osama bin Laden, the Taliban, and international terror-ism. Musharraf noted that the United States had won United Nations support and confided to the nation that neighbouring India had offered its armed facilities to the United States in the hopes of isolating Pakistan and getting it declared a terrorist state. Musharraf made it clear to his countrymen that Pakistan had to assist the United States; otherwise four vital interests of Pakistan would be in jeopardy—its sovereignty, its economy, its strategic (nuclear and missile) assets, and its cause in Kashmir. Musharraf and his advisors apparently drew the line, however, at inserting Pakistani armed forces into Afghanistan.

Despite concerns about a violent domestic backlash from political parties and groups that had links with the Taliban as well as the threat of al-Qaeda or Taliban attacks across the border, Pakistan thus committed itself almost overnight to give the United

States valuable flight corridors over its territory and access to stage U.S. search and rescue forces at facilities near Karachi in the south and closer to Afghanistan at the Pakistani armed airfield near Jacobabad. Pakistani forces also provided backstopping for U.S. operations against al-Qaeda and the Taliban later, by attempting to seal the mountainous borders so as to prevent hostile units fleeing across the border into Pakistan. Pakistani intelligence and security forces also cooperated with covert U.S. forces in efforts to hunt down those al-Qaeda and Taliban elements that succeeded in entering Pakistan to take refuge, or to slip out of the country.

Operation Enduring Freedom against al-Qaeda and Taliban forces in Afghanistan began with air strikes on October 7, 2001. Saudi Arabia had vetoed U.S. use of amenities on its soil for the attack and Iran denied access through its airspace. This put a much greater burden on U.S. aircraft carriers and other naval forces that assembled in the Arabian Sea, on bombers that had been flown to Diego Garcia and some that flew all the way from the United States, and on the prodigious use of aircraft refueling capabilities. But to the surprise of most observers, Russian President Putin gave his blessing to the U.S. counterterrorist effort and the leaders of three post-Soviet Central Asian states neighbouring Afghanistan—Uzbekistan, Tajikistan, and Kyrgizstan—provided the United States air access and staging facilities near Afghanistan in the north and west. Use of these facilities greatly eased U.S. cooperation with the Afghan Northern Alliance and the Uzbek elements that had reestablished a presence under General Rashid Dostum and that would retake Mazar-i-Sharif.

As a result, not merely was the United States able to use its own infiltrated ground spotters and air strikes to destroy exposed Taliban armed assets and installations—there were relatively few big targets— but it was also able to use airborne firepower to break down the front lines of the Taliban forces opposite the Northern Alliance, enabling the alliance and the other anti-Taliban forces that reemerged to advance, taking Mazar-i-Sharif, Kabul, Herat and Konduz in succession. Mazar-i-Sharif fell on November 9. Kabul was retaken on November 12, and Herat fell the same day. Konduz, where a combined force of about twenty thousand al-

Qaeda and Taliban forces put up a fierce resistance, fell on November 24.

A thousand U.S. marines were airlifted on November 26 into a remote landing strip (dubbed Camp Rhino) fifteen miles southeast of Kandahar to provide protection for a buildup of helicopters, armored personnel carriers, and the entry of additional special operations units.

This also provided the United States with a staging area inside Afghanistan to pursue operations in the Pushtun areas to the north and east, including near the border with Pakistan. Coupled with well-targeted air raids, the ground presence of U.S. combat forces helped break the main, residual Taliban resistance in the south, stimulated defections, and forced the hard core to disperse into hiding. Kandahar fell on December 7.

Aided by the Rome political process of negotiating a new Afghan government, Hamid Karzai's leadership had begun by this time to make significant headway among Pushtun elements in the south and east that could absorb defectors and accommodate the Northern Alliance in forming a new government in Kabul. The U.S.-assisted Afghan meetings in Rome helped negotiate agreed steps to constitute a new, representative government in stages—and made the level of international commitment to rehabilitating Afghanistan clearer.

Special combat operations shifted once Kandahar had fallen to the White Mountains, near Khost, adjoining Pakistan, where al-Qaeda and Taliban forces had taken refuge in fortified and well-provisioned mountain caves and bunkers. The Tora Bora operations heavily bombed the cave complexes and ground units then cleared most of them on the ground by early January 2002. Several hundred al-Qaeda and Taliban prisoners were taken, with many shipped to Guantanamo Bay in Cuba for interrogation. A significant number of the al-Qaeda Arabs at Tora Bora evidently slipped through into Pakistan, however. In March, U.S. and allied forces gathered in Operation Anaconda to attack a well-dug-in al-Qaeda/Taliban force of about 1,500 fighters in the Shah-e-Kot Mountains south of Gardez in northeastern Afghanistan. Anaconda produced the largest number of U.S. casualties in a single Afghan operation, but apparently took a heavy toll on the enemy, killing an estimated four hundred to eight hundred opponents. Again, some of the fighters melted away into Pakistan, although in this case Pakistani forces intercepted and fought small units, capturing and turning over a number of al-Qaeda members to the United States for interrogation.

In roughly six months U.S. and allied armed intervention, coupled with the residual anti-Taliban forces in Afghanistan, had radically transformed the situation. Momentum increasingly favored the formation of a new Afghan government—although it was clear that such a government would be hard put to establish order throughout the country and develop the capacity, even with international assistance, to conduct a far-reaching economic and social rehabilitation program. Pockets of Taliban and al-Qaeda resistance remained, with a capacity to harass the emerging Karzai government and foment perceptions of disorder, but by summer 2002, these isolated elements no longer held the capacity to counter-attack the U.S. and allied presence in any major way.

During that armed campaign, the radical Islamic backlash that the Musharraf government had feared would erupt within Pakistan launched a handful of demonstrations but then largely subsided during the remainder of 2001. Considerable anti-American feeling and anger with Musharraf's decisions percolated below the surface but potentially massive, violent agitation was contained. Meanwhile, the level of violence in Kashmir rose to a degree. Then on December 13, 2001, halfway through the armed campaign, terrorists struck the Indian parliament and precipitated a full Indian armed mobilization against Pakistan.

7

Al-Badr (Jammu and Kashmir)

INTRODUCTION

Al-Badr is an Islamic militant group operating in the Jammu Kashmir region, run by Jasniel Rihal. The group was allegedly formed by the Pakistani Inter-Services Intelligence (ISI) in June 1998. It is believed the group was encouraged by the ISI to operate independently from their previous umbrella group, Hizb-ul-Mujahideen (HM).

Prior to the groups separation from HM, they participated in the fighting in Afghanistan in 1990 as part of Gulbuddin Hekmatyar's Hizb-l-Islami (HIG) alongside other anti-Soviet Afghan mujihadeen.

FOUNDATION AND SEPARATION

The group was originally led by Arfeen Bhai, also known as Jannisar or Lukmaan, when it separated in 1998 and is currently led by Bahkt Zameen Khan. In 2002, Zameen declared jihad against the U.S. forces in Afghanistan after being responsible for prior attacks against coalition forces there beginning in 2001.

Al-Badr went on further in 2002 to order all women police in the Rajouri District of Kashmir to quit their jobs by mid-January the next year. The group has stated membership in the United Jihad Council (UJC), a coalition of Pakistan-based militants who are active in the Jammu Kashmir region. They have been linked to Jamaat-e-Islami and alleged to have connection with al-Qaeda. The groups stated purpose is to liberate the Indian states of Jammu and Kashmir to be merged with Pakistan. Al-Badr opposes negotiations to end the violence in Kashmir and opposes the Line of Control (LoC) and calls for the strengthening of the jihad.

DESIGNATION AS TERRORIST ORGANIZATION

Al-Badr was banned by India under The Unlawful Activities (Prevention) Act, 2004. On April 27, 2005 State Department of United States Government identified Al-Badr as a terrorist organisation in its list of 40 Foreign Terrorist Organizations. Al-Badr is currently on the U.S. State Department list of Designated Foreign Terrorist Organizations.

TRAINING CAMP

The Islamic fundamentalist group Al-Badr operates one or more covert Al Badr training camps in Pakistan to train Pakistani civilians to serve as fighters in the conflict in Kashmir. In the 90s, militants trained at al-Badr camp in the use of RDX and C4 explosives. Shaukat Ahmed Khan, the author of an article about the camps, in the *Times of India,* said he was kidnapped from his home in India by recruiters for the camp; and that when he made clear he wasn't interested in fighting on behalf of Al Badr those running the camp cut out his tongue, and cut off his right hand. He said they spared his life because he was a fellow Muslim.

AL-BADR LEADERS

Ashrafuz Zaman Khan

Ashrafuz Zaman Khan is one of the convicted masterminds of 1971 killing of Bengali intellectuals. In 1971, he was a member of the Central Committee of the Islami Chhatra Sangha. After liberation he went to Pakistan and worked for Radio Pakistan. Later, he moved to New York and presently heads the Queens branch of Islamic Circle of North America (ICNA). He was sentenced to death in absentia by the International War Crimes Tribunal for killing 18 Bengali intellectuals during the last days of the 1971 Liberation War of Bangladesh.

Activities as a Commander of Al Badr

Ashrafuzzaman Khan shot to death 7 teachers of Dhaka University in the killing zones at Mirpur. Mofizzuddin, who drove the vehicle that carried those hapless victims to Mirpur, clearly identified Ashrafuzzaman as the "chief killer" of the intellectuals.

After 1971 War

After Liberation, Ashrafuzzaman's personal diary was recovered from his residence, 350 Nakhal Para. Two pages of his diary registered names and residential addresses of 19 teachers as well as the name of the medical officer of Dhaka University. Of those 20 persons, 8 were missing on December 14: Munier Chowdhury (Bengali), Dr. Abul Khair (History), Ghiasuddin Ahmed (History), Rashidul Hasan (English), Dr. Faizul Mohi (IE R) and Dr. Murtaza (Medical Officer). Mofizuddin confessed that Ashrafuzzaman himself shot all of them. As per Mofizuddin's description, the decomposed bodies of those unfortunate teachers were recovered from the swamps of Rayer Bazar and the mass grave at Shiyal Bari at Mirpur. There were also other names in the diary including:

- Dr. Wakil Ahmed (Bengali),
- Dr. Nilima Ibrahim (Bengali),
- Dr. Latif (IE R),
- Dr. Maniruzzaman (Geography),
- K M Saaduddin (Sociology),
- AMM Shahidullah (Math),
- Dr. Sirajul Islam (Islamic History),
- Dr. Akhtar Ahmed (Education),
- Zahirul Huq (Psychology),
- Ahsanul Huq (English),
- Serajul Islam Chowdbury (English), and
- Kabir Chowdhury (English).

Another page of his diary recorded the names of 16 collaborating teachers of Dhaka university. Apart from that there were also names of Chowdbury Moinuddin, the chief of operation for elimination of the intelligentsia, and Shawkat Imran, a member of the central Al-Badr command, and the head of Dhaka Al-Badr forces.

The diary also contained names and addresses of several other prominent Bengalis. All of them lost their lives at the hands of Al-Badr forces. On a small piece of paper the name of the member finance of the Pakistan Jute Board, Abdul Khalek, was written down. On December 9, 1971, the Al-Badr forces kidnapped Mr. Khalek from his office.

They demanded Taka 10,000 as ransom. They saw Mrs. Khalek for ransom money. But at that time she was unable to pay the kidnappers more than 450 taka. She promised that she would give them the rest of the money later, and begged them her husband's life. But Mr. Khalek never came back.

Ashrafuzzaman has also been implicated in the murder of some journalists. It was Ashrafuzzaman who kidnapped the shift-in- charge of the Purbadesh, and the literary editor, Mr. Golam Mustafa.

Activities in USA

Reportedly, he is currently the President of the Islamic Circle of North America, ICNA, New York Chapter and the local Imam. Nowadays, he promotes anti-war movement.

Recent Development

After the Bangladesh Government announced of conducting war crime trial, a story about this alleged cold blooded killer was published in Bangladesh's Bengali daily Sangbad a few months ago. A Virginia based on-line journal republished the same story in English Mr. Khan's people saw the published report and gave a stern warning to the journal editors through a legal entity.

The message said something like this: *the law office represented Ashrafuzzaman Khan and was referring to the article where Mr. Khan was labelled as war criminal and mastermind of intelllectual killing of 1971. The law office wanted all evidence to substantiate same. If the News Bangla authority failed to do so, the paper was asked to retract such remarks and confirm same with the office.* The News Bangla editorial board hired a local lawyer. He was given all the documentation about Ashrafuzzaman Khan in electronic and print version. The law firm representing News Bangla communicated to Khan's law office with some of the papers and told the other party that NEWS BANGLA story was simply an English translation of the original text in Bengali daily SANGBAD from Dhaka. Quite interestingly, Khan's attorney did not respond to this message. The case was closed apparently. Consequently, NEWS BANGLA did not have to retract or apologize to the alleged mastermind of 1971's intellectual killing in Bangladesh.

Arrest warrant

On April 25, 2013, the International Crimes Tribunal submitted formal charges against Ashrafuz Zaman Khan on the charge of killing 18 intellectuals towards the end of the Bangladesh liberation war 1971, as the "chief executor" of the Al-Badr force. A total of 16 charges of crimes against humanity have been brought against him under five categories, and an arrest warrant against him has been issued by the tribunal.

Verdict

On 3 November 2013 International war crimes tribunal sentenced Ashrafuz Zaman to death after the tribunal found him guilty of torture and murder of 18 intellectuals including nine Dhaka University teachers, six journalists and three doctors during 1971 Liberation war of Bangladesh. According to International Crimes Tribunal, the prosecution proved all the charges against Ashrafuz beyond doubt.

The tribunal also said that Ashrafuz Zaman and his ally Chowdhury Mueen-uddin at times, carried out the murders, sometimes they instigated and encouraged them and the two had complete control over the Al Badr during the 1971 War.

List of victims killed by Ashrafuz Zaman and Chowdhury Mueen-uddin

A court found Ashrafuz Zaman and Chowdhury Mueen-uddin to be guilty for the murder of following 18 Bengali intellectuals: Dhaka University Professors Ghyasuddin Ahmed, Rashidul Hasan, Anwar Pasha, Faizul Mahi, famous playwright and Professor Munier Chowdhury, Mufazzal Haider Chaudhury, Dr Abul Khair, Dr Santosh Chandra Bhattacharyya and Dr Sirajul Haque Khan, Professor of Cardiology Mohammed Fazle Rabbee, eminent eye specialist AFM Alim Chowdhury, Physician Mohammad Martuza,

Novelist and Journalist Shahidullah Kaiser, Journalist and Poet Selina Parvin, Journalists Serajuddin Hossain, Syed Nazmul Haque, ANM Golam Mostafa, and Nizamuddin Ahmed, in between 10 to 15 December 1971.

Chowdhury Mueen-Uddin

Chowdhury Mueen-Uddin (born 27 November 1948), is one of the convicted war criminal for killing Bengali intellectuals in collaboration with Pakistan army at the time of Bangladesh liberation war. After the liberation of Bangladesh, Chowdhury escape from Bangladesh and took British citizenship.

Chowdhury is a trustee (former Chairman) of Muslim Aid, and a director of Muslim spiritual care provision in the United Kingdom's National Health Service (NHS).

On 3 November 2013, the International Crimes Tribunal which is set up by the government of Bangladesh to judge international crimes committed during 1971 Bangladesh Liberation War, sentenced Mueen-Uddin, in absentia, to death for killing 9 teachers of Dhaka University, 6 journalists and 3 doctors in 1971. Mueen has remained in the United Kingdom since leaving Bangladesh shortly after its independence in 1971. Mueen-Uddin denies the charges.

He was alleged war criminal long before creation of International Crimes Tribunal (Bangladesh). In 1972, *The New York Times* reported that he "has been identified as the head of a secret, commando-like organization of fanatic Moslems", In In 1995, a documentary film made by David Bergman, named *War Crimes File* was aired on British television channel Channel 4 showing his involvement in 1971 Bangladesh genocide.

Career

In 1971, Mueen-Uddin was a journalist at the *Daily Purbodesh*. In 1972, *The New York Times* reported that he "has been identified as the head of a secret, commando-like organization of fanatic Moslems", in connection with the Bangladesh liberation war. He fled Bangladesh shortly after its independence in 1971, and went to the United Kingdom via India, Nepal and Pakistan In the United Kingdom he was able to create a new life.

He was a special editor of the London-based weekly *Dawat* and a leader of the London-based Jamaat organization Dawatul Islam.

Mueen-Uddin is a director of Muslim Spiritual Care Provision in the United Kingdom's National Health Service (NHS), a member of Multi Faith Group for Health care Chaplaincy (MFGHC), and a trustee of Muslim Aid. He is currently a citizen of the UK.

Since moving to the UK in the early 1970s, Mueen-Uddin has taken British citizenship and built a career as a community activist and Muslim leader.

In 1989 he was a key leader of protests against the Salman Rushdie book, The Satanic Verses. Around the same time he helped to found the extremist Islamic Forum of Europe, Jamaat-e-Islami's European wing, which believes in creating a sharia state in Europe and in 2010 was accused by a Labour minister, Jim Fitzpatrick, of infiltrating the Labour Party.

Tower Hamlets' directly-elected mayor, Lutfur Rahman, was expelled from Labour for his close links with the IFE. Until 2010 Mr Mueen-Uddin was vice-chairman of the controversial East London Mosque, controlled by the IFE, in which capacity he greeted Prince Charles when the heir to the throne opened an extension to the mosque. He was also closely involved with the Muslim Council of Britain, which has been dominated by the IFE. He was chairman and remains a trustee of the IFE-linked charity, Muslim Aid, which has a budget of £20 million. He has also been closely involved in the Markfield Institute, the key institution of Islamist higher education in the UK.

War crimes trial

In 1995, a documentary film *War Crimes File* by David Bergman was aired on British television channel Channel 4 about the 1971 Bangladesh genocide. In the film, Mueen-Uddin was accused of being a member of the pro-Pakistan paramilitary force Al-Badr during the 1971 Bangladesh Liberation War, and of being involved in war crimes.

In 2012, Bangladesh law minister Shafique Ahmed stated that Mueen-Uddin would be charged for war crimes. However, the prosecution has delayed submitting charges. He is accused of being a top member of the notorious paramilitary force Al-Badr and of the fundamentalist Jamaat-e-Islami political party, which fought for the country to remain part of Pakistan. Mueen-Uddin has denied all allegations.

Arrest warrant and extradition conditions

On 2 May 2013, Bangladesh's International Crimes Tribunal brought war criminal charges against Mueen-Uddin and Ashrafuz Zaman Khan. The United Kingdom does not have an extradition agreement with Bangladesh, and the UK was reluctant to extradite Mueen-Uddin without assurances of a fair trail, plus assurances that there would be no death penalty in the event of a guilty verdict.

Although Scotland Yard said in the 1990s that Bangladesh had primary jurisdiction for prosecuting Mueen for the 1971 killings, Britain could reconsider its decision to not prosecute.

Both Mueen and Khan were charged with committing a war crime by killing 18 intellectuals who were Dhaka University Professors Ghyasuddin Ahmed, Rashidul Hasan, Anwar Pasha, Faizul Mahi, famous playwright and Professor Munier Chowdhury, Mufazzal Haider Chaudhury, Dr Abul Khair, Dr Santosh Chandra Bhattacharyya and Dr Sirajul Haque Khan, Professor of Cardiology Mohammed Fazle Rabbee, eminent eye specialist AFM Alim Chowdhury, Physician Mohammad Martuza, Novelist and Journalist Shahidullah Kaiser, Journalist and Poet Selina Parvin, Journalists Serajuddin Hossain, Syed Nazmul Haque, ANM Golam Mostafa, and Nizamuddin Ahmed, in between 10 to 15 December 1971.

An arrest warrant also issued for them. Both of them was most wanted after Bangladesh liberation war. According to prob report *Chowdhury Mueen-Uddin* was "operation-in-charge of Al-Badr".

Allegations from the relatives of the victims

The widow of one victim, Dolly Chaudhury, claims to have identified Mr Mueen-Uddin as one of three men who abducted her husband, Mufazzal Haider Chaudhury, a prominent scholar of Bengali literature, on the night of 14 December 1971. "I was able to identify one [of the abductors], Mueen-Uddin," she said in video testimony. "He was wearing a scarf but my husband pulled it down as he was taken away. When he was a student, he often used to go to my brother in law's house. My husband, my sister-in-law, my brother-in-law, we all recognised that man." Professor Chaudhury was never seen again.

The widow of another victim, claims that Mr Mueen-Uddin was in the group that abducted her husband, Sirajuddin Hussain, another journalist, from their home on the night of 10 December 1971. "There was no doubt that he was the person involved in my husband's abduction and killing," said Noorjahan Seraji.

"I have waited 40 years to see the trial of the war criminals," said the widow, Noorjahan Seraji. "I have not spent a single night without suffering and I want justice."

One of the other members of the group, who was caught soon afterwards, allegedly gave Mr Mueen-Uddin's name in his confession.

Another reporter on Purbodesh, Ghulam Mostafa, also disappeared. The vanished journalist's brother, Dulu, said he appealed to Mr Mueen-Uddin for help and was taken around the main Pakistani Army detention and torture centres by Mr Mueen-Uddin. Dulu Mostafa said that Mr Mueen-Uddin appeared to be well known at the detention centres, gained easy admission to the premises and was saluted by the Pakistani guards as he entered. Ghulam was never found.

Mueen-Uddin's then editor at the paper, Atiqur Rahman, said that Mr Mueen-Uddin had been the first journalist in the country to reveal the existence of the Al-Badr Brigade and had demonstrated intimate knowledge of its activities. After his colleagues disappeared, he said, Mueen-Uddin had asked for his home address.

Fearing that he too would be abducted, the editor gave a fake address. Rahman's name, complete with the fake address, appeared on an Al-Badr death list found just after the end of the war. "I gave that address only to Chowdhury Mueen-Uddin, and when that list appeared it was obvious that he had given that address to Al Badr," Rahman said in statements given to the investigators. "I'm sure I gave the address to no-one else." Rahman then published a front-page story and picture about Mueen-Uddin, who had by that stage left the city, naming him as involved in "disappearances."

This brought forward two further witnesses, Mushtaqur and Mahmudur Rahman, who claim they recognised the picture as somebody who had been part of an armed group looking for the BBC correspondent in Dhaka during the abductions. The group was unsuccessful because the BBC man had gone into hiding.

Verdict

On 3 November 2013, the International Crimes Tribunal - a special Bangladeshi court set up by the government - sentenced Mueen-uddin to death after the tribunal found him guilty *in absentia* of torture and murder of 18 intellectuals during 1971 Liberation war of Bangladesh. According to *The Daily Star*, lawyers called no defence witnesses, whereas the prosecution brought in 25 witnesses, due to non-cooperation from Mueen-Uddin's family. Those sentenced in absentia are not eligible to challenge the court's verdict. Chowdhury Mueen-Uddin denied the charges in an interview aired by Al Jazeera in August, 2013.

The tribunal also said that Mueen-Uddin sometimes carried out the murders, and sometimes instigated and encouraged them. They ruled that he and his allies had complete control over the Al Badr during the 1971 War.

Reaction of trial from defence

However, the trial was criticized by Bangladesh Jamaat-e-Islami, the party he was served and which opposed the creation of Bangladesh and took part in committing war crime in 1971, stated that the trials were politically motivated. They also accused the current government of trying to destroy the opposition party by sentencing its leadership to death. However, the political motivation against Mueen-Uddin is unclear as he is living in the UK for more than 40 years. Mueen-Uddin's Legal Counsel described the verdict as *"farcical"*. He further alleged *"serious judicial and prosecutorial misconduct and the collusion of the Government with members of the judiciary and prosecution"*, and condemned the entire trial as a "show trial".

John Cammegh, a barrister in chambers at 9 Bedford Row, London, which represents Mueen-Uddin, in an op-ed piece, stated that the trial *"made mockery of that principle* [of international law], and that it served as *"a terrible warning of the way in which the ideals of universal justice and accountability can be abused"*.

Reaction from victims' relatives about verdict

Relatives of the victims voiced their satisfaction at the verdicts. Professor Rashiddudin Ahmad, whose brother Giasuddin Ahmed, a university teacher at the time was amongst those killed, said: *"We have waited 40 years for this. It is some sort of justice, even though the sentence may never be carried out."*

Europe's reaction to the trial

The UK said on Jan 22, 2013 that it supported the war crimes trial in Bangladesh but always opposed capital punishment while Germany and France termed the trial an internal affair of the country. They gave their reactions a day after the International Crimes Tribunal-2 awarded death sentence to Abul Kalam Azad for genocide and crimes against humanity during the Liberation War.

Warren Daley, spokesperson of the British high commission in Dhaka, said: *"The UK has made clear its support for Bangladesh's efforts to bring to justice those accused of atrocities committed in 1971. Along with our EU partners, we are however opposed to the application of the death penalty in all circumstances."*

Muhammad Kamaruzzaman

Muhammad Kamaruzzaman is the senior assistant secretary general of the political party Bangladesh Jamaat-e-Islami convicted of war crimes during the 1971 Liberation war of Bangladesh. He is also the editor of the *Weekly Sonar Bangla*.

On 9 May 2013 the International Crimes Tribunal sentenced him to death after it found Kamaruzzaman guilty of crimes against humanity including genocide, killing, rape, looting, arson, and deportation of people during the Bangladesh Liberation War. However, he denied the charges and said that the trial was politically motivated.

Early life

Kamaruzzaman was born on 4 July 1952, at Sajbarkhila village in Sherpur, Bangladesh (at the time East Pakistan). His father Moulavi Insan Ali Sarker, was a businessman. Kamaruzzaman obtained Master's degree in journalism in 1976 from Dhaka University. He has 5 sons. His wife's name is Nurun Nahar.

Career

In 1971, Kamruzzaman was the leader of the Islami Chattra Sangha (Islamic students organization) in Mymensingh. He was the chief organizer of the Al-Badr, a paramilitary force formed to assist the Pakistan army to thwart the freedom struggle of Bangladesh in 1971, of greater Mymensingh region.

An article in the Daily Sangram on August 16, 1971, said, "A rally and symposium were organized in Mymensingh by the Al-Badr to celebrate the 25th independence day of Pakistan. The chief organizer of the Al-Badr, Mouhammed Kamruzzaman presided over the symposium held at the local Muslim Institute."

Kamaruzzaman was a two-time President of Islami Chhatra Shibir the student wing of Bangladesh Jamaat-e-Islami. Kamaruzzaman became a journalist at the Weekly Sonar Bangla in the 1980s, later taking the role of editor.

He also worked for *The Daily Sangram* as Executive Editor. In four successive elections between 1991 and 2008 Kamaruzzaman unsuccessfully contested the seat Sherpur-1 for Jamaat-e-Islami, losing the last three times to the Awami League candidate Md. Atiur Rahman Atik. Under pressure from Shahbag protesters, Kamaruzzaman's membership of the National Press Club was cancelled on 13 February 2013.

A Strategy for Change

Kamuruzzaman is a leading progressive voice within Jamaat. Well aware of the stigma that the party face and the impediments this stigma caused for the Islamic Movement in Bangladesh, he advocates the establishment of a new party unlinked to any figures, or the families of any figures, accused of crimes in the 1971 Bangladesh War. In his 2010 paper "A Strategy for Change" he outlined how the new party should not use the student front Islami Chatro Shibir for its own purposes and feature women as an integral part from the highest decision making levels down. The document also calls on the illogical gender segregation policies to be revoked.

War crimes trial

Kamuruzzaman was initially arrested on 13 July 2010 and detained for over a year without being formally informed of charges. In November 2011 the United Nations Working Group on Arbitrary Detention adopted the opinion that the detention was disproportional and breached human rights conventions.

Kamaruzzaman, along with nine other senior members from Jamaat-e-Islami, was charged on seven counts of crimes against humanity during the Bangladesh Liberation War in 1971, including genocide, killing, rape, looting, arson, and deportation of unarmed civilians.

He denied all charges.

Charges

- Killing of Badiuzzaman by Al-Badr, led by Kamaruzzaman on Jun 29, 1971.
- Torture of Lecturer Abdul Hannan by Kamaruzzaman and his associates on May in 1971.
- Genocide of 120 men and rape of the women of the village Shohaghpur on July 25, 1971, planned and advised by Kamaruzzaman.
- Murder of Golam Mostafa by Al-Badr on Kamaruzzaman's orders on Aug 23, 1971.
- Killing of eight people from Chawkbazar by Al-Badr in presence of Kamaruzzaman at Sherpur in the middle of the Ramadan during the war.
- Repression of Didar and others in Mymensingh district on November 1971.
- Murder of five on the 27th day of Ramadan by the Al-Badr members following the orders of Kamaruzzaman.

Controversies

Though the government and ICT have stated that justice was the priority, opposition parties Jamaat-e-Islami and the BNP accused the prime minister Sheikh Hasina of using the tribunal to persecute them. In December 2012, conversations and e-mails between the judge and a Brussels-based lawyer were published, which according to *The Economist* revealed that the government wanted a quick verdict from the International Crimes Tribunal. In response, an application was submitted on behalf of Kamaruzzaman for a retrial, which was rejected. Following the revelations, the controversial chief Justice Nizamul Huq resigned from the post and Fazle Kabir was appointed there.

Conviction

The final arguments of the trial closed on 14 April 2013. On 9 May 2013 the International Crimes Tribunal found him guilty of five out of seven counts of charges including torture, genocide, killing, rape, looting, arson, and deportation of unarmed civilians during the 1971 Liberation war of Bangladesh and sentenced him to death by hanging on two of the charges. Kamaruzzaman denied the charges and said that the trial was politically motivated.

RECENT ACTIVITY

It is believed the group has been weakened in recent years due to increased presence of Indian security forces along the Line of Control (LoC) that separates India from Pakistan. Indian security forces gauge the strength of al-Badr to be between 200-300 strong with 30 per cent of those forces being foreign mercenaries. Al-Badr is currently one of only two Kashmiri separatist groups that employ suicide squads as a tactic, the other being Lashkar-e-Tayyeba.

On 27 October 2006, two members of al-Badr were apprehended in Mysore in what Indian police are calling a foiled terror attack. Mohd Ali Hussain and Mohd Fahad were captured carrying a laptop, chemicals often used for creating improvised explosive devices (IEDs), detonators, an AK-47 rifle, a pistol, a cell phone, a digital camera and passports as well as sketches of the state legislature building, 'Vidhan Soudha'.

THREAT GROUP PROFILE META DATA & ANALYSIS

Group Alias: al-Badhr, Al Badr Mujahidin

Intel Analysis: Al Badr was formed with the intention of strengthening the Kashmiri freedom struggle and to liberate the Indian state of Jammu and Kashmir. Al Badr traces it origins to 1971 and operated as part of faction of Hizb-e-Islami led by warlord Gulbuddin Hekmatyar (Group Profile) in Afghanistan during the 1980's.

The outfit has also sought to enforce Islamist lifestyles in the areas in which it operates. For instance, reports of August 2003 indicated that the Al Badr ordered women in the rural areas of J&K to quit police jobs, wear veils, give up studies after the age of 14 and not to venture out without a male escort. Posters carrying these diktats were seen pasted on street walls and mosques in the Thannamandi and Darhal areas of Rajouri district. The posters, written in Urdu, warned of unspecified consequences if women failed to comply. This group, as set forth in The Unlawful Activities (Prevention) Amendment Ordinance, 2004, was deemed a terrorist organization by the government of India.

Group Activities: Al Badr has pledged continued resistance against the Indian army and has launched or attempted to launch attacks against Indian military installations and personnel. The group, initially called Hizb-ul-Mujahideen (Group Profile), was active in the 70's, ceased operations in the 80's, and reappeared as Al-Badr in the late 90's. Members have been actively planning attacks against Indian military and government personnel and have stated their resistance to the cease-fire on the Kashmiri Line of Control declared by India and Pakistan in 2003. Al Badr also seeks to influence extremist Islamic values and has used terror and murder to demonstrate and to impose their beliefs. In 2002, Al Badr terrorists killed three women in the Jammu region because they were attending college.

Individuals Involved: Bakht Zameen: chief commander of the outfit Arfeen Bhai: chief commander in Jammu and Kashmir Ifran: deputy supreme commander Zahid Bhai: publicity chief Jasm Bhat: communication in charge

Operating Region: Jammu & Kashmir, India and Pakistan

Strength: Al Badr is believed to have approximately 200 fighters, including 120 foreign mercenaries.

External Aid: The Pakistani government formally supported Al Badr forces, but in 1998 the ISI urged the Pakistani government to let Al Badr operate independently. Before the fall of the Taliban (Group Profile), al Badr secured weapons and ideological training in many camps throughout Afghanistan The Al Badr is part of the United Jehad Council (UJC), a coalition of Pakistan-based terrorist groups active in Jammu and Kashmir

CHRONOLOGY OF MAJOR KILLINGS IN JAMMU AND KASHMIR

Following is the chronology of major killings in Jammu and Kashmir since 1997 (in reverse chronological order):

Year 2003

- March 24, 2003: 24 Hindus killed in Nadimarg, Kashmir.

Year 2002

- January 7, 2002: 17 Hindus killed in Ramsoo area in Jammu.
- February 17, 2002: 8 Hindus killed in Rajouri area in Jammu.
- March 30, 2002: 12 Hindu temple-goers killed in Raghunath Temple in Jammu.
- May 14, 2002: 32 Hindus killed in Kaluchak, Jammu.
- July 13, 2002: 20 Hindus killed in Kasim Nagar, Jammu.
- August 6, 2002: Nine Amarnath pilgrims killed and 29 others injured at Nunwan base camp in Pahalgam area of Anantnag district in south Kashmir.
- August 24, 2002: 10 Hindus killed in Rajouri district of J&K State.
- November 24, 2002: 14 Hindu temple-goers killed in Raghunath Temple in Jammu.

Year 2001

- February 3, 2001: Six Sikhs gunned down in Mahjoornagar in Srinagar.
- Feb 11, 2001: 15 members of nomad (Gujjar) families

Massacred in Kot-Chadwal in Rajouri district of Jammu.

- Mar 2, 2001: 15 policemen and two medical assistant killed in Manjkote area of Rajouri.
- March 17, 2001: Eight people massacred near Atholi in Doda.
- July 21, 2001: 13 people, including seven Amarnath pilgrims killed at Sheshnag in Anantnag.
- July 22, 2001: 12 people massacred in Cheerji and Tagood in Doda district of Jammu.
- August 4, 2001: 15 villagers killed in Ludder-Sharotid Har area of Doda.

Year 2000

- February 28, 2000: Five Hindu drivers killed near qazigund in Anantnag district of Kashmir.
- Mar 20, 2000: 35 Sikhs massacred at Chatisinghpora in Anantnag.
- August 1, 2000: 31 people including Amarnath yatris killed At Pahalgam in Anantnag.
- August 1-2, 2000: 27 labourers gunned down in Qazigund and Achabal in Anantnag.
- August 2, 2000: Seven family members killed in frontier District of Kupwara in North Kashmir.
- August 2, 2000: 11 Hindus killed in Doda district of Jammu.

Year 1999

- Feb 20, 1999: Four Hindus killed at Muraputta-Rajouri, nine at Barlyara-Udhampur and seven at Bllala-Rajouri in Jammu.
- June 30, 1999: Fifteen Hindu labourers killed in Anantnag district of south Kashmir.
- July 19, 1999: 15 HHindus killed at Layata in Doda district Of Jammu.

Year 1998

- April 18, 1998: 27 Hindus killed in Prankote in Udhampur district in Jammu region.

- June 19, 1998: 25 Hindus killed in Chapnari area Of Doda district in Jammu region.
- July 28, 1998: 16 Hindus killed in two villages of Doda District in Jammu region.
- August 8, 1998: 35 labourers killed in Kalaban on Jammu-Himachal Pradesh border.

Year 1997

- Jan 25/26,1997: 25 Kashmiri Pandits killed at Wandhama-Ganderbal, Srinagar
- Mar 20, 1997: Seven Kashmiri Pandits killed in Sangrampura (Budgam).

LEADERSHIP, COMMAND STRUCTURE AND CADRE

During the time of its formation, the Al Badr was led by Lukmaan, a resident of Pakistan occupied Kashmir (PoK).

Bakht Zameen, a resident of Punjab province in Pakistan, is the present 'chief commander' of the outfit.

Arfeen Bhai alias Lukmaan alias Jannisar is reported to be the 'chief commander' of Al Badr in Jammu and Kashmir.

Among the other leaders of Al Badr are: 'launching commander' Irfan; 'deputy supreme commander' Zahid Bhai; 'publicity chief' Jasm Bhat; 'communication in-charge' Abu Mawai.

Al Badr is reported to possess a cadre strength of approximately 200, including 120 foreign mercenaries.

Headquarters and Areas of Operation

The outfit is headquartered at Mansehra in Pakistan. It is also reported to have a camp office in Muzaffarabad, PoK.

Reportage of the past five years has indicated that the Al Badr is active in the Anantnag, Baramulla, Budgam, Srinagar and Kupwara districts of the Kashmir Valley. It also has a presence in the Poonch and Rajouri districts of Jammu region.

Operational Dynamics

The Al Badr is part of the United Jehad Council (UJC), a coalition of Pakistan-based terrorist groups active in Jammu and Kashmir.

It is reported to have training camps in the Manshera area of North West Frontier Province (NWFP) in Pakistan, Kotli and Muzaffarabad in PoK.

It has launched or threatened to launch attacks targeting Indian military installations and prominent government officials in Jammu and Kashmir.

Al Badr cadres are reported to have taken an active part, under the ISI tutelage, in the Kargil intrusion of 1999. The outfit's 'chief commander' Bakht Zameen was reportedly based in Skardu during the intrusion to monitor the movement of his cadres from Pakistan to Skardu and its forward areas.

The outfit, which was defunct for some time towards the end of the 1990s, had, with increasing frequency, begun to claim responsibility for several acts of terrorist violence in J&K during year 2000.

Official sources indicated that several terrorists killed in the year 2000 were Al Badr cadres. In one such incident, five terrorists, allegedly part of an Al Badr suicide squad, were killed when troops raided their hideout at Theuru near Ganderbal.

The outfit has opposed the cease-fire on the Line of Control (LoC) declared by India and Pakistan in November 2003. Al Badr has consistently been opposed to any process of dialogue between India and Pakistan. For instance, the outfit's chief Bakht Zameen said in an interview on September 5, 2001, that India was not sincere about holding a dialogue for the amicable settlement of the Kashmir issue. While urging Pakistan to concentrate upon strengthening *Jehad* instead of "wasting further time seeking a negotiated settlement," he also asked the military regime to refrain from initiating any steps that would undermine the 'freedom movement' in Jammu and Kashmir.

The outfit has also sought to enforce Islamist lifestyles in the areas in which it operates. For instance, reports of August 2003 indicated that the Al Badr ordered women in the rural areas of J&K to quit police jobs, wear veils, give up studies after the age of 14 and not to venture out without a male escort.

Posters carrying these diktats were seen pasted on street walls and mosques in the Thannamandi and Darhal areas of Rajouri district. The posters, written in Urdu, warned of unspecified consequences if women failed to comply. Earlier on December 20, 2002, in a major terrorist act against women across Jammu region, terrorists killed three young girls, including two college students, at Hasiot village in Rajouri district. The separate incidents were reportedly carried out by a group of three Pakistani terrorists belonging to the Al Badr led by the outfit's 'area commander' Zubair Gul.

The outfit launched a monthly Urdu magazine 'Al Badr' from Karachi and Rawalpindi in January 1999.

Linkages

The Al Badr is reported to have close linkages with the Inter Services Intelligence and Jamaat-e-Islami in Pakistan. During the regime of the Taliban militia in Afghanistan, the outfit's cadres secured weapons and ideological training in many camps across that country.

The Lahore-based *Daily Times* reported on December 27, 2003, that security agencies were investigating the Hizb-ul-Mujahideen and Al Badr's links with the Al Qaeda, Taliban and Gulbuddin Hekmatyar's Hizb-e-Islami. There were reports that the two organisations' former *Mujahideen* were recruiting *Jihadis* for the Taliban and the Hizb-e-Islami from the North-West Frontier Province (NWFP) and Baluchistan.

INCIDENTS INVOLVING AL BADR

2012

November 27: Replying to a question, Union Minister of State for Home Affairs R. P. N Singh told Lok Sabha (Lower House of Parliament) that various terrorist groups, including Lashkar-e-Toiba (LeT), Indian Mujahideen (IM) and Jaish-e-Mohammed (JeM) are engaged in terrorist activities in the country. "As per available information, militants/terrorists active in India are often supported by their parent outfits based abroad, particularly in Pakistan," he said. Singh said other terrorist outfits which are active in India include Harkat-ul-Mujahideen (HuM), Al-Umma, Al Badr, Harkat-ul-Jehadi-Islami (HuJI), Hizb-ul-Mujahideen (HM), Babbar Khalsa

International (BKI), Khalistan Zindabad Force (KZF) and Khalistan Tiger Force (KTF).

June 11: A 'divisional commander' of Al-Badar, Munir Ahmad Bukhari *alias* Sajad Baloch *alias* Hamza alias Amir alias Ghazi alias Sajad was arrested by the Police from Sopore area in Baramulla District.

2011

October 27: Salahuddin and Al Badr Mujahideen leader Bakht Zameen, too opposed Pakistan's decision in principle to grant MFN-status to India.

January 10: Five militants, including a local 'commander', were killed when two rival militant outfits clashed in Zangi area of Kurram Agency in Federally Administered Tribal Areas (FATA). Sources said that the killed militants belonged to Al Badr outfit. The slain militants were identified as Zuber Khan, Ismail Khan, Kamal Khan, Habibur Rehman and 'commander' Yahya. Sources said that various militant outfits developed differences with each other over extortion and ransom money.

2010

May 26: Security Forces (SFs) in Jammu and Kashmir are fighting a "dozen-odd Hindu militants", according to a document prepared by Police. The dozen-odd surviving Hindu militants are with the Hizb-ul-Mujahideen (HM), Al Badr, Lashkar-e-Toiba (LeT) and the Harkat-ul-Ansar (HuA), they are active in the Jammu Districts of Rajouri, Kishtwar, Doda and Reasi.

May 17: A trial court sent Al Badr militant Sheikh Sajjad, who was arrested on charges of possessing communication equipment, meant for Kashmiri terrorists, to 14-day judicial custody. He was reportedly detained there for possessing as well as allegedly sending hi-tech communication equipment, including satellite phones, to militants in Jammu and Kashmir. Police said during interrogation it was revealed that he was a major supplier of satellite phones to suspected terrorists.

April 27: Ajay Maken, the Minister of State for Home Affairs told Lok Sabha in a written reply. The Minister also said some of the prominent groups which pose a serious threat include LeT,

Jaish-e-Mohammed (JeM), Hizb-ul-Mujahideen (HM), Harkat-ul-Jehad-al-Islami (HuJI), Harkat-ul Mujahideen (HuM), Al Badr, Babbar Khalsa International (BKI), Khalistan Zindabad Force (KZF), Khalistan Commando Force (KCF), International Sikh Youth Federation (ISYF), United Liberation Front of Asom (ULFA) and Communist Party of India -Maoist (CPI-Maoist).

March 12: Chidambaram blamed Pakistan for sponsoring terrorism against India, vowing "swift and decisive" response if a fresh terror attack was found to have been directed from within Pakistan. "It is no secret that every militant organisation that is based in Pakistan is supported by ISI [Inter-Services Intelligence]. Lashkar [Lashkar-e-Toiba], Hizb-ul-Mujahideen (HM), Jama'at-ud-Da'awa (JuD), Al Badr every one of them is supported by ISI.

January 10: A militant of the Pakistan-backed Al-Badr terrorist outfit was arrested from Gopalpura, near Srinagar. Acting on specific information, the SFs arrested Syed Muneer Bukhari alias 'Muna', a resident of Nowpora-Sopore at Gopalpura, a Police spokesman said. He said a pistol, its one magazine, five rounds and one grenade were recovered from his possession.

2009

September 17: The Defence Ministry sources reports that around 300 militants are waiting across the Line of Control (LOC) in Pakistan-occupied Kashmir (PoK) for an opportunity to infiltrate into India, prompting the Army to strengthen its anti-insurgency security grid. Security Forces have killed at least 25 terrorists while foiling these infiltration attempts in August 2009 and these encounters took place at the points along the LoC. Most of these terrorists come from militant outfits such as the Lashkar-e-Toiba (LeT), Al Badr and HM.

August 23: The Special Operations Group of Jammu and Kashmir Police arrested the 'chief commander' of Al Badr militant outfit in the Sopore area of Baramulla District. Zeenat-ul-Islam, a resident of Shopian District in south Kashmir, was operating under various codenames, including Zahid and Junaid, during his four-year stint as the operations chief of the outfit, official sources said. Zeenat-ul-Islam Shah was active in militancy since 2005 and was operating in the Lolab area of Kupwara District, the Inspector General of Police (Kashmir), Farooq Ahmed, said. He is reported to have shifted to Shopian only two months back. He used to report to top Al-Badr commander Yusuf Baloch in Pakistan. He was reportedly trained in Lolab by Pakistan trainer Sikander in 2005.

March 19: Shawaz Ismail (27), a former Pakistan Rangers soldier, who was apparently headed for Kashmir to 'revive' the Al-Badr militant group was arrested in the vicinity of Writers' Buildings in Kolkata, capital of West Bengal. This is the second such arrest in the city in less than a fortnight. Earlier on March 6, Lashkar-e-Toiba (LeT) explosives expert Abu Taher was arrested from the Sealdah railway station.

Shawaz Ismail is reported to have confessed to having served with the Pakistani border guards - service number R39409. He also admitted to be an Al Badr operative. Security sources said he was going to replace the outfit's head of operations in Kashmir. Investigation has revealed that Ismail was sent from Karachi to Bangladesh a few months ago. From Dhaka, he moved to the India-Bangladesh border a couple of days ago and sneaked in through the Rajshahi-Malda corridor on March 18. After entering India, Ismail boarded a Howrah-bound train from Murshidabad. Security Forces arrested him in the busy BBD Bag area on March 19. Additional Commissioner of Police (STF), Rajeev Kumar, said Ismail was supposed to take a train from Howrah to Jammu and Kashmir.

January 15: A suspected Al-Badr 'commander' was killed in an encounter with the Security Forces in the Handwara area of Kupwara District. Official sources said the slain militant was identified as self-styled commander Abu Tamim. One AK 47 rifle, five AK magazines, 80 AK rounds, one pouch, two Chinese grenades and one satellite phone were recovered from his possession.

2008

October 25: Two persons, Mohd Shafi Seer and Mohammad Yousuf Bhat, who were asked by militant groups to carry out grenade attack during polls, were arrested by the SFs from

Handwara area of Kupwara district. One hand grenade each was recovered from them. While Seer was operating for Al Badr, Bhat was carrying out the assignment for LeT outfit. They were asked to lob hand grenades at public places to thwart people's participation in upcoming elections.

October 12: In a joint operation, troops and Jammu and Kashmir Police arrested two most wanted Al-Badr militants from Handwara area of Kupwara district. The militants were identified as Nissar Ahmad Thoker alias Abu Wikas and Imtiyaz Ahmad Dar alias Abu Maaz. One AK 47, one AK 56, six AK magazines, 108 rounds of AK ammunition, six grenades, two pouches and one bag have been recovered from their possession

September 3: Police arrested two locally trained militants belonging to Al-Badr and LeT from the Wader and Mawar areas of Handwara.

July 20: SFs killed two militants in an encounter that ensued after a cordon-and-search operation at Chali Wan in the Bandipora district. The slain militants were later identified as 'launching commander' Abu Zaid alias Abu Zarr alias Abu Zubair, a foreign militant of the LeT in Bandipora, and Gowhar Ahmad alias Akash, a local militant of the Al Badr outfit.

July 15: Police in Shopian district arrested one over ground worker of the Al Badr outfit. Muzaffar Ahmad Chopan of Reshipora was detained along with 126 rounds of Pika rifle.

May 23: The SFs arrested an Al-Badr militant, identified as Mohammad Ashraf Bhat alias Jamshed, arrested from Shopian in the Pulwama district. One Chinese pistol with one magazine, eight rounds of ammunition and two hand grenades were recovered from his possession.

April 9: SFs shot dead three militants, including a Pakistan national, in the Lolab area of Kupwara district. Three more militants of the group, however, managed to escape from the incident site. One of the slain militants has been identified as Ali Bhai, a 'company commander' of the Al-Badr Mujahideen, who, official sources said, was responsible for the killing of two constables in Kupwara on April 4.

March 25: A militant of the Al Badr Mujahideen outfit,

identified as Ahmed Ganai, was arrested in the Budgam district along with two hand grenades.

March 2: Two Al-Badr militants, identified as district commander Janabaz Ahmed Khan, a Pakistani national, and Imtiyaz Ahmed Dar, were killed in an encounter with the SFs in the Chewdara area of Budgam district.

February 29: BSF personnel arrested a militant of the Al-Badr outfit, identified as Mushtaq Ahmad Bhat, in the Kupwara district along with one Chinese pistol.

8

Islamic State of Iraq and the Levant (ISIS)

The Islamic State (IS) also known as the Islamic State of Iraq and the Levant (ISIL) and the Islamic State of Iraq and Syria (ISIS) is a jihadist group, widely regarded as a terrorist organisation. In its self-proclaimed status as a caliphate, it claims religious authority over all Muslims across the world and aspires to bring much of the Muslim-inhabited regions of the world under its direct political control, beginning with territory in the Levant region, which includes Jordan, Israel, Palestine, Lebanon, Cyprus, and an area in southern Turkey that includes Hatay. The group has been officially designated as a foreign terrorist organization by the United States, the United Kingdom, Australia, Canada, Indonesia, and Saudi Arabia, and has been widely described as a terrorist group by Western and Middle Eastern media sources.

The group, in its original form, was composed of and supported by a variety of Sunni Arab terrorist insurgent groups, including its predecessor organizations, Al-Qaeda in Iraq (AQI) (2003–2006), Mujahideen Shura Council (2006–2006) and the Islamic State of Iraq (ISI) (2006–2013), other insurgent groups such as Jeish al-Taiifa al-Mansoura, Jaysh al-Fatiheen, Jund al-Sahaba and Katbiyan Ansar Al-Tawhid wal Sunnah, and a number of Iraqi tribes that profess Sunni Islam.

ISIS grew significantly as an organization owing to its participation in the Syrian Civil War and the strength of its leader, Abu Bakr al-Baghdadi. Economic and political discrimination against Arab Iraqi Sunnis since the fall of the secular Saddam Hussein also helped it to gain support. At the height of the 2003–2011 Iraq War, its forerunners enjoyed a significant presence in the Iraqi governorates of Al Anbar, Nineveh, Kirkuk, most of Salah ad Din, parts of Babil, Diyala and Baghdad, and claimed Baqubah as a capital city. In the ongoing Syrian Civil War, ISIS has a large presence in the Syrian governorates of Ar-Raqqah, Idlib and Aleppo.

ISIS is known for its extreme and brutally harsh interpretation of the Islamic faith and sharia law and has a record of horrifying violence, which is directed at Shia Muslims, indigenous Assyrian/Chaldean/Syriac Christians and Armenian Christians, Yazidis, Druze, Shabakis and Mandeans in particular. It has at least 4,000 fighters in its ranks in Iraq who, in addition to attacks on government and military targets, have claimed responsibility for attacks that have killed thousands of civilians. ISIS had close links with al-Qaeda until 2014, but in February of that year, after an eight-month power struggle, al-Qaeda cut all ties with the group, reportedly for its brutality and "notorious intractability".

ISIS's original aim was to establish a caliphate in the Sunni-majority regions of Iraq. Following its involvement in the Syrian Civil War, this expanded to include controlling Sunni-majority areas of Syria. A caliphate was proclaimed on 29 June 2014, Abu Bakr al-Baghdadi—now known as Amir al-Mu'minin Caliph Ibrahim—was named as its caliph, and the group was renamed the Islamic State.

LEADERSHIP

Osama bin Laden and Zawahiri believed AQI's indiscriminate attacks on fellow Muslims would erode public support for al-Qaeda in the region, and in July 2005 they questioned Zarqawi's strategy in written correspondence. Fishman said the relationship collapsed when Zarqawi ignored al-Qaeda instructions to stop attacking Shiite cultural sites.

A U.S. air strike that killed Zarqawi in June 2006 marked a victory for U.S. and Iraqi intelligence and a turning point for AQI. In its aftermath, Abu Ayyub al-Masri, an Egyptian-born explosives expert and former Zawahiri confidant, emerged as AQI's new leader. In October 2006, Masri adopted the alias Islamic State of

Iraq (ISI) to increase the group's local appeal, which suffered just as Zawahiri had feared, and embody its territorial ambitions; it later came to be known as ISIS, reflecting its broadened ambitions as instability in neighboring Syria after the 2011 uprising there created new opportunities to exploit. ISIS is currently led by Abu Bakr al-Baghdadi, also known as Abu Du'a. The U.S. government believes he resides in Syria.

Funding

Supporters in the region, including those based in Jordan, Syria, and Saudi Arabia, are believed to have provided the bulk of past FUNDING. Iran has also financed AQI, crossing sectarian lines, as Tehran saw an opportunity to challenge the U.S. military presence in the region, according to the U.S. Treasury and documents confiscated in 2006 from Iranian Revolutionary Guards operatives in northern Iraq. In early 2014, Iran OFFERED to join the United States in offering aid to the Iraqi government to counter al-Qaeda gains in Anbar province.

The bulk of ISIS's financing, experts say, comes from sources such as smuggling, extortion, and other crime. ISIS has relied in recent years on funding and manpower from internal recruits [PDF]. Even prior to ISIS's takeover of Mosul, Iraq's second-largest city, in June 2014, the group extorted taxes from businesses small and large, netting upwards of $8 million a month, according to some estimates.

Staying Power

Heavy-handed actions taken by Maliki to consolidate power in the wake of the U.S. withdrawal have alienated much of the Sunni minority, and ISIS has since exploited the "failed social contract," said former CFR press fellow Ned Parker. Maliki's Shiite-dominated government was reluctant to integrate Awakening militias into the national security forces, and critics say he has persecuted Sunni political rivals and stoked sectarian polarization for political gain.

Sunnis who felt marginalized by the Maliki government began protesting for reforms in Anbar province in December 2012, andprominent Shiite clerics such as the Grand Ayatollah Ali Sistani and Moqtada al-Sadr acknowledged the legitimacy of their grievances, Parker wrote. According to a report by the nonpartisan Congressional Research Service [PDF], there were roughly a dozen days in 2012 on which ISIS executed multi-city attacks that killed at least twenty-five Iraqis. On at least four of those days, coordinated attacks left more than a hundred Iraqis dead.

In April 2013, Iraqi security forces raided a protest camp at al-Hawijah, provoking an escalation in Sunni militancy. Car bombings and suicide attacks intensified, with coordinated attacks regularly targeting Shiite MARKETS, cafes, and mosques.

In 2013, 7,818 civilians (including police) were killed in acts of terrorism and violence, more than double the 2012 death toll, according to United Nations figures. An additional 17,891 were injured, making 2013 Iraq's bloodiest year since 2008. At the end of 2013, security forces sought to clear a protest camp in Ramadi. The move provoked an uprising in which security forces pulled out of the city as well as nearby Fallujah, and ISIS moved to fill the void.

Meanwhile, the civil war in neighboring Syria has drawn Sunni jihadists into the rebellion against the regime of Bashar al-Assad, which is dominated by the Alawite sect, an offshoot of Shiite Islam.

While al-Qaeda-linked groups in Syria have fought among themselves and with the secular opposition, the Free Syrian Armysigned a truce with ISIS in late September, an acknowledgment of their efficacy on the battlefield. But divisions within the Islamist opposition camp remain stark.

ISIS declared a merger with Jabhat al-Nusra, an al-Qaeda affiliate that has greater indigenous legitimacy in Syria, in April 2013. But Zawahiri, who succeeded bin Laden as head of so-called "core al-Qaeda," annulled the merger, ruling that Baghdadi's group's operations be limited to Iraq. Baghdadi rejected Zawahiri's ruling and questioned his authority, his group's pledge of fealty to al-Qaeda notwithstanding. Various rival Islamist militant groups coalesced in late 2013 as the Mujahedeen Army with the common goal of forcing ISIS to cede territory and leave Syria.

At odds with al-Qaeda's aims, ISIS has since expanded its territorial control, establishing a "de facto state in the borderlands of Syria and Iraq" that exhibits some of the traditional markers of sovereignty, note Douglas A. Ollivant and Fishman. Beyond fielding a militia, it provides limited services and administers its ultraconservative brand of justice. Much of Anbar province has remained outside the central government's authority since January 2014, and in mid-2014, a Sunni insurgency wrested control of Mosul and its environs after the predominantly Shiite army, hobbled by desertions and cronyism, retreated overnight. ISIS is at the vanguard of the insurgency, but the tactical alliances it has formed with non-jihadi Sunnis, including former members of the Ba'athist regime, have led analysts and policymakers to question how long it can rule over a population concerned by ISIS's extremism.

The takeovers highlighted Baghdad's weakness: In Fallujah, Maliki called on Sunni tribesmen to resist ISIS, and in Mosul, which had been considered a model for the surge and Awakening, he called on the Kurdish security forces, the peshmerga, to do the same. Maliki has also mobilized Shiite militias implicated in sectarian killings, and Iraqi forces are accused of indiscriminate airstrikes. Meanwhile, ISIS gains in the country's north set back the peshmerga and have created a humanitarian crisis for thousands of Iraqi Christians and Yezidis, who are among religious and ethnic minorities targeted by ISIS.

Insurgents' consolidation of territorial control is a concern for the United States, which believes such areas outside of state authority may become safe havens for those jihadis with ambitions oriented toward the "far enemy"—the West. The Obama administration has responded to the regional resurgence by increasing the CIA's support for the Maliki government, including assistance to elite counterterrorism units that report directly to the prime minister, and providing Hellfire missiles and surveillance drones. After Iraqi forces retreated from Mosul, the insurgents who routed them released more than one thousandprisoners and picked up troves of U.S.-supplied matériel.

NAME AND NAME CHANGES

The group has had a number of different names since its formation in early 2004 as *Jamâ*ع*at al-Taw per cent*ع*îd wa-al-Jihâd*, "The Organization of Monotheism and Jihad" (JTJ). These names are underscored in the following paragraphs. In October 2004, the group's leader Abu Musab al-Zarqawi swore loyalty to Osama bin Laden and changed the name of the group to *Tan*✈*îm Qâ*✈*idat al-Jihâd fi Bilâd al-Râfidayn,* "The Organization of Jihad's Base in the Country of the Two Rivers", more commonly known as "Al-Qaeda in Iraq" (AQI). Although the group has never called itself "Al-Qaeda in Iraq", this name has frequently been used to describe it through its various incarnations.

In January 2006, AQI merged with several smaller Iraqi insurgent groups under an umbrella organization called the "Mujahideen Shura Council". This was little more than a media exercise and an attempt to give the group a more Iraqi flavour and perhaps to distance al-Qaeda from some of al-Zarqawi's tactical errors, notably the 2005 bombings by AQI of three hotels in Amman. Al-Zarqawi was killed in June 2006, after which the group's direction shifted again.

On 12 October 2006, the Mujahideen Shura Council joined four more insurgent factions and the representatives of a number of Iraqi Arab tribes, and together they swore the traditional Arab oath of allegiance known as *$*✈*ilf al-Mum*✈*ayyabîn* ("Oath of the Scented Ones"). During the ceremony, the participants swore to free Iraq's Sunnis from what they described as Shia and foreign oppression, and to further the name of Allah and restore Islam to glory.

On 13 October 2006, the establishment of the *Dawlat al-*✈*Iraq al-Islâmîyah,* "Islamic State of Iraq" (ISI) was announced. A cabinet was formed and Abu Abdullah al-Rashid al-Baghdadi became ISI's figurehead emir, with the real power residing with the Egyptian Abu Ayyub al-Masri. The declaration was met with hostile criticism, not only from ISI's jihadist rivals in Iraq, but from leading jihadist ideologues outside the country. Al-Baghdadi and al-Masri were both killed in a US–Iraqi operation in April 2010. The next leader of the ISI was Abu Bakr al-Baghdadi, the current leader of ISIS.

On 9 April 2013, having expanded into Syria, the group adopted the name "Islamic State of Iraq and the Levant", also known as "Islamic State of Iraq and al-Sham". The name is abbreviated as ISIS or alternately ISIL. The final "S" in the acronym ISIS stems from the Arabic word *Shâm* (or *Shaam*), which in the context of global jihad refers to the Levant or Greater Syria. ISIS was also known as *al-Dawlah* ("the State"), or *al-Dawlah al-Islâmîyah* ("the Islamic State"). These are short-forms of the Arabic name for the "Islamic State of Iraq and al-Sham"; it is similar to calling "the United States of America" "the States".

ISIS's detractors, particularly in Syria, refer to the group as *"Da'ish"* or *"Daesh"*,, a term that is based on an acronym formed from the letters of the name in Arabic, *al-Dawla al-Islamiya fi Iraq wa al-Sham*. The group considers the term derogatory and reportedly uses flogging as a punishment for people who use the acronym in ISIS-controlled areas.

On 14 May 2014, the United States Department of State announced its decision to use "Islamic State of Iraq and the Levant" (ISIL) as the group's primary name. The debate over which acronym should be used to designate the group, ISIL or ISIS, has been discussed by several commentators. Ishaan Tharoor from *The Washington Post* concluded: "In the larger battlefield of copy style controversies, the distinction between ISIS or ISIL is not so great."

On 29 June 2014, the establishment of a new caliphate was announced, with Abu Bakr al-Baghdadi named as its caliph, and the group formally changed its name to the "Islamic State".

IDEOLOGY AND BELIEFS

ISIS is an extremist group that follows al-Qaeda's hard-line ideology and adheres to global jihadist principles. Like al-Qaeda and many other modern-day jihadist groups, ISIS emerged from the ideology of the Muslim Brotherhood, the world's first Islamist group dating back to the late 1920s in Egypt. ISIS follows an extreme anti-Western interpretation of Islam, promotes religious violence and regards those who do not agree with its interpretations as infidels and apostates. Concurrently, ISIS (now IS) aims to establish a Salafist-orientated Islamist state in Iraq, Syria and other parts of the Levant.

ISIS's ideology originates in the branch of modern Islam that aims to return to the early days of Islam, rejecting later "innovations" in the religion which it believes corrupt its original spirit. It condemns later caliphates and the Ottoman empire for deviating from what it calls pure Islam and hence has been attempting to establish its own caliphate. However, there are some Sunni commentators, Zaid Hamid, for example, and even Salafi and jihadi muftis such as Adnan al-Aroor and Abu Basir al-Tartusi, who say that ISIS and related terrorist groups are not Sunnis at all, but Kharijite heretics serving an imperial anti-Islamic agenda.

Salafists such as ISIS believe that only a legitimate authority can undertake the leadership of jihad, and that the first priority over other areas of combat, such as fighting against non-Muslim countries, is the purification of Islamic society. For example, when it comes to the Israeli–Palestinian conflict, since ISIS regards the Palestinian Sunni group Hamas as apostates who have no legitimate authority to lead jihad, it regards fighting Hamas as the first step towards confrontation with Israel.

GOALS

From its beginnings the establishment of a pure Islamic state has been one of the group's main goals. According to journalist Sarah Birke, one of the "significant differences" between Al-Nusra Front and ISIS is that ISIS "tends to be more focused on establishing its own rule on conquered territory". While both groups share the ambition to build an Islamic state, ISIS is "far more ruthless... carrying out sectarian attacks and imposing sharia law immediately". ISIS finally achieved its goal on 29 June 2014, when it removed "Iraq and the Levant" from its name, began to refer to itself as the Islamic State, and declared the territory which it occupied in Iraq and Syria a new caliphate.

In mid-2014, the group released a video entitled "The End of Sykes–Picot" featuring an English-speaking Chilean national named Abu Safiyya. The video announced the group's intention to eliminate all modern borders between Islamic Middle Eastern countries; this was a reference to the borders set by the Sykes–Picot Agreement during World War I.

ISIS LEADERSHIP STRUCTURE (2014)

ISIS Organisational Structure in Iraq and Syria

The ISIS is composed of 16 wilayats (read provinces/ administrative districts), in both Iraq and Syria and is reflected in the following map:

LIST OF AREAS THE ISLAMIC STATE CLAIMS IT CONTROLS AFTER THIS WEEK'S OFFENSIVE IN NINEWA, FROM AUG. 7, 2014 STATEMENT ON TWITTER:

1. All of Sinjar municipality and the areas belonging to it.
2. All of Talkif municipality and the areas belonging to it.
3. All of al-Hamdaniya municipality and the areas belonging to it.
4. All of Makhmour municipality and the areas belonging to it.
5. Zammar township and all the villages belonging to it.
6. Rabee'ah township and all the villages belonging to it.
7. Bartala township and all the villages belonging to it.
8. Karam Lays township and all the villages belonging to it.
9. Al-Kweir township and all the villages belonging to it.
10. Wana township and all the villages belonging to it.
11. Large areas in Filfeel township.
12. Large areas of Ba'ashiqa township.
13. Some of the al-Shalalat areas in Mosul.
14. The Sada and Ba'wiza area of Mosul.
15. The oil-rich 'Ayn Zalah area.
16. The strategic Mosul dam
17. The large Tumarat base.

THE ISLAMIC STATE OF IRAQ AND THE SHAM'S 16 WILAYATS ARE:

IN IRAQ:

- Southern Division (based in Babil province, south of Baghdad)
- Diyala Division
- Baghdad Division
- Kirkuk Division
- Salahuddin Division
- Anbar Division (is the largest and most active wilayat in Iraq)
- Ninewa Division

IN SYRIA:

- Al Barakah Division (Hasaka)
- Al Kheir Division (Deir al Zour)
- Al Raqqah Division
- Al Badiya Division
- Halab [Aleppo] Division
- Idlib Division
- Hama Division
- Damascus Division
- Coast [Al Sahel] Division

Areas of Operation in Iraq

Anbar Province

The ISIS stronghold is in the Anbar province, as seen in the operation of training camps coupled with attacks on Government security personnel, a case in point being various suicide bomb attacks in a single day targeting local police in Rawa. In addition, the ISIS gained control in areas of Ramadi and Fallujah, following the withdrawal of the Iraqi army due to widespread Sunni rejection of attempts to dismantle the Ramadi camp protest site. Their presence in these areas were also seen in Anbar with mortar attacks at the Sahwa leader Abu Risha's estate and fighting with security forces in various Anbar urban locations, such as the al-Mal'ab quarter in Ramadi and the al-Khaldiya area near Fallujah.

Mosul, Baiji, Babil, and Baghdad

Beyond Anbar, the group has enacted frequent attacks on the Iraqi army in various districts of Mosul as well as target specific bomb attacks in the Baiji area of Salah ad-Din province, Jurf al-Sakhr in northern Babil province (just south of Baghdad), and the Tarmiya area of northern Baghdad province, where assaults have been launched on "Sahwa" forces, resulting in incidents such as the execution of 18 Sunnis suspected of being "Sahwa militia" during November 2013.

Kurdistan

During 2013, ISIS operations expanded to Iraqi Kurdistan, as seen in the Arbil bombings in September 2013, that the ISIS referred to as retaliation due to the Kurdistan Regional Government's alleged support for the "PKK" in Syria.

ISIS in Syria

In April 2013, ISIS attempted to morph into the creation of the Islamic State of Iraq and the Levant (ISIS/ISIL) but the formation of a new group was rejected by the al-Nusra Front. ISIS's leader, Abu Bakr al-Baghdadi, known as Abu Dua, nevertheless pressed ahead with expanding its operations into Syria. In August 2013, US intelligence assessed that he was based in Syria and commanded as many 5,000 fighters, many of them foreign jihadists. The group is active mostly in northern and eastern provinces of Syria. It has assumed joint control of municipalities in Aleppo, Idlib and Raqqa provinces. In November 2013 Al-Qaeda chief Ayman al-Zawahiri ordered the disbanding of the main jihadist faction in Syria, the ISIL, in an audio message aired on Al-Jazeera. The tape appeared to confirm a letter posted by Al-Jazeera in June 2013, claimed to have been written by Zawahiri and addressed to the leaders of Al-Qaeda factions in both countries. The head of Al-Qaeda also stressed that the Al-Nusra Front was the branch of the global jihadist group in Syria.ISIL's extremism has resulted in the deaths of more than 1,000 rebels in the last 3-4 weeks alone.

ISIS in Lebanon

The ISIS reach into Lebanon is seen in the following most recent developments:

On 3 January 2014, a leader in the Jordanian Salafi movement said the ISIS has decided officially to infiltrate Lebanon militarily, by stating that "the leader of al-Nusra Front Abu Muhammad al-Goulani and the prince of "ISIL" Abu Baker al-Baghdadi have decided to enter Lebanon militarily".

The ISIS claimed credit for the suicide bombing Haret Hreik in the southern suburb of Beirut on 22 January 2014, which killed 5 people. In the statement released via Twitter, the ISIS stated that the group has the capacity to violate Hezbollah security measures and that the suicide bombing is "a first small payment from the heavy account that is awaiting those criminals."

The above announcement was followed by the Lebanon-focused A'isha Media Center announcement of an online campaign to support the ISIS in the conflict with Syrian militant factions.

On 25 January 2013 a video recording declared the creation of a Lebanese division for the ISIS. In the recording, Abu Sayyaf al-Ansari (further details unknown) swears allegiance to Abu Bakr al-Baghdadi, the Iraqi leader of ISIS. He also called on Sunnis to abandon the Lebanese crusader" army, supportive of continued allegations by Sunni Islamists that the armed forces are "backed by Hezbollah." The recording surfaced amid escalating tensions in Lebanon linked to the war in neighbouring Syria. While the Lebanon's Shiite Hezbollah has deployed troops to Syria to back President Bashar al-Assad, many Sunnis are opposed to Assad and any support to his government. In the five-minute recording, al-Ansari indicated that "a spokesman for ISIS in Lebanon" identified as Abu Omar al-Muhajir would soon make a statement of his own.

ISIS in Gaza Strip/West Bank

During February 2014, the ISIS released a video that showed ISIS fighters announcing plans to wage a jihad in Gaza. A spokesperson in the video announced that DAESH (ISIS) now has "lions and armies in the environs of Jerusalem" and called on Muslims to support the group in their jihad against the enemies of Islam and "Arab tyrants." The ISIS regards Hamas as to moderate and not committed in the fight against Israel. The ISIS announcement is the first indication of presence within Gaza Strip/ West Bank as well as a direct challenge to the Palestinian Islamist movement Hamas. The extent of support for the ISIS from Gaza culminated in the formation of an ISIS Syrian brigade comprised and dedicated to fighters from Gaza, referred to as the "Sheikh Abu al-Nur al-Maqdisi Brigade," named after the founder of the Jund Ansar Allah group in Gaza- Abdel Latif Moussa, who was killed in clashes with Hamas in 2009.

PROPAGANDA AND SOCIAL MEDIA

The group is also known for its effective use of propaganda. In November 2006, shortly after the creation of the Islamic State of Iraq, the group established the al-Furqan Institute for Media

Production, which produced CDs, DVDs, posters, pamphlets, and web-related propaganda products. ISIS's main media outlet is the I'tisaam Media Foundation, which was formed in March 2013 and distributes through the Global Islamic Media Front (GIMF). In 2014, ISIS established the Al Hayat Media Center, which targets a Western audience and produces material in English, German, Russian and French. In 2014 it also launched the Ajnad Media Foundation, which releases jihadist audio chants.

ISIS's use of social media has been described by one expert as "probably more sophisticated than [that of] most US companies". It regularly takes advantage of social media, particularly Twitter, to distribute its message by organizing hashtag campaigns, encouraging Tweets on popular hashtags, and utilizing software applications that enable ISIS propaganda to be distributed to its supporters' accounts. Another comment is that "ISIS puts more emphasis on social media than other jihadi groups.... They have a very coordinated social media presence." Although ISIS's social media feeds on Twitter are regularly shut down, it frequently recreates them, maintaining a strong online presence. The group has attempted to branch out into alternate social media sites, such as Quitter, Friendica and Diaspora; Quitter and Friendica, however, almost immediately removed ISIS's presence from their sites.

FINANCES

A study of 200 documents—personal letters, expense reports and membership rosters—captured from Al-Qaeda in Iraq and the Islamic State of Iraq was carried out by the RAND Corporation in 2014. It found that from 2005 until 2010, outside donations amounted to only 5 per cent of the group's operating budgets, with the rest being raised within Iraq. In the time-period studied, cells were required to send up to 20 per cent of the income generated from kidnapping, extortion rackets and other activities to the next level of the group's leadership. Higher-ranking commanders would then redistribute the funds to provincial or local cells that were in difficulties or needed money to conduct attacks. The records show that the Islamic State of Iraq was dependent on members from Mosul for cash, which the leadership used to provide additional funds to struggling militants in Diyala, Salahuddin and Baghdad.

In mid-2014, Iraqi intelligence extracted information from an ISIS operative which revealed that the organization had assets worth US$2 billion, making it the richest jihadist group in the world.

About three quarters of this sum is said to be represented by assets seized after the group captured Mosul in June 2014; this includes possibly up to US$429 million looted from Mosul's central bank, along with additional millions and a large quantity of gold bullion stolen from a number of other banks in Mosul. However, doubt was later cast on whether ISIS was able to retrieve anywhere near that sum from the central bank, and even on whether the bank robberies had actually occurred.

ISIS has routinely practised extortion, by demanding money from truck drivers and threatening to blow up businesses, for example. Robbing banks and gold shops has been another source of income. The group is widely reported as receiving funding from private donors in the Gulf states, and both Iran and Iraqi Prime Minister Nouri al-Maliki have accused Saudi Arabia and Qatar of funding ISIS, although there is reportedly no evidence that this is the case.

The group is also believed to receive considerable funds from its operations in Eastern Syria, where it has commandeered oilfields and engages in smuggling out raw materials and archaeological artifacts. ISIS also generates revenue from producing crude oil and selling electric power in northern Syria. Some of this electricity is reportedly sold back to the Syrian government.

Since 2012, ISIS has produced annual reports giving numerical information on its operations, somewhat in the style of corporate reports, seemingly in a bid to encourage potential donors.

TIMELINE OF EVENTS

2014 events:

- *3 January:* ISIS proclaimed an Islamic state in Fallujah. After prolonged tensions, the newly formed Army of Mujahedeen, the Free Syrian Army and the Islamic Front launched an offensive against ISIS-held territory in the Syrian provinces of Aleppo and Idlib. A spokesman for the rebels said that rebels had attacked ISIS in up to 80 per cent of all ISIS-held villages in Idlib and 65 per cent of those in Aleppo.

- *4 January:* ISIS claimed responsibility for the car-bomb attack on 2 January that killed four people and wounded dozens in the southern Beirut suburb of Haret Hreik, a Hezbollah bastion.
- By 6 January, Syrian rebels had managed to expel ISIS forces from the city of Ar-Raqqah, ISIS's largest stronghold and capital of Ar-Raqqah province. Several weeks later ISIS took the city back.
- *8 January:* Syrian rebels expelled most ISIS forces from the city of Aleppo. However, ISIS reinforcements from Deir ez-Zor province managed to retake several neighbourhoods of the city of Ar-Raqqah. By mid-January ISIS fighters had retaken the entire city of Ar-Raqqah, while rebels expelled ISIS fighters fully from Aleppo city and the villages west of it.
- *25 January:* ISIS announced the creation of its new Lebanese arm, pledging to fight the Shia militant group Hezbollah and its supporters in Lebanon.
- *29 January:* Turkish aircraft near the border fired on an ISIS convoy inside Aleppo province in Syria, killing 11 ISIS fighters and one ISIS emir.
- *30 January:* ISIS fired on border patrol soldiers in Turkey. The Turkish Army retaliated with Panter howitzers and destroyed the ISIS convoy.
- In late January, it was confirmed that Syrian rebels had assassinated ISIS's second-in-command, Haji Bakr, who was al-Qaeda's military council head and a former military officer in Saddam Hussein's army.
- *3 February:* Al-Qaeda's general command broke off its links with ISIS, reportedly to concentrate the Islamist effort on unseating President Bashar al-Assad.
- By mid-February, Al-Nusra Front had joined the battle in support of rebel forces, and expelled ISIS forces from Deir ez-Zor province in Syria.

- By March, ISIS forces had fully retreated from Syria's Idlib province after battles against the Syrian rebels.
- *4 March:* ISIS retreated from the Aleppo province–Turkey border town of Azaz and nearby villages, choosing instead to consolidate around Ar-Raqqah in anticipation of an escalation of fighting with Al-Nusra.
- *8 March:* During an interview with French television channel France 24, Iraqi Prime Minister Nouri al-Maliki accused Saudi Arabia and Qatar of openly funding ISIS.
- *20 March:* In Niðde city in Turkey, three ethnic Albanian members of ISIS—Benjamin Xu, Çendrim Ramadani and Muhammed Zakiri—opened fire while hijacking a truck which killed one police officer and one gendarmerie officer and wounded five people. Shortly after their arrest, Polis Özel Harekat teams launched a series of operations against ISIS in Ýstanbul. Police found documents and an ISIS flag in one place and two Azerbaijanis were arrested.
- *27 April:* Iraqi military helicopters reportedly attacked and destroyed an ISIS convoy of eight vehicles inside Syria. This may be the first time that Iraqi forces have struck outside their country since the Gulf War.1 May: ISIS carried out a total of seven public executions in the city of Ar-Raqqah, northern Syria. Pictures that emerged from the city show how ISIS had been carrying out public crucifixions in areas under its control. In most of these crucifixions, the victims were shot first and their bodies then displayed, but there were also reports of crucifixions preceding the victims being shot or decapitated. In one case a man was said to have been "crucified alive for eight hours", but there was no indication of whether he died.
- In early June, following its large-scale offensives in Iraq, ISIS was reported to have seized control of most of Mosul, the second most populous city in Iraq, a large part of the surrounding Nineveh province, and the city of Fallujah. ISIS also took control of Tikrit, the administrative center of the Salah ad Din Governorate, with the ultimate goal of capturing Baghdad, the Iraqi capital. ISIS was believed to have only 2,000–3,000 fighters up until the Mosul

campaign, but during that campaign it became evident that this number was a gross underestimate.

- Also in June, there were reports that a number of Sunni groups in Iraq that were opposed to the predominantly Shia government had joined ISIS, thus bolstering the group's numbers. However, the Kurds—who are mostly Sunnis—in the northeast of Iraq were unwilling to be drawn into the conflict, and there were clashes in the area between ISIS and the Kurdish Peshmerga.
- *5 June:* ISIS militants stormed the city of Samarra, Iraq, before being ousted from the city by airstrikes mounted by the Iraqi military.
- *6 June:* ISIS militants carried out multiple attacks in the city of Mosul, Iraq.
- *7 June:* ISIS militants took over the University of Anbar in Ramadi, Iraq and held 1,300 students hostage before being ousted by the Iraqi military.
- *9 June:* Mosul fell to ISIS control. The militants seized control of government offices, the airport and police stations. Militants also looted the Central Bank in Mosul, reportedly absconding with US$429 million. More than 500,000 people fled Mosul to escape ISIS. Mosul is a strategic city as it is at a crossroad between Syria and Iraq, and poses the threat of ISIS seizing control of oil production.
- *11 June:* ISIS seized the Turkish consulate in the Iraqi city of Mosul and kidnapped the head of the diplomatic mission and several staff members. ISIS seized the Iraqi city of Tikrit.
- *12 June:* Human Rights Watch, an international human rights advocacy organization, issued a statement about the growing threat to civilians in Iraq.
- *13 June:* Navi Pillay, UN High Commissioner for Human Rights, expressed alarm at reports that ISIS fighters "have been actively seeking out—and in some cases killing—soldiers, police and others, including civilians, whom they perceive as being associated with the government".
- *15 June:* ISIS militants captured the Iraqi city of Tal Afar

in the province of Nineveh. ISIS claimed that 1,700 Iraqi soldiers who had surrendered in the fighting had been executed, and released many images of mass executions via its Twitter feed and various web sites.

- *22 June:* ISIS militants captured two key crossings in Anbar, a day after seizing the border crossing at Al-Qaim, a town in a province which borders Syria. According to analysts, capturing these crossings could aid ISIS in transporting weapons and equipment to different battlefields.
- *24 June:* The Syrian Air Force bombed ISIS positions in Iraq. Iraqi Prime Minister Nouri al-Maliki stated: "There was no coordination involved, but we welcome this action. We welcome any Syrian strike against Isis because this group targets both Iraq and Syria."
- *25 June:* Al-Nusra Front's branch in the Syrian town of al-Bukamal pledged loyalty to ISIS, thus bringing to a close months of fighting between the two groups.
- *25 June:* In an interview with the BBC Arabic service, Prime Minister Nouri al-Maliki said that Iraq had purchased used Sukhoi fighter jets from Russia and Belarus to battle ISIS militants after delays in the delivery of F-16 fighters purchased from the US. "[If] we had air cover, we would have averted what happened", he said.
- *26 June:* Iraq launched its first counterattack against ISIS's advance with an airborne assault designed to seize back control of Tikrit University.
- *28 June:* The Jerusalem Post reported that the Obama administration had requested US$500 million from the US Congress to use in the training and arming of "moderate" Syrian rebels fighting against the Syrian government, in order to counter the growing threat posed by ISIS in Syria and Iraq.
- *29 June:* ISIS announced the establishment of a new caliphate. Abu Bakr al-Baghdadi was appointed its caliph, and the group formally changed its name to the Islamic State.
- *2 July:* Abu Bakr al-Baghdadi, the self-proclaimed caliph

of the new Islamic State, said that Muslims should unite to capture Rome in order to "own the world". He called on Muslims the world over to unite behind him as their leader.

- *3 July:* ISIS captured Syria's largest oilfield from rival Islamist fighters, Al-Nusra Front, who put up no resistance to the attack. Taking control of the al-Omar oilfield gave ISIS access to potentially useful crude oil reserves.
- *17 July:* Syria's Shaer gas field in the Homs Governorate was seized by the Islamic State. According to the Syrian Observatory for Human Rights, at least 90 National Defence Force guards defending the field were killed, as were 21 ISIS fighters. The SOHR later put the death toll from the fighting and executions at 270 soldiers, militiamen and staff, and at least 40 ISIS fighters.
- *19 July:* ISIS claimed responsibility for a suicide bombing which killed 33 people and left more than 50 wounded. The explosion occurred in Baghdad's Kadhimiya district, which is the site of a major Shia shrine.
- *24 July:* ISIS blew up the Mosque and tomb of the Prophet Yunus (Jonah) in Mosul, with no reported casualties. Residents in the area said that ISIS had erased a piece of Iraqi heritage.
- *26 July:* ISIS blew up the Nabi Shiyt (Prophet Seth) shrine in Mosul. Sami al-Massoudi, deputy head of the Shia endowment agency which oversees holy sites, confirmed the destruction and added that ISIS had taken artifacts from the shrine to an unknown location.
- *28 July:* To mark the Muslim holy festival of Eid al-Fitr, which ends the period of Ramadan, ISIS released and circulated a 30-minute video showing graphic scenes of mass executions.
- The UN reported that of the 1,737 fatal casualties of the Iraq conflict during July, 1,186 were civilians.
- *1 August:* The Indonesian BNPT (id) declared ISIS a terrorist organization.
- *2 August:* The Iraqi Army confirmed that 37 loyalist fighters

had died during combat with Islamic State militants south of Baghdad and in Mosul. The Patriotic Union of Kurdistan (PUK) claimed that "hundreds" of IS militiamen had died in the action.

- *3 August:* IS fighters occupied the city of Zumar and an oilfield in the north of Iraq, after a battle against Kurdish forces.
- *5 August:* Al Jazeera reported that an IS offensive in the Sinjar area of northern Iraq had forced 30,000–50,000 Yazidis to flee into the mountains fearing they would be killed by the IS. They had been threatened with death if they refused conversion to Islam. A UN representative said that "a humanitarian tragedy is unfolding in Sinjar".
- *6 August:* The Islamic State kidnapped 400 Yazidi women in Sinjar to sell them as sex slaves.
- *7 August:* IS fighters took control of the town of Qaraqosh in the province of Nineveh in northern Iraq, which forced its large Christian population to flee.
- *7 August:* President Obama authorized targeted airstrikes in Iraq against ISIS, along with airdrops of aid. The UK offered the US assistance with surveillance and refuelling, and planned humanitarian airdrops to Iraqi refugees.
- *8 August:* The US asserted that the systematic destruction of the Yazidi people by the Islamic State was genocide. The US military launched indefinite airstrikes targeting Islamic State fighters, equipment and installations, with humanitarian aid support from the UK and France, in order to protect civilians in northern Iraq. The Islamic State had advanced to within 30 km of Erbil in northern Iraq. The UK is also considering joining the US in airstrikes.
- *10 August:* France's Foreign Minister Laurent Fabius said that Iraq's Kurds must be equipped to fight against ISIS and indicated that France would consider providing arms aid "in liaison with the Europeans". Islamic State militants buried alive an undefined number of Yazidi women and children, in an attack that killed 500 people, in what has been described as ongoing genocide in northern Iraq.

- *11 August:* The Arab League accused the Islamic State of committing crimes against humanity. The UK decided not to join the US in airstrikes and instead stepped up its humanitarian aid to the refugees.
- *12 August:* The US announced that it would not extend its airstrikes against the Islamic State to areas outside northern Iraq, emphasizing that the objective of the airstrikes was to protect US diplomats in Erbil. The US and the UK airdropped 60,000 litres of water and 75,000 meals. The Vatican called on religious leaders of all denominations, particularly Muslim, to unite and condemn IS for what it described as "heinous crimes" and the use of religion to justify them.
- *13 August:* Jihadists from the Islamic State (IS) group have taken control of a string of villages in the northern Syrian province of Aleppo, a monitoring group said on Wednesday.The Britain-based Syrian Observatory for Human Rights said the extremist group had managed to seize the six villages north of the city of Aleppo, and not far from the border with Turkey."
- *14 August:* Brochures urging Muslims to leave Britain and join ISIS were handed out to shoppers in Oxford Street in central London. Men were described as standing in front of posters declaring "the dawn of a new era has begun" and handing out pro-ISIS brochures. "The khilafah (Caliphate) has been established", one leaflet read, in reference to territories gained in Iraq and Syria after ISIS waged its lightning offensive in recent weeks. Another leaflet said: "We have been living in a constant state of ignorance, our lands separated, resources stolen, ummah disunited, honour humiliated and the laws of shirk established over us."

2013 events:

- Starting in April 2013, the group made rapid military gains in controlling large parts of Northern Syria, where the Syrian Observatory for Human Rights described them as "the strongest group".

- *11 May:* Two car bombs exploded in the town of Reyhanlý in Hatay Province, Turkey. At least 51 people were killed and 140 injured in the attack. The attack was the deadliest single act of terrorism ever to take place on Turkish soil. Along with the Syrian intelligence service, ISIS was suspected of carrying out the bombing attack.
- By 12 May, nine Turkish citizens, who were alleged to have links with Syria's intelligence service, had been detained. On 21 May 2013, the Turkish authorities charged the prime suspect, according to the state-run Anatolia news agency. Four other suspects were also charged and 12 people had been charged in total. All suspects were Turkish nationals whom Ankara believed were backed by the Syrian government.
- In July, Free Syrian Army battalion chief Kamal Hamami—better known by his nom de guerre Abu Bassir Al-Jeblawi—was killed by the group's Coastal region emir after his convoy was stopped at an ISIS checkpoint in Latakia's rural northern highlands. Al-Jeblawi was traveling to visit the Al-Izz Bin Abdulsalam Brigade operating in the region when ISIS members refused his passage, resulting in an exchange of fire in which Al-Jeblawi received a fatal gunshot wound.
- Also in July, ISIS organised a mass break-out of its members being held in Iraq's Abu Ghraib prison. British newspaper *The Guardian* reported that over 500 prisoners escaped, including senior commanders of the group. ISIS issued an online statement claiming responsibility for the prison break, describing the operation as involving 12 car bombs, numerous suicide bombers and mortar and rocket fire. It was described as the culmination of a one-year campaign called "destroying the walls", which was launched on 21 July 2012 by ISIS leader Abu Bakr al-Baghdadi; the aim was to replenish the group's ranks with comrades released from the prison.
- In early August, ISIS led the final assault in the Siege of Menagh Air Base.

- In September, members of the group kidnapped and killed the Ahrar ash-Sham commander Abu Obeida Al-Binnishi, after he had intervened to protect members of a Malaysian Islamic charity; ISIS had mistaken their Malaysian flag for that of the United States.
- Also in September, ISIS overran the Syrian town of Azaz, taking it from an FSA-affiliated rebel brigade. ISIS members had attempted to kidnap a German doctor working in Azaz. In November 2013, *Today's Zaman*, an English-language newspaper in Turkey, reported that Turkish authorities were on high alert, with the authorities saying that they had detailed information on ISIS's plans to carry out suicide bombings in major cities in Turkey, using seven explosive-laden cars being constructed in Ar-Raqqah.
- From 30 September, several Turkish media web sites reported that ISIS had accepted responsibility for the attack and had threatened further attacks on Turkey.
- In November, the Syrian Observatory for Human Rights stated: "ISIS is the strongest group in Northern Syria—100 per cent—and anyone who tells you anything else is lying."
- In December, there were reports of fighting between ISIS and another Islamic rebel group, Ahrar ash-Sham, in the town of Maskana, Aleppo in Syria.

9

Hezbollah

A Shia'ist militant group based in Lebanon, they are considered to be more powerful than the Lebanese army. Founded by Muslim clerics (speared by Ayatollah Khomeini) the Hezbollah was founded mainly to counter Israeli occupation of Lebanon (1982). Their objective was well defined in that they wanted to expel any sort of western presence (especially American) from Lebanon, along with western allies. Hezbollah is known to receive training and funding from Iran and is also backed by Syria. The 1983 bombings on the US Embassy in Lebanon, the Lebanon hostage crisis from 1982 to 1992, the London Israeli Embassy attack in 1994, the AC flight 901 attack in 1994 in Panama, and many many more terrorist activities have been credited to this terrorist group.

Hezbollah is a Shiite Muslim political party and militant group that the United States and European Union consider a terrorist organization. With significant support from Iran and Syria, Hezbollah maintains an extensive security apparatus, political organization, and social services network in Lebanon, where the group is often described as a "state within the state." Hezbollah's raison d'etre, resistance to Israel and Western involvement in the Middle East, has made it an effective proxy for Iranian foreign policy while earning the group some support from beyond its Shiite base. But as it has become increasingly embroiled in the Syrian civil war, where its fighters have fought for the Assad regime, it has alienated some of its Lebanese constituents and reportedly prompted deadly reprisals in Beirut from partisans of the predominantly Sunni Muslim Syrian rebels. The U.S.

government and its European allies consider Hezbollah a global terrorist threat and a menace to Mideast stability.

What are Hezbollah's origins?

Hezbollah (or "Party of God") emerged during Lebanon's fifteen-year-long civil war (1975–1990) in the aftermath of Israel's invasion in 1982 and subsequent occupation. Israel aimed to expel Palestinian militants operating in southern Lebanon, but the move galvanized a faction of disenfranchised Shiites to take up arms in support of an Iranian-style clerical regime. In its infancy, the movement obtained critical financial support and training from Iran's Revolutionary Guards. Suicide attacks on the U.S. embassy and Marine Corps barracks in Beirut in October 1983 (258 Americans killed) furthered the group's image as leaders of the Shiite resistance. Just months later, President Ronald Reagan withdrew U.S. Marines who had been deployed to Lebanon as part of a multinational peacekeeping force.

Hezbollah issued its founding manifesto in 1985, around the time that analysts believe the group coalesced into a unified organization. The platform vowed Hezbollah's loyalty to Iran's supreme leader, Ayatollah Ruhollah Khomeini; urged the establishment of an Islamic regime; and called for the expulsion of the United States, France, and Israel from Lebanese territory, as well as for the destruction of the Israeli state. The manifesto states:

"Our primary assumption in our fight against Israel states that the Zionist entity is aggressive from its inception, and built on lands wrested from their owners, at the expense of the rights of the Muslim people. Therefore our struggle will end only when this entity is obliterated. We recognize no treaty with it, no cease-fire, and no peace agreements, whether separate or consolidated."

What is Hezbollah's leadership and organizational structure?

Hezbollah's top commander, the general secretary, is chosen by a seven-member shura council, which in turn oversees five sub-councils: 1) the political assembly, 2) jihad assembly, 3) parliamentary assembly, 4) executive assembly, and 5) judicial assembly. Hassan Nasrallah has led Hezbollah as general secretary since 1992, following Israel's targeted killing of the group's cofounder Abbas al-Musawi. Nasrallah was a member of Hezbollah's ideological predecessor, al-Dawa al-Islamiya (The Islamic Call), a militant group that followed the teachings of prominent Iraqi cleric Mohammed Baqir al-Sadr. Other ranking Hezbollah members include Naim Qassem, second-in-command, and Hussein al-Khalil, a top political adviser to Nasrallah.

For more than twenty years, Imad Fayez Mugniyah was considered Hezbollah's top planner of worldwide terrorist operations, and was on several U.S. and international most wanted lists. Experts say Mugniyah joined Hezbollah in its early days and quickly rose to a senior position in the organization. He was killed in a car bombing in Damascus in February 2008 that Hezbollah officials accused Israel of orchestrating. The Israeli government has denied involvement.

Iran bankrolls Hezbollah with up to $200 million a year, Matthew Levitt, a senior fellow at the Washington Institute for Near East Policy, said at a CFR meeting in October 2013. It is a particularly substantial investment, considering the economic stress of international sanctions that Iran has been under, Levitt said.

The U.S. government and its European allies consider Hezbollah a global terrorist threat and a menace to Mideast stability.

Where is Hezbollah active?

Hezbollah's base is in Lebanon's Shiite-dominated areas, including parts of Beirut, southern Lebanon, and the Bekaa Valley, an important farming region in the east. Israel withdrew from Lebanon in 2000 after years of fighting Hezbollah guerrillas there.

Hezbollah continued to periodically shell Israeli forces in the disputed Shebaa Farms border zone. Periodic conflict between militants and Israeli forces erupted in a month-long war during the summer of 2006, in which Hezbollah launched thousands of rockets into Israeli territory. The group's use of sophisticated anti-ship and anti-armor weaponry, which Western officials suspect was supplied by Iran, surprised many Israeli commanders. Though Lebanon suffered heavy losses, the campaign bolstered Hezbollah's resistance credentials, analysts say. A UN-brokered cease-fire was formalized in August of that year, but Israel-Hezbollah tensions remain high.

"Its recent involvement in Syria has raised the question: is it a Lebanese nationalist organization, or a group more interested in protecting Shiite interests throughout the Middle East?" —Robert Danin, Council on Foreign Relations

In mid-2013, Nasrallah publicly pledged his forces to the survival of Syria's Assad regime, Hezbollah's longtime ally. "This battle is ours... and I promise you victory," he said in a televised address. Some Western analysts say the influx of Hezbollah fighters has been critical to his survival so far.

At that time, more than a thousand Hezbollah fighters helped Syrian forces retake the strategic city of Qusayr. They have since helped government forces secure supply corridors in the Bekaa Valley, alongside the Lebanese border. Analysts estimate that Iran and Hezbollah are marshaling several thousand fighters in support of the Assad regime.

"The decision to send expeditionary forces to Syria marked a major turning point for Hezbollah, leaving southern Lebanon potentially exposed to Israel," says CFR's Robert Danin. "This move has left many Shiites in Lebanon worried that Hezbollah has overreached and forsaken its commitment to Lebanon in favor of its larger alliance with Iran and Assad's Syria."

Israel is believed to have conducted multiple air strikes in Syria to destroy shipments of advanced weaponry to Hezbollah. The United States and the European Union have accused Iran's Quds Force, an elite unit of the Revolutionary Guard Corps, of providing material support to Hezbollah and Syrian forces. Israeli officials believe Quds Force commander Qassem Suleimani has traveled to Damascus to manage operations.

Where else does Hezbollah operate?

The U.S State Department designated Hezbollah a Foreign Terrorist Organization in October 1997, and believes the group operates terrorist cells in Europe, Africa, Asia, and Latin America. In 2010, the Obama administration described Hezbollah as "the most technically capable terrorist group in the world." With Iranian unseen since the 1990s," said a 2013 State Department fact sheet. Several major terrorist operations across the globe have been attributed to Hezbollah or its affiliates, though the group disputes involvement in many. Incidents include:

- the 1983 suicide attacks on U.S. facilities in Beirut
- the 1985 hijacking of TWA flight 847
- the 1992 car bombing of the Israeli embassy and 1994 bombing of a Jewish community center in Argentina (disputed)
- the 1996 Khobar Towers bombing in Saudi Arabia (disputed)
- the 2005 assassination of Lebanese prime minister Rafik Hariri (disputed)
- the 2012 bombing of bus carrying Israeli tourists in Bulgaria (disputed)

Since 2012, alleged Hezbollah operatives have been detained in Nigeria, Thailand, and Cyprus, where a court convicted a Swedish-Lebanese man for plotting multiple attacks on Israeli targets. Hezbollah disputed these charges. In July 2013, the European Union labeled the group's armed wing a terrorist organization after considerable debate among the bloc's members. Some governments feared such a move would bruise relations with Lebanon and fuel Mideast instability.

What is Hezbollah's role in Lebanese politics?

Under Lebanon's 1943 National Pact, the prime minister must be Sunni, the president a Maronite Christian, and the speaker of parliament a Shiite—a system designed to accommodate the country's primary religious groups, whose coexistence has long required delicate balancing.

Hezbollah joined the Lebanese political process in the early 1990s following the 1989 Taif agreement—brokered by Saudi Arabia and Syria—which addressed some of Lebanon's deep-seated sectarian challenges and brought an end to its civil war. However, the agreement allowed Hezbollah to remain armed, and Syrian troops stayed to keep the peace. Israel occupied southern Lebanon until 2000, while Syria eventually withdrew its forces in 2005.

Hezbollah won eight parliamentary seats (out of 128 total) competing in national elections for the first time in 1992. Analysts note the group's political strength grew significantly in May 2008 after Hezbollah was effectively granted veto power in the cabinet via the so-called Doha agreement. The accord helped bring an end to an eighteen-month-long political crisis that culminated in Hezbollah's takeover of West Beirut.

Hezbollah won ten parliamentary seats in the 2009 national elections. Just months later, the group's leader, Hassan Nasrallah, updated Hezbollah's manifesto and expounded on the merits of democracy. "Even Hezbollah has had to accommodate its fundamentalist religious messaging to a pluralistic culture in which piety and modernity exist side-by-side. This has required a gradual shift from the group's Khomeinist roots toward a more contemporary Islamist nationalist approach," wrote the nonpartisan U.S. Congressional Research Service in a 2011 report.

Nasrallah restated Hezbollah's rejection of an Israeli state in 2009: "This stand is firm, permanent, and final, and it does not tolerate any retreat or compromise even if the entire world recognizes Israel."

In recent years, Hezbollah has continued to play a consequential role in Lebanese politics. The group brought down the government of Saad Hariri, a Saudi-backed Sunni, in 2011. And though Hezbollah helped usher in a replacement in Prime Minister Najib Mikati, it forced his departure from office and a collapse of the government in March 2013 in a dispute over the Lebanese security forces.

Hezbollah's ongoing military engagement in Syria has invited reprisals from Sunni militants fighting the Assad regime, who threatened attacks in Beirut as long as Hezbollah remains active in Syria.

In November, Hezbollah rival Future Bloc said it would only form a cabinet if "Hezbollah returns from Syria"; Nasrallah called this an "impossible condition," and as of January 2014, the government remained gridlocked while Beirut appeared to be turning into a proxy battleground for the neighboring civil war.

"Hezbollah is at a critical juncture in its political evolution. Its recent involvement in Syria has raised the question: is it a

Lebanese nationalist organization, or a group more interested in protecting Shiite interests throughout the Middle East?" says CFR's Danin. "In many ways, the war in Syria and Iran's future posture in the region will determine Hezbollah's fate. It could emerge from the Syrian war empowered and emboldened and able to play a dominant role in Lebanese politics. Conversely, it could emerge weakened, tarnished, and without a solid base even amongst Lebanon's large Shiite community."

FOUNDING & FIRST LEBANON WAR (1982-2000)

Hezbollah's origins and ideology stem from the Iranian Revolution. The revolution called for a religious Muslimgovernment that would represent the oppressed and downtrodden. According to Hezbollah, the United States was to blame for many of the country's problems. Israel was seen as an extension of the United States and a foreign power in Lebanon. The organization itself started in 1982 as part of the Iranian government's Revolutionary Guard Corps. Led by religious clerics, the organization wanted to adopt an Iranian doctrine as a solution to Lebanese political malaise. This doctrine included the use of terror as a means of attainting political objectives.

Toward the end of 1982, Iran sent fighters to assist in the establishment of a revolutionary Islamic movement in Lebanon. Iran's hope was that the new members would participate in the *Jihad*, or Holy War, against Israel. These forces, which were located in the area of Ba'albek in the northern Beqa'a valley, brought Iranian-Islamic influence to the area and constituted the core of the Hezbollah organization in Lebanon.

As the organizational infrastructure developed, Hezbollah, with Iranian and Syrian assistance, began to establish an extensive military network in the Ba'albek area. Its militias have since spread into the Shi'ite neighborhoods in southern and western Beirut as well as into southern Lebanon.

Thousands of Hezbollah activists and members are located in the Beqa'a valley, Beirut and southern Lebanon. These areas also offer a base for the recruitment of additional activists and fighters among the local Shi'ite populations. After Israel's war in Lebanon, the organization gained strength as it fought against the presence of French and American peacekeepers who remained in Lebanon after Israeli forces withdrew from Beirut. In 1985, the IDFwithdrew from Lebanon, with the exception of a security zone created to protect Israel's northern border. For the next five years Israeli troops worked with the South Lebanese Army to defend the border. Meanwhile, Hezbollah stockpiled weapons and and recruited many new members, all with the goal of driving the Israelis out of Lebanon.

To gain support from the local population in South Lebanon, Hezbollah donated money, equipment, and medical supplies. In October 1997, the U.S. State Department added Hezbollah to its list of terrorist organizations.

Following Israel's unilateral withdrawal from southern Lebanon in 2000, Hezbollah continued to mount terrorist operations against Israel. It accused Israel of continuing to hold Shaba'a Farm lands (which Israel and the UN agree are not part of Lebanon) and refusing to release Lebanese prisoners in Israeli jails.

In response, Hezbollah, with the help of a UN peacekeeping force, kidnapped three IDF soldiers. A prisoner swap was not agreed upon until 2004, four years after the kidnapping.

Building its Arsenal (2000-2005)

The "Al-Aqsa intifada" in Israel created additional opportunities for Hezbollah to perform acts of violence against the Jewish state. The organization funded the Palestinian Authority (PA) and collaborated with other terrorist organizations, including Hamas, to systematize attacks on Israel. It stepped up its recruitment in order to more efficiently infiltrate Israel's international borders. It also continued to smuggle arms and advanced weapons into Lebanon from Syria and Iran and the PA.

In 2002, the IDF intercepted a Palestinian Authority-owned ship, the *Karine-A,* carrying 50 tons of weapons, including anti-tank missiles, Katyusha rockets, and long range mortar bombs. Many of the weapons were made in Iran. A senior Hezbollah member was responsible for loading the weapons onto the ship.

During this time, Iran and Syria both financially supported Hezbollah, facilitating its military growth to help enable it to fight Israel with more precision and lethality.

Second Lebanon War & Aftermath

On July 12, 2006, the military and financial support that Hezbollah had been receiving from Iran and Syria was put to the test when its guerrilla's perfidiously attacked an IDF patrol on the Israel-Lebanon border and abducted two soldiers, Ehud Goldwasser and Eldad Regev. Simultaneously, Hezbollah units inside Lebanon began firing katyusha rockets to pound northern Israel and create panic and fear.

After more than a weeklong campaign of artillery and air fire to suppress Hezbollah targets, the IDF invaded southern Lebanon at the end of July with the mission to destroy Hezbollah's military capability and kill as many of its terrrorists and fighters as possible. Though the war is widely considered to have ended in a stalemate, with neither side producing a decisive victory, Israel maintains that it killed nearly 600 Hezbollah guerrilla's and destroyed tons of their illegal weaponry.

Hezbollah leader Hassan Nasrallah mentioned in various interviews that he did not expect such a high level response and invasion by the IDF following the initial attack but that he believes his forces acted heroically and not only withstood the Israeli assault but inflicted their own damage, killing more than 120 Israeli soldiers.

In the aftermath of the month-long war in 2006, the United Nations was tasked with maintaining a UNIFIL force both on Israel's border with Lebanon to prevent future skirmishes, but also on Lebanon's border with Syria to prevent further arms smuggling into the Hezbollah stronghold areas. Unfortunately, UNIFIL's mission has been compromised either by a lack of desire on the part of its soldiers to interfere or a lack of ability to stop the smuggling.

Israeli intelligence now believes that Hezbollah has completely rearmed itself from the 2006 war and has even enhanced its weapons stock further, despite UNIFIL's presence. It is believed that Hezbollah's weapons stores hold at least 10,000 katyusha and other short to medium-range rockets. In January 2012, the IDF further updated its operational assessment of Hezbollah to say that it believed the terrorist organization now had long-range surface-to-air missile systems imported from Syria that can match Israel's aerial dominance. The upheaval in Syria during the winter of 2011/2012 enabled Hezbollah to obtain the weapons systems in addition to other various Russian-made air-defense units.

While Hezbollah is known to have a large quantity of shoulder-launched anti-aircraft missiles, the IDF now assumes that the Lebanese Islamist group has received the SA-8, a truck-mounted Russian tactical surface- to-air missile system reported to have a range of 30 kilometers. In addition to the possible transfer of air-defense systems, Hezbollah is also believed to have received several dozen more M600 long-range missiles, as well as additional 302 mm. Khaibar-1 rockets, which have a range of about 100 kilometers.

In November 2013, security officials learned that Hezbollah had close to 200 Iranian-made unmanned aerial vehicles (UAV), including those that can track movement from high altitude and "kamikazes" that can avoid capture by radar and fire or drop munitions from low altitudes.

On October 7, 2014 an explosive device was detonated on the Israel controlled side of the Israeli-Lebanon border. Hezbollah immediately took responsibility for the attack less than 4 hours after it happened, which is surprising considering their record of denying any attacks against Israel that they have been accused of. This marks the first time that Hezbollah has claimed responsibility for an attack against Israel since the the Second Lebanon War in 2006. The explosive device was detonated in the area of Sheeba Farms, an area that Lebanon believes is unrightfully occupied by Israel, and that Syria also claims the rights to. The explosion seriously injured 2 Israeli soldiers and was supposedly a retaliatory attack in response to an incident on Sunday in which IDF soldiers witnessed individuals attempting to illegally cross from Lebanon into Israel. The IDF soldiers opened fire at these individuals and caused them to retreat back to Lebanese territory. According to Lebanese sources this is not how the confrontation proceeded, and they claim that Israeli soldiers fired on their military positions, injuring one soldier. According to IDF spokesman Lt Colonel Peter Lerner, this attack was a "blatant breach of Israel's sovereignty". In response to this attack, the Israeli military fired artillery at two Hezbollah positions in Southern Lebanon, no injuries were reported. In a rare televised appearance on November 4 2014, Hezbollah leader Hassan Nasrallah warned of a third Lebanon war and stated that Israel should close "all of your airports and your ports" in the event of a third Lebanon war. Nasrallah threatened Israel and claimed that "there is no place on the land of occupied Palestine that the resistance's rockets cannot reach".

Israeli warplanes struck multiple positions in Damascus on Sunday December 7 2014 in an attempt to thwart weapons transfers to Hezbollah in Lebanon. These strikes hit a storage facility that was housing anti-aircraft missiles and drone fighters that were going to be sold to Hezbollah

Policies & Politics

Hezbollah has consistently tried to paint itself as a moderate national liberation organization aimed at "introducing theIslam that is confident in achieving justice, as well as introducing the Islam that protects all human rights." It tries to portray an image as a group who would rather not commit acts of terror, but must for the benefit of the Arab world.

After expressing written statements against terrorist attacks, the Secretary General of Hezbollah, Hassan Nasrallah, communicated to a Lebanese audience at a memorial for a Hezbollah suicide bomber that "we must continue the path of resistance and the path of the First and Second Intifada."

Hezbollah is an active participant in Lebanese politics. In 1992, it participated in elections for the first time, winning 12 out of 128 seats in parliament. It won 10 seats in 1996, and 8 in 2000. In the general election of 2005, it won 23 seats nationwide. An alliance between Amal and Hezbollah won all 23 seats in Southern Lebanon.

Operations

Hezbollah's main tactic is the use of suicide bombers. Hezbollah uses these human weapons to create mental and physical suffering for the Israelis and to force the Israelis to retreat out of "Islamic land."

Shi'a Islam international bases are used to buy and sell weapons for organized attacks. Asia is a key target for Hezbollah, and

Hezbollah has been pulling Malaysians and Indonesians into the organzation to expand operations and terrorist attacks around the world.

Hezbollah extended its operations across the globe throughout the 1980s, kidnapping individuals in a attempt to gain political leverage.

Hezbollah operates a satellite television station from Lebanon, *Al-Manar TV* ("the Lighthouse") as well as a radio station, *al-Nour* ("the light"). *Qubth Ut Alla* ("The Fist of God") is the monthly magazine of Hezbollah's paramilitary wing. They are widely viewed by West Bank and Gazan Palestinians as well as some Lebanese.

Leadership

The spiritual father of the movement in Lebanon is Sheikh Muhammed Hussein Fadlallah who acts as chief Mujtahid (arbiter of Islamic law) of the Shi'ite community in Lebanon.

The current Secretary General of Hezbollah is Hassan Nasrallah. At the start of the 1980s he was responsible for the Beqa'a area on behalf of the AMAL movement. He left the organization in 1982 and affiliated with Hezbollah, taking with him many of his followers. Following the death of Abbas Musawi, Nasrallah was unanimously elected to be his successor.

Ideology & Support

The organization views an Islamic republic, modeled after Iran, to be the ideal form of a state. Lebanon remains a religiously and ideologically heterogeneous society.

According to their published political platform in 2003, Hezbollah claims to favor the introduction of an Islamic government in Lebanon by peaceful democratic means. According to the United States Department of State and reports submitted to Defense Technical Information Center, the organization is seeking to create an fundamentalist Iranian-style Islamic republic and removal of all non-Islamic influences.

Hezbollah supports the destruction of the state of Israel and co-operates with other militant Islamic organizations such as Hamas in order to promote this goal. Hamas actually maintains its own "embassy" in Tehran. In 1992, Iran, Hezbollah, and Hamas signed an official agreement of cooperation. As recently as 2002, it has been known that Iran was directly involved in numerous attempts to launch rockets into Israel through members of Hamas and Islamic Jihadwho were trained by Hezbollah in Iranian camps.

A relationship has also developed between Hezbollah and Al-Qa'ida, according to a former Al-Qa'ida member who was captured and convicted of bombing U.S. embassies in Kenya and Tanzania. Ali Muhammad said that "Hezbollah provided explosives training for Al-Qa'ida," and that he personally arranged a meeting between Hezbollah's chief and Osama bin Laden in Sudan. In 2002, leaders of Hezbollah, Al-Qa'ida, and Hamas met formally in Lebanon to discuss future joint terrorist attacks against America, Britain, and Israel.

Syria backs Hezbollah morally and has also supplied it with money and arms. In return, Hezbollah protects Syria's political and military interests in Lebanon.

Hezbollah also receives financial aid, training, weapons, and explosives from Iran. Iran also contributes political, diplomatic, and organizational aid. According to Iran's official budget, Iran gave $500 million in support of radical Islamic organizations around the world in the 1990s. Of that money, Hezbollah was reported to receive at least $250 million.

It is also suspected that Hezbollah has received financial and military aid from Russia in the past. Russia did not denounce Hezbollah as a terrorist organization until approximately twelve years after its establishment.

Hezbollah has a number of illicit fund-raising rings operating in the United States. In 2003, the Drug Enforcement Administration discovered the existence of an organized drug smuggling operation that was funneling money to Hezbollah from Chicago and Detroit. In Charlotte, North Carolina, the Bureau of Alcohol, Tobacco, and Firearms investigated a multi-million dollar cigaretter smuggling ring that gave over $2 million to Hezbollah over a period of 8 years. The money received from the Charlotte operation allowed Hezbollah to purchase advanced military technology and global positioning systems. In March 2003, the leader of the cigarette smuggling ring, Mohamed Hammoud, received a 155-year sentence for racketeering and providing material support for Hezbollah.

Activities Around the World

Hezbollah is believed to have kidnapped and tortured to death U.S. Army colonel William R. Higgins and the CIA Station Chief in Beirut, William Buckley, and to have kidnapped around 30 other Westerners between 1982 and 1992.

Hezbollah was suspected of involvement in numerous anti-US and anti-Israeli terrorist attacks. The organization was responsible for the suicide truck bombings of the U.S. Embassy and U.S. Marine barracks in Beirut in October 1983, in which 241 American servicemen were killed (220 Marines, 18 Navy personnel and 3 Army soldiers) and the U.S. Embassy annex in Beirut in September 1984. The bombing at the Marine barracks in Beirut was the deadliest single-day death toll for the United States Marine Corps since the Battle of Iwo Jima (2,500 in one day) of World War II and the deadliest single-day death toll for the United States military since the 243 killed on 31st January 1968 — the first day of the Tet offensive in the Vietnam war. The attack remains the deadliest single attack on Americans overseas since World War II.

Three members of Hezbollah, Imad Mughniyah, Hasan Izz-al-Din, and Ali Atwa, are on the FBI's list of 22 Most Wanted Terrorists for the hijacking in 1985 of TWA Flight 847 during which a U.S. Navy diver was murdered. Elements of the group were responsible for the kidnapping and detention of Americans and other westerners in Lebanon in the 1980s.

In 1992 and 1994, Hezbollah is claimed to have carried out the Israeli Embassy Bombing and the AMIA Bombing in Buenos Aires, Argentina. Eight days after the AMIA Bombing the Israeli Embassy in London was car bombed by two Palestinians linked to Hezbollah.

In January 2000, Hezbollah assassinated the commander of the South Lebanon Army Western Brigade, Colonel Aql Hashem, at his home in the security zone. Hashem had been responsible for day to day operations of the South Lebanon army.

On June 16, 2004, two Palestinian girls — aged 14 and 15 — were arrested by the IDF for plotting a suicide bombing. According to IDF statement, the two minors were guided by Hezbollah. On June 23, 2004, another allegedly Hezbollah-funded suicide bombing attack was foiled by the Israeli security forces.

In February 2005, the Palestinian Authority accused Hezbollah of attempting to derail the truce signed with Israel. Palestinian officials and former militants described how Hezbollah promised an increase in funding for any cell able to carry out a terrorist attack

Since the Second Lebanon War, Hezbollah operatives have been seen and, at times, even arrested in the Caribbean,Central America, South America and Asia.

"There are parts of the Caribbean where we've seen some, certainly some travel," said Henry Crumpton, the State Department's counter-terrorism coordinator said. "There are parts of Central America where we've seen some operatives, where we've seen transactions – financial transactions – in the Caribbean. In the southern part of the Caribbean, next to Venezuela, in Colombia, we've seen some activity there."

In January 2012, one Hezbollah suspect was arrested and another managed to avoid capture, in Thailand's capital city, Bangkok, where security services believe they were working in a cell planning to attack areas commonly frequented by Israeli tourists. The attacks were thought to have been planned in coordination with the anniversary of the assassination of Hezbollah operations chief Imad Mughniyeh on February 12. Israeli counter-terror experts warned that Hezbollah's long arm was begining to extend even further than many believed it could.

On October 7, 2014 an explosive device was detonated on the Israel controlled side of the Israeli-Lebanon border. Hezbollah immediately took responsibility for the attack less than 4 hours after it happened, which is surprising considering their record of denying any attacks against Israel that they have been accused of. This marks the first time that Hezbollah has claimed responsibility for an attack against Israel since the the Second Lebanon War in 2006. The explosive device was detonated in the area of Sheeba Farms, an area that Lebanon believes is unrightfully occupied by Israel, and that Syria also claims the rights to. The explosion seriously injured 2 Israeli soldiers and was supposedly a retaliatory attack in response to an incident on Sunday in which IDF soldiers witnessed individuals attempting to illegally cross from Lebanon into Israel. The IDF soldiers opened fire at these individuals and caused them to retreat back to Lebanese territory. According to Lebanese sources this is not how the confrontation proceeded, and they claim that Israeli soldiers fired on their military positions, injuring one soldier. According to IDF spokesman Lt Colonel Peter Lerner, this attack was a "blatant breach of Israel's sovereignty". In response to this attack, the Israeli military fired artillery at two Hezbollah positions in Southern Lebanon, no injuries were reported.

Drug Smuggling to Fund Terrorism

Hezbollah FINANCES its terrorism using a sophisticated drug-trafficking operation and continues to profit from its drug sales despite the world's objections.

Hezbollah primarily earns its profits through drug sales in Latin America, but its activities have been traced across multiple continents. The group combines its drug profits with proceeds from legitimate used-car sales in West Africa. Until it was uncovered by officials, this global money-laundering scheme effectively masked Hezbollah's earnings.

In 2001, international intelligence sources identified Lebanese residents operating for Hezbollah in South America's tri-border area (Argentina, Paraguay and Brazil). That area is a major source of funding for Hezbollah's terror activities. In October 2008, investigators took down a cocaine smuggling operation in Colombia, noting that "profits from the sales of drugs went to FINANCE Hezbollah."

In January 2010, German officials arrested two suspects in Frankfurt's airport after linking four Lebanese individuals to nearly 10 million euros in drug profits. Officials accused the suspects of trading drugs and sending the proceeds to relatives directly connected to top Hezbollah officials.

In 2011, the U.S. government seized drug profits linked to Ayman Joumaa, a drug trafficker and money launderer, linked to Hezbollah. His network was earning as much as $200 million per month. In April 2013, the United States Treasury Department took action against Hezbollah for working as a drug cartel and also blacklisted two Lebanese financial institutions, accusing them of transferring tens of millions of dollars to the terror group. American officials later confirmed that one of the banks agreed to pay the United States $102 million to settle a lawsuit involving Hezbollah's money laundering scheme. In June 2013, four Lebanese men were sanctioned for effectively acting as "ambassadors" for Hezbollah in West Africa.

10

Abu Nidal Organization

The Abu Nidal Organization (ANO) is the most common name for the Palestinian group Fatah–The Revolutionary Council (*Fatah al-Majles al-Thawry*), also known as Black June, the Arab Revolutionary Brigades, the Revolutionary Organization of Socialist Muslims, and sometimes operating as Black September (not to be confused with the Black September Organization). The ANO is named after its founder Abu Nidal. It was created by a split from Yasser Arafat's Fatah faction of the PLO in 1974. It is regarded as a terrorist organization by the United States, Israel, and the European Union.

FORMATION AND BACKGROUND

The ANO was originally formed as a result of the 1974 Rejectionist Front split in the PLO, after Arafat's Fatah had pushed through amendments of the PLO's goals, which were seen as a step towards compromise with Israel. Abu Nidal then moved to Ba'th-ruled Iraq where he set up the ANO, which soon began a vicious string of terrorist attacks. It has not clearly defined its ideological position, but was clearly opposed to any form of compromise or negotiation with Israel. It is known as one of the most uncompromisingly militant Palestinian groups ever. It had an estimated membership of several hundred, but its strength today is not known.

ABU NIDAL ORGANIZATION INTERNAL EXECUTIONS

The Abu Nidal Organization internal executions were the mass executions of members of the Abu Nidal Organization and their families by Abu Nidal and key associates during 1987–1988. The executions took place at a number of locations in Syria, Lebanon and Libya. The number of people executed – mostly Palestinians – is estimated at 600.

Background

The Abu Nidal Organization was established by Sabri Khalil al-Bannah (Abu Nidal), a Palestinian Arab nationalist and a former Ba'ath party member. Al-Bannah established his faction within the PLO, just prior the Black September in Jordan, and following internal disagreements within the PLO. During Fatah's Third Congress in Damascus in 1971, he emerged as the leader of a leftist alliance against Arafat.

Abu Nidal's first independent operation took place on September 5, 1973, when five gunmen using the name *Al-Iqab* ("The Punishment") seized the Saudi embassy in Paris, taking 11 hostages and threatening to blow up the building if Abu Dawud was not released from jail in Jordan, where he had been arrested in February 1973 for an attempt on King Hussein's life. Following the incident, Mahmud Abbas of the PLO took flight to Iraq to meet Abu Nidal. In the meeting Abbas became so angry, that he stormed out of the meeting, followed by the other PLO delegates, and from that point on, the PLO regarded Abu Nidal as a mercenary.

Two months later, just after the October 1973 Yom Kippur War, during discussions about convening a peace conference in Geneva, the Abu Nidal Organization (ANO) hijacked a KLM airliner, using the name of the Arab Nationalist Youth Organization. The operation was intended to send a signal to Fatah not to send representatives to any peace conference. In response, Arafat officially expelled Abu Nidal from Fatah in March 1974, and the rift between the two groups, and the two men, was complete.

Abu Nidal's organization was engaged in a series of international terrorist incidents aimed at Israel and Western countries. Setting himself up as a freelance contractor, Abu Nidal is believed by the United States Department of State to have ordered attacks in 20 countries, killing or injuring over 900 people. The ANO group's most notorious attacks were on the El Al ticket counters at Rome and Vienna airports in December 1985, when

Arab gunmen high on amphetamines opened fire on passengers in simultaneous shootings, killing 18 and wounding 120. Patrick Seale, Abu Nidal's biographer, wrote of the attacks that their "random cruelty marked them as typical Abu Nidal operations."

Executions within the organization

"According to ANO members who were able to escape, recruits were buried alive, fed through a tube forced into their mouths, then finally killed by a bullet fired down the tube. Some had their genitals placed in skillets of boiling-hot oil.—Duane 'Dewey' Clarridge "

The ANO's official newspaper *Filastin al-Thawra* regularly carried stories announcing the execution of traitors within the movement. Each new recruit of the ANO was given several days to write his entire life story by hand – including names and addresses of family members, friends, and lovers – and was then required to sign a paper agreeing to his execution if anything was found to be untrue. Every so often, the recruit would be asked to rewrite the whole story. Any discrepancies were taken as evidence that he was a spy and he would be made to write it out again, often after days of being beaten and nights spent forced to sleep standing up.

1987 events

By 1987, Abu Nidal had turned the full force of his paranoia and terror tactics inwards on the ANO itself. Members were routinely tortured by the "Committee for Revolutionary Justice" until they confessed to betrayal and disloyalty. Men would be hanged naked for hours and whipped until they lost consciousness, then revived with salt or chili powder rubbed into their wounds. A naked prisoner would be forced into a car tire with his legs and backside in the air, then whipped, wounded, and salted. Plastic melted under a flame would be dripped onto prisoners' skin. According to recruits who were able to escape, prisoners' genitals would be placed in skillets of boiling-hot oil and fried while the men were held down. Between interrogations, prisoners would be confined alone in tiny cells, bound hand and foot. If the cells were full, a prisoner might be buried alive, with a steel pipe in his mouth to allow him to breathe. Water would be poured into it occasionally. When word came that Abu Nidal wanted the prisoner executed, a bullet would be fired down the tube instead, then the pipe removed and the hole filled in.

Perpetrators

In one year from 1987–1988, around 600 were killed, between a third and a half of the membership of the ANO. Abu Nidal even had the elderly wife of a veteran member, Al-Hajj Abu Musa, thrown in jail and killed on a charge of lesbianism. The killings were mostly the work of four men: Mustafa Ibrahim Sanduqa of the Justice Committee; Isam Maraqa, Abu Nidal's deputy, who was married to his wife's niece; Sulaiman Samrin, also known as Dr. Ghassan al-Ali, the ANO's first secretary; and Mustafa Awad, also known as Alaa, the head of the Intelligence Directorate. Most of the decisions to kill, said Abu Dawud, a long-time member of the ANO, were taken by Abu Nidal "in the middle of the night, after he [had] knocked back a whole bottle of whiskey".

THE ARAB REVOLUTIONARY BRIGADES, OR THE REVOLUTIONARY ORGANIZATION OF SOCIALIST MUSLIMS

Abu Nidal is a terrorist organization widely known for deadly attacks in the 1980s on Western, Palestinian, and Israeli targets. They were attempting to derail diplomatic relations between the Palestinian Liberation Organization (PLO) and the West, while advocating for the destruction of Israel. The organization was named for a former member of the PLO who split off in a dispute over establishing diplomatic ties with Israel. Abu Nidal has been on the U.S. list of terrorist organizations for more than twenty years but is largely considered to be inactive, according to the 2008 State Department Country Reports on Terrorism.

What is the Abu Nidal Organization?

The Abu Nidal Organization—named for its leader Sabri al-Banna, a veteran Palestinian terrorist known by the *nom de guerre* Abu Nidal—is a secular international terrorist group that has been sponsored by Syria, Libya, and Iraq, and has attacked a wide range of Western, Israeli, and Arab targets. Over the years, the Abu Nidal

Organization (ANO) mounted terrorist operations in twenty countries, killing about three hundred people and wounding hundreds more. In the mid-1980s, the group was seen as the world's most dangerous terrorist organization, but some experts say the group is inactive and no longer poses much of a threat. The ANO—also called the Fatah Revolutionary Council, the Arab Revolutionary Brigades, or the Revolutionary Organization of Socialist Muslims—remains on the U.S. State Department's list of foreign terrorist organizations.

Who is Abu Nidal?

Abu Nidal, which means "father of the struggle" in Arabic, is the alias of Sabri al-Banna, who was born in 1937 into a landowning family in British-ruled Palestine. During the 1948 Arab-Israeli War, Banna's family fled, ending up in the West Bank. In the 1950s, he joined the Arab nationalist Baath Party, and in 1967 he got involved with the PLO. Abu Nidal represented al-Fatah—the dominant faction of the PLO, led by Yasir Arafat—in Sudan and later Iraq. He split with the PLO in 1974 after it proposed the creation of a national authority in the West Bank and Gaza Strip as a step toward Palestinian statehood. Abu Nidal, who continued to advocate Israel's destruction, accused the PLO of selling out by pursuing diplomatic relations with the state of Israel and set up his own organization, the Fatah Revolutionary Council—signifying that he saw his group as the true heir to Arafat's Fatah movement.

Abu Nidal was sentenced to death in absentia by the PLO in 1974 for attacks against fellow Palestinians and again in 2001 by Jordan for the 1994 assassination of a Jordanian diplomat in Beirut. In August 2002, Abu Nidal was reported dead in Iraq.

What terrorist activities has the Abu Nidal Organization undertaken?

Many of the group's targets have been Israelis, PLO officials, and representatives of Arab governments it dislikes. Westerners were also targeted until the late 1980s. Among the group's best-known attacks are:

- the 1994 assassination of the senior Jordanian diplomat Naeb Imran Maaytah in Beirut;

- the January 1991 assassination of Abu Iyad, the PLO's second-in-command after Arafat, and another PLO official in Tunis;
- a September 1986 shooting at the Neve Shalom synagogue in Istanbul, Turkey, that killed twenty-two;
- the December 1985 attempted hijacking of a Pan Am flight in Karachi, Pakistan, in which twenty-two people died;
- the December 1985 simultaneous attacks on U.S. and Israeli airport counters in Rome and Vienna, which killed eighteen people and injured 111;
- the June 1982 attempt to assassinate Israeli ambassador Shlomo Argov in London, which helped trigger Israel's invasion of Lebanon.

Although no major attack has been attributed to the group since Abu Nidal's reported death, Jordanian officials reported the apprehension of an ANO member suspected of planning attacks in Jordan in 2008.

What are the Abu Nidal Organization's goals?

The group wants the state of Israel to be eliminated, preferably through an international Arab revolution, and therefore supports "armed struggle" against Israel. It bitterly opposes Arab-Israeli peace negotiations, as well as the United States, the PLO, and moderate Arab regimes in Jordan, Egypt, and the Persian Gulf states. It has also served as a mercenary terrorist force for radical Arab regimes.

Has the Abu Nidal Organization received state support?

Yes. Iraq, Syria, and Libya have all harbored the group and given it training, logistical support, and funding, often using the ANO as guns for hire. Abu Nidal began working with Iraqi intelligence while representing Fatah in Baghdad, experts say. He formed his organization with Iraq's help and began by attacking Syria and the PLO. In 1983, Iraqi President Saddam Hussein expelled Abu Nidal and his group in an attempt to win U.S. military support for Iraq's 1980s war with neighboring Iran. Once the war ended, Iraq resumed its support of Abu Nidal.

After being expelled from Iraq, the organization moved to Syria, where it worked to undermine peace plans involving Jordan, Israel, and the PLO. In turn, Syria expelled the Abu Nidal Organization in 1987, probably under U.S. pressure to distance itself from terrorists, at which point Libya took it in. In 1999, in an attempt to rid itself of international sanctions, Libya kicked out the Abu Nidal Organization. The group's current access to resources are unclear; however, the decline of state support is thought to have severely curtailed operations and capabilities.

Where does the group now operate?

The organization is largely considered inactive. In 1999, Egypt and Libya closed down ANO offices in their countries. Current and former leaders and associates are now thought to be in Iraq, with cells in Palestinian refugee camps in Lebanon.

ANO ATTACKS

The ANO carried out attacks in 20 countries, killing or injuring almost 900 persons. Targets include the United States, the United Kingdom, France, Israel, moderate Palestinians, the PLO, and various Arab and European countries. The group has not attacked Western targets since the late 1980s.

Major attacks included the Rome and Vienna Airport Attacks in December 1985, the Neve Shalom synagogue in Istanbul and the Pan Am Flight 73 hijacking in Karachi in September 1986, and the *City of Poros* day-excursion ship attack in Greece in July 1988. The ANO has been especially noted for its uncompromising stance on negotiation with Israel, treating anything less than all-out military struggle against Israel as treachery. This led the group to perform numerous attacks against the PLO, which had made clear it accepted a negotiated solution to the conflict. Fatah-RC is believed to have assassinated PLO deputy chief Abu Iyad and PLO security chief Abu Hul in Tunis in January 1991. It assassinated a Jordanian diplomat in Lebanon in January 1994 and has been linked to the killing of the PLO representative there. Noted PLO moderate Issam Sartawi was killed by the Fatah-RC in 1983. In the late 1970s, the group also made failed assassination attempt on the present Palestinian president and PLO chairman, Mahmoud Abbas. These attacks, and numerous others, led to the PLO issuing a death sentence *in absentia* against Abu Nidal. In the early 1990s, it made an attempt to gain control of a refugee camp in Lebanon, but this was thwarted by PLO organizations.

SUPPORTING FACTORS

The group has at various stages received funding from Iraq, Libya, and (until 1987) Syria. Initially, it was closest to the Iraqi regime, but near the end of the 1970s, it moved closer to Libya. From the early 1980s, some viewed it as a Libyan proxy. As Gadaffi came under increasing pressure from Western governments for his involvement in international terrorism, Libyan backing dwindled, and the group seems to have been forced by the authorities to remain quiet from the late 1980s.

The ANO's operations in Libya were finally stopped by local authorities in 1999, but by then most of the organization had already left for, or fled to, Sudan and other Arab countries. The choking of funding from Middle Eastern governments caused the organization to slip away in obscurity. Abu Nidal's failing health also seems to have contributed to this. Abu Nidal lived in Baghdad from the 1990s. He was found dead in 2002 by agents of the Iraqi regime. According to the Iraqi government he shot himself in the mouth when security services came to arrest him, but the ANO issued a statement from Beirut, stating their belief that Abu Nidal had been murdered.

The group has repeatedly been accused, not least by other Palestinians, of acting as a mercenary terrorist force rather than as part of a national liberation movement. Many of its attacks are seemingly unrelated to the Palestinian struggle, and international terrorism experts point out that it tended to attack Libya's enemies during periods of Libyan support, Iraqi enemies during periods of backing from Saddam Hussein, etc.

ATTACKS ATTRIBUTED TO ABU NIDAL

Abu Nidal (Sabri al-Banna) was regarded as the most dangerous of the Palestinian political leaders. Abu Nidal, whose pseudonym means "father of struggle" (Abu meaning father and Nidal, a secular term, meaning "struggle" or "effort" in Arabic) was primarily active in the 1970s and 1980s in the left-wing of the Palestine Liberation Organization and later the secular/rejectionist front, and was accused by Western and Arab sources of acting as a mercenary for various Arab governments. Most of its targets were Arab politicians, rivals, and activists they felt were soft on the Israeli issue, but Jews of all nationalities, as well as political representatives of Western nations were also targets, especially those involved in the peace process in the Middle East. The following list has been compiled from a variety of sources. It is not complete and may contain errors. Some of these attacks have been claimed by several groups, some of them by no group, and others may have been falsely claimed by or attributed to Abu Nidal's organization.

1972:

- *September 5, 1972:* Abu Nidal is believed to have been involved in the planning of the Munich massacre at the 1972 Summer Olympics.

1973:

- *September 5, 1973:* Occupation of the Saudi embassy in Paris, in order to gain the release of Abu Daoud, then imprisoned in Jordan.
- *November 25, 1973:* KLM flight from Beirut to New York and Tokyo hijacked over Iraqi airspace and diverted to Nicosia, Cyprus, then Valletta, Malta. Passengers and crew released. Claimed by the Arab Nationalist Youth Organization.

1974:

- *September 8, 1974:* Bombing of TWA Flight 841. All 79 passengers died.
- *October 1974:* Aborted assassination attempt on Yasser Arafat and Mahmoud Abbas. Following this he is sentenced to death in absentia by the PLO council. It is at this point that he founds the independent Abu Nidal Organisation.
- *November 22, 1974:* British Airways Vickers VC-10 flight from London to the Far East hijacked in Dubai and diverted to Tunis. One passenger was killed. The hijackers were allowed to fly to Libya.

1976:

- *September 1976:* Attack and takeover of the Semiramis Hotel, Damascus, Syria. Three of the captured attackers were later hanged in public.
- *October 11, 1976:* Attacks on the Syrian embassies in Islamabad, Pakistan, and Rome, Italy.
- *November 17, 1976:* ANO fighters stormed the Intercontinental Hotel in Amman, Jordan, taking several hostages. The hotel was stormed in turn by Jordanaian security forces, and three gunmen, two soldiers and two civilians were killed. The remaining attackers were executed shortly afterwards.
- *December 1, 1976:* Syrian foreign minister Abdul Halim Khaddam is shot and wounded in an attack on his car in Damascus.
- *December 13, 1976:* Foiled attack on the Syrian embassy in Istanbul.

1977:

- *October 1977:* Second assassination attempt on Khaddam at Abu Dhabi airport, during which the foreign minister of the United Arab Emirates is killed by accident.
- *November 15, 1977:* Assassination of the director of the Arab Library, Paris.

1978:

- *January 4, 1978:* Assassination of Said Hammami, PLO representative in London, Great Britain
- *February 18, 1978:* Egyptian journalist Youssef al-Seba'i killed whilst acting as president of the Conference of the Organization for the Solidarity with the Peoples of Africa, Asia and Latin America.
- *1978:* Assassination of PLO representative in Brussels, Belgium.
- *June 15, 1978:* Assassination of Ali Yassin, PLO representative in Kuwait.
- *August 3, 1978:* Izz al-Din al-Kalak, PLO representative to Paris, France is assassinated along with an assistant.

- *August 5, 1978:* PLO offices in Islamabad, Pakistan are attacked.
- *1978:* Assassination of PLO representative in Rome, Italy.
- *1978:* Assassination of PLO representative in Madrid.

1980:

- *January 17, 1980:* Yussouf Mubarak, director of the Palestinian library-shop, is assassinated in Paris, France.
- *July 27, 1980:* Attack with 2 hand grenades on Jewish group of boys going to Aguda Holiday Camp Antwerp, Belgium. (Killing one 14 year old and wounding over 20 boys)
- *July 27, 1980:* Claims responsibility for murder of Israeli commercial attaché in Brussels.

1981:

- *February 6, 1981:* Hisham Muheissen, the Jordanian charge d'affairs in Beirut was kidnapped and three of his bodyguards killed by unidentified attackers, later believed to be ANO. Mulheissen was released unharmed 67 days later.
- *May 1, 1981:* Assassination of councilman Heinz Nittel in Vienna, Austria. Nittel was President of the Austrian-Israeli Friendship Association and had been involved in the peace process in Israel.
- *June 1, 1981:* Killing of Naim Khader, the PLO's representative in Belgium.
- *August 1, 1981:* A series of bombings damage several French banks and businesses, the Air France office and the Saudi Arabian embassy in Beirut, but no one is seriously hurt.
- *August 29, 1981:* 1981 Vienna synagogue attack Three men attacked a Vienna synagogue with machine guns. Two civilians were killed and 23 wounded, including 3 policemen. The attackers were arrested and imprisoned.
- *September 4, 1981:* The French ambassdor to Lebanon, Louis Delamare was assassinated on a Beirut street in a bungled kidnap attempt.
- *September 23, 1981:* Five Greek Cypriots are injured in a grenade attack on shipping offices in Limassol.

- *October 6, 1981:* PLO officer Majed Abu Sharar was assassinated by a bomb hidden in his hotel room in Rome, Italy. ANO claimed he was compromising the principles of the revolution.
- *November 7, 1981:* A kidnap attempt on a Saudi Arabian diplomat is foiled in Beirut.

1982:

- *June 3, 1982:* Attempted assassination in London of Shlomo Argov, Israeli ambassador to the United Kingdom. The Israeli government blamed the PLO for the attack, and this was one of the incidents which provoked a large-scale invasion of Lebanon on June 6. Argov was permanently disabled and died of his injuries 21 years later.
- *June 4, 1982:* A Kuwaiti diplomat is assassinated outside his home in New Delhi, India.
- *July 7, 1982:* A Jordanian diplomat was assassinated and another seriously injured in an attack on an Athens street in Greece.
- *August 9, 1982:* Gun and grenade attack on Goldenberg Restaurant in Jewish quarter of Paris, France leaves six dead, 22 wounded.
- *August 26, 1982:* Two failed assassination attempts - on the United Arab Emirates consul in Bombay and a Kuwaiti diplomat in Karachi, Pakistan.
- *1982:* Assassination of PLO official in Madrid, Spain.
- *September 16, 1982:* Kuwaiti diplomat Najeed Sayed al-Rafaia is assassinated in Madrid, Spain when he was mistaken for the ambassador.
- *September 18, 1982:* Four people are wounded when a synagogue in Brussels is attacked in a "shoot and run" incident.
- *October 9, 1982:* 1982 Great Synagogue of Rome attack: five elegantly dressed attackers threw at least three hand grenades and sprayed a crowd of people with submachine fire, as they were leaving the central synagogue in Rome, Italy. A 2-year-old toddler (Stefano Gaj Taché) was killed in the attack, and 37 people were injured.

1983:

- *April 10, 1983:* Noted PLO dove and Arafat aide Issam Sartawi is killed at the Socialist International conference in Albufeira, Portugal.
- *1983:* Attack on the Jordanian ambassador to Italy, in Rome, who survives.
- *August 29, 1983:* A French aircraft was hijacked from Vienna, Austria and taken to Tehran. No one was hurt in the incident.
- *September 23, 1983:* Bombing of Gulf Air Flight 771. 117 people killed.
- *October 26, 1983:* Jordanian ambassador to India was shot six times in an ambush in New Delhi, but survived his injuries.
- *October 27, 1983:* Jordanian ambassador to Italy, Taysir AlaEddin Toukan, was shot and wounded along with his driver during an ambush by two gunmen in Rome. Both men survived.
- *November 7, 1983:* Attack on the Jordanian embassy in Athens, Greece. A guard is killed.
- *December 26, 1983:* Two people are injured by a bomb explosion outside a Marks and Spencers department store in London, England. The Provisional Irish Republican Army are blamed, but it later emerges that the ANO is responsible.
- *December 1983:* Accused of responsibility for the bombing of the French Cultural Center in Ýzmir, Turkey.
- *December 29, 1983:* The Jordanian ambassador to Spain is assassinated in Madrid.

1984:

- *1984:* Assassination of Jordanian ambassador in India.
- *1984:* Assassination of Jordanian ambassador in Spain.
- *1984:* Assassination of Jordanian ambassador in Italy.
- *February 8, 1984:* The United Arab Emirates' ambassador to France, Khalifa Abdel Aziz al-Mubarak, was assassinated on a Paris street.

- *March 7, 1984:* Three were killed and nine injured in the bombing of a civilian bus in Ashdod, Israel.
- *March 24, 1984:* In Amman, a bomb was found and removed at the Intercontinental Hotel, coinciding with the visit of Queen Elizabeth II to Jordan.
- *March 28, 1984:* British Cultural Attache and British Council representative Kenneth Whitty was assassinated on an Athens street in Greece by a single gunman, coinciding with the start of a European tour of *A School For Scandal,* to celebrate the British Councils 50th anniversary, which opened in Athens three days later on 31 March.
- *April 2, 1984:* 48 people are wounded by a machine gun attack on a crowded shopping mall in Jerusalem, Israel.
- *May 24, 1984:* Bomb explodes in an Athens restaurant, no one is hurt.
- *June 5, 1984:* Assassination attempt on Israeli diplomat in Cairo, Egypt.
- *October 4, 1984:* A car bomb exploded in the Israeli embassy car park in Nicosia, Cyprus. One person was hurt
- *October 4, 1984:* An Israeli intelligence agent was killed with four other people in an ambush on a Beirut street.
- *October 26, 1984:* The attempted assassination of a senior UAE diplomat in Rome, Italy, leaves him in a coma and a woman bystander dead.
- *November 28, 1984:* Percy Norris, British Deputy High Commissioner in Bombay, India, is shot and killed by an unidentified gunman as he drove through traffic.
- *November 29, 1984:* British Airways' offices in Beirut, Lebanon, are bombed.
- *November 1984:* Attempted assassination of Jordanian diplomat in Greece.
- *December 4, 1984:* Kills a Jordanian diplomat in Bucharest, Romania, using the name Black September.
- *December 26, 1984:* Bombing of the home of veteran Fatah and PLO leader Hani al-Hassan (a.k.a. Abu Tariq, Abu al-Hassan), in Amman, Jordan. Uses the name Black September.

- *December 29, 1984:* Assassination in Amman, Jordan of former Hebron mayor and West Bank moderate Fahd Qawasma, who had previously been deported by Israel for alleged incitement to violence; in Amman, Jordan; uses the name Black September.

1985:

- *March 25, 1985:* British journalist Alec Collett, working for the UN, was kidnapped in Beirut, Lebanon along with an Austrian who was soon released. On 23 April 1986, he was hanged in revenge for Operation El Dorado Canyon.
- *1985:* Bombing of British Airways office in Madrid, Spain, killing one.
- *1985:* Attack on resort hotel in Athens, Greece. 13 wounded.
- *March 21, 1985:* Bombing of the Royal Jordanian Airlines (ALIA) offices in Rome, Italy, under the name Black September.
- *March 21, 1985:* Bombing of the Royal Jordanian Airlines (ALIA) offices in Athens, Greece, under the name Black September.
- *March 21, 1985:* Bombing of the Royal Jordanian Airlines (ALIA) offices in Nicosia, Cyprus, under the name Black September.
- *April 3, 1985:* Rocket attack on ALIA airliner taking off from Athens Airport. No casualties.
- *April 4, 1985:* Rocket attack against Jordanian embassy in Italy.
- *May 1, 1985:* An assassination attempt on a Kuwaiti newspaper editor believed to be soft on Israel failed.
- *July 11, 1985:* Eleven people were killed and 90 injured in two large bomb explosions in cafés in Kuwait City. Amongst the dead was the target of the bombings, the head of Kuwait's investigative branch of the police. A third bomb was successfully defused.
- *July 7, 1985:* A yacht carrying French and Belgian Jews was hijacked off the Gaza Strip and sailed to Libya with eight civilian hostages. These people are then used as "bargaining chips" in Libyan dealings with France, and Abu Nidal

dealing with Belgium, until they are all released in 1990. Abu Nidal takes responsibility for this act in November. 1987 (Silco incident).

- *July 22, 1985:* Failed bombing of the US embassy in Egypt.
- *July 21, 1985:* A Kuwati Airlines office was destroyed in Beirut. No one was hurt.
- *July 24, 1985:* Jordanian diplomat Zayed Sati was assassinated in Istanbul, Turkey.
- *July 1985:* Bombing of the British Airways office in Madrid, Spain. One person was killed, 27 wounded. Near simultaneous attack on ALIA offices nearby, with two wounded.
- *September 16, 1985:* Grenades were thrown into a popular tourist attraction, the Cafe de Paris in Rome, Italy, wounding 38 people.
- *November 1985:* Hijacking of EgyptAir Flight 648 at Malta. Resolved after Egyptian commandos stormed the plane, slaying 1 of the 3 hijackers, one of which had been killed in an in-flight shootout with a sky marshal, although 58 of the 91 passengers died.
- *October 7, 1985:* Eleven people were injured by a bomb which exploded in a residential building in Jerusalem.
- *November 20, 1985:* Two Palestinians were assassinated in Jordan by ANO because they were apparently associated with Yasser Arafat.
- *December 19, 1985:* A courtroom in Nantes. France was held hostage by a gunman for several hours in a symbolic protest. No one was hurt.
- *December 27, 1985:* Attacks on Israeli El Al airport counters in Rome and Vienna. 18 dead, 111 wounded.

1986:

- *March 28, 1986:* Two professors working in Beirut, Leigh Douglas, British and Philip Padfield, American, were kidnapped by ANO operatives. Both were executed on the 17 April in a reprisal for Operation El Dorado Canyon.
- *April 2, 1986:* Four people are killed in the bombing of TWA Flight 840 over Corfu.

- *April 17, 1986:* British journalist John McCarthy was kidnapped in Beirut in response to Operation El Dorado Canyon. He was released in 1991.
- *April 27, 1986:* British tourist Paul Appelby was abducted and murdered in Jerusalem.
- *May 27, 1986:* One person was killed and five injured in six bomb attacks on Saudi Airlines and Pan Am offices in Karachi, Pakistan.
- *June 21, 1986:* A rocket attack on the Iraqi embassy in Vienna, Austria was foiled.
- *September 5, 1986:* 19 people killed during the hijacking of Pan Am Flight 73 in Karachi.
- *September 6, 1986:* Gunmen stormed the Neve Shalom synagogue in Istanbul, Turkey during the Sabbath. They shot 22 people dead and set fire to the building before being killed in the (possibly deliberate) detonation of a grenade.
- *September 11, 1986:* Syrian executive of the International Lions Club, Victor Kano, was kidnapped in Beirut, but later released unharmed.
- *November 5, 1986:* Rockets hit the Romanian embassies in Bahrain and Lebanon in protest at the Romanian support for the peace process. No one was hurt.

1987:

- *January 19, 1987:* Two Israeli youths were non-fatally stabbed in Jerusalem, apparently after stumbling upon some ANO operatives by accident.
- *March 5, 1987:* Two Palestinian men were abducted and hanged in Turkey on unproven "charges" of being Jordanian secret agents.

1988:

- *1988:* Car bomb outside the Israeli embassy in Cyprus. Three dead.
- *February 5, 1988:* Two Scandinavian aid workers were kidnapped in Beirut and released a month later.
- *March 23, 1988:* A man fired on a bus in Bombay, India,

which was carrying an Alitalia flight crew. One person wounded. Two days later, grenades were discovered and removed from the Saudi Arabian consulate in the city.

- *May 15, 1988:* Simultaneous gun and grenade attacks on the Acropole Hotel and the Sudan Club in Khartoum aimed at Western diplomats and their families. Four Britons, three Americans and two Sudanese killed, 21 people wounded.
- *May 11, 1988:* A large truck bomb explodes close to the Israeli embassy in Nicosia, Cyprus. The driver is one of the three people killed, apparently when an accomplise remotely detonated the device early. 19 people were injured.
- *July 11, 1988:* A car bomb explodes prematurely at a pier in Athens, killing two ANO members. This is followed by an attack on the cruise ship *City of Poros*, which leaves nine dead and 98 wounded.
- *August 20, 1988:* 25 people are injured in a hand grenade explosion at a shopping centre in Haifa, Israel.
- *November 17, 1988:* A Swiss Red Cross worker was kidnapped in Sidon, Lebanon, and held for a month before being released unharmed.

1989:

- *January 4, 1989:* A Saudi diplomat, Salah Al-Maliki, is killed and another man injured near the embassy in Bangkok, Thailand
- *March 29, 1989:* Two Muslim clerics opposed to the Salman Rushdie fatwah were assassinated in a mosque in Brussels, Belgium.
- *October 4, 1989:* Dr Joseph Wybran, a Belgian Jew and peace activist was assassinated in Brussels.
- *October 6, 1989:* Two Swiss Red Cross workers were kidnapped in Beirut. Both were released unharmed in August 1990.
- *1989:* Orders a purge of the ANO/Fatah-RC. 150 members are believed to have been tied up and machine-gunned.

1990:

- *July 25, 1990:* A prominent member of the Israeli community in Lima, Peru was seriously wounded in an assassination attempt.

- *October 12, 1990:* An Egyptian politician was shot and killed in Cairo. Egyptian and Iraqi backed ANO forces believed responsible.

1991:

- *January 14, 1991:* Assassination in Tunis of Abu Iyad, a top-ranking Fatah leader, who was Arafat's closest aide and the PLO's second-in-command. Also killed is the PLO Western (Israel) Sector commander Abu Hul and one of their bodyguards.
- *October 29, 1991:* A rocket struck the US Embassy compound in Beirut. No one was hurt.

1992:

- *June 8, 1992:* PLO officer Atef Bseiso was assassinated in Paris. ANO claimed credit, but PLO statement accused Mossad.
- *June 30, 1992:* Four PLO fighters were assassinated in a co-ordinated ambush in Sidon, Lebanon. One of the dead was Anwar Madi, PLO commander in Southern Lebanon.

1993:

- *November 15, 1993:* A PLO official was assassinated in Sidon, Lebanon.

1994:

- *January 29, 1994:* Assassination of Naeb Imran Maaytah, Jordanian diplomat, on a Beirut street. Jordanian authorities hinted that the ANO conducted this attack on behalf of Libya.

1997:

- *1997:* Killing of two ANO/Fatah-RC members in Lebanon over accusations of embezzlement.
- *1997:* Accused of assassinating Egyptian Islamist Sheikh Moutaleb in Yemen.

11

Boko Haram

A militant Islamist group in Nigeria, this group is known to receive funding from Al-Qaeda. Extremely vocal about their intolerance towards western education, Boko Haram had recently been in the news for the abduction of around 200 Nigerian girls. Boko Haram literally means "western education is sin". Boko Haram has been alleged to have on their hands a 5000-civilians kill number between 2009 and 2014. Boko Haram, originally founded as a Sunni Islamic group, have been advocating the extremely intolerant Sharia law in places of their stronghold. Threatening to overthrow the government, which they as becoming extremely open to the western culture, Boko Haram is known to spread terror by killing people who indulge in non-islamic practices, eg drink alcohol.

The founder of the sect, Mohammed Yusuf, had said in an interview that the theory about the Earth being round should be rejected as it had been propagated by the west. An incapability on the Nigerian government's part to deal with their growing militancy, Boko Haram has also been responsible for bombing the UN headquarters in Abuja in June, 2011.

Boko Haram (usually translated as "Western education is a sin"), is a militant Islamist movement based in north-east Nigeria which seeks to establish an Islamic state. The group was designated by the US Department of State as a terrorist organisation in November 2013. Membership is estimated to number in the hundreds to a few thousand. The group has received training and funds from al Qa'ida in the Islamic Maghreb.

By June 2014 Boko Haram had killed more than 5000 civilians, including at least 2000 in the first half of 2014. 650,000 people had fled their homes by August 2014, an increase of 200,000 since May. Corruption and mismanagement in the Nigerian security forces and human rights abuses perpetrated by them have hampered efforts to counter the insurgency.

Name

Jama'atu Ahlis Sunna Lidda'Awati Wal-Jihad, a.k.a. Jama'atu Ahlus-Sunnah Lidda'Awati Wal Jihad, a.k.a. Jama'atu Ahlus-Sunna Lidda'Awati Wal Jihad, meaning "People Committed to the Prophet's Teachings for Propagation and Jihad".

They are generally known as "Boko Haram", meaning "Western education is forbidden", from the Arabic *harâm*, (as opposed to *halâl*), meaning "forbidden"; and the Hausa word *boko* [the first vowel is long, the second pronounced in a low tone] meaning, roughly, "fake" (defined as "(a) Doing anything to create impression that one is better off, or that thing is of better quality or larger in amount than is the case, (b) anything so treated... etc.")

Western education has always been dismissed as *ilimin boko*, "fake education" (according to another source, *karatun boko*); a school that teaches Western education is *makaranta boko*. The uncompromising hostility of the northern Nigerian Muslims towards anything remotely perceived as foreign, a mindset of *boko haram* that has in the past been applied even towards vocal recitation of the Quran, has historically been a source of friction with the Muslims from the middle of the country.

Ideology

Boko Haram was founded as a Sunni Islamic sect advocating a strict form of Sharia law and developed into a Salafist-jihadi group in 2009, influenced by the Wahhabi movement. It seeks the establishment of an Islamic state in Nigeria, and opposes the Westernising of Nigerian society that has concentrated the wealth of the country among a small, mainly southern, Christian elite; 90 per cent of Nigeria's population of 155 million (in 2009) live on less than $2 a day. The Sharia law imposed by local authorities, beginning with Zamfara in January 2000 and covering 12 northern states by late 2002, was considered by the group to have been corrupted by politicians.

Boko Haram kills people who engage in practices seen as un-Islamic such as drinking alcohol. In a 2009 interview, the founder of the sect, Mohammed Yusuf, stated his belief that the theory that the Earth is round is contrary to Islamic teaching and should be rejected. Many of the group's senior radicals were reportedly inspired by Mohammed Marwa (known as "Maitatsine").

History

Background

Nigeria was governed by a series of ruthless military dictatorships from its independence in 1960 until the advent of democracy in 1999. Ethnic militancy is thought to have been one of the causes of the 1967-70 civil war; religious violence reached a new height in 1980 in Kano, the largest city in the north of the country, where the Muslim fundamentalist sect Yan Tatsine ("followers of Maitatsine") instigated riots that resulted in 4000 casualties. In the ensuing military crackdown Maitatsine was killed, causing a backlash of increased violence which spread among other northern cities over the course of the next 20 years.

Mohammed Yusuf founded the sect that became known as Boko Haram in 2002 in Maiduguri, the capital of the north-eastern state of Borno., establishing a religious complex with a school that attracted poor Muslim families from across Nigeria and neighbouring countries. The center had the political goal of creating an Islamic state, and became a recruiting ground for jihadis. By denouncing official state corruption, Yusuf attracted followers from unemployed youths. Disenfranchisement and inequality in Nigeria have been driving forces behind the conflict. Local politicians have the authority to grant 'indigeneship', which has far-reaching consequences, determining whether citizens can participate in politics, own land, work, or attend school. The system has been widely abused for political gain.

Boko Haram conducted its operations more or less peacefully during the first seven years of its existence. In 2009 the Nigerian government launched an investigation into the group's activities following reports that its members were arming themselves. Prior to that the government had repeatedly ignored warnings about the increasingly militant character of the organization. Clashes with security forces in 2009 in Maiduguri led to the deaths of an estimated 700 people. Yusuf was arrested, and executed by police "while trying to escape". He was succeeded as leader by Abubakar Shekau, formerly his second-in-command.

Terror campaign

Having regrouped under their new leader, in September 2010 Boko Haram broke 105 of its members out of prison in Maiduguri along with over 600 other prisoners. They went on to launch bold attacks in several areas of northern Nigeria, raising tensions between Christians and Muslims. As had been the case decades earlier in the wake of the 1980 Kano riots, the government's reliance on a purely military strategy, once again executing the leader of a militant group, would have unintended consequences.

Under Shekau's leadership, the group continuousy improved its operational capabilities. After launching a string of IED attacks against soft targets, and its first vehicle-borne IED attack in June 2011, killing 6 at the Abuja police HQ, in August of that year Boko Haram bombed the UN HQ in Abuja, the first time they had struck a Western target. A spokesman claiming responsibility for the attack, in which 11 UN staff members died as well as 12 others with more than 100 injured, warned of future planned attacks on US and Nigerian government interests. Speaking soon after the US embassy's announcement of the arrival in the country of the FBI, he went on to announce Boko Haram's terms for negotiation - the release of all imprisoned members. The increased sophistication of the group led many observers to believe that Boko Haram had linked up with al Qaeda's North African wing, which was known to be active in Niger.

The group have maintained a steady rate of attacks since 2011, striking a wide range of targets, multiple times per week. Targets have included schools, media, and politicians as well as the country's security infrastrucure. The tactic of suicide bombing, used in the two attacks in the capital on the police and UN HQs, was new to Nigeria, and alien to its mercenary culture; in Africa as a whole, it had only been utilised by al-Shabab in Somalia and, to a lesser extent, al-Qa'ida in the Islamic Maghreb. Since late 2012 Boko Haram have carried out a number of kidnappings in association with the splinter group Ansaru, which has drawn them a higher level of international attention. They have also ventured into neighbouring countries, further increasing their notoriety.

Within hours of President Goodluck Jonathan's inauguration for his first full four-year term of office in May 2011, the group carried out a series of bomb blasts in Bauchi, Abuja and Zaria. The most successful of these was the attack on the army barracks in Bauchi. A spokesman for the group told BBC Hausa that the attack had been carried out, as a test of loyalty, by serving members of the military hoping to join the group; a claim later emphatically denied by an army spokesman, who asserted "This is not a banana republic". However, on January 8, 2012 President Jonathan would announce that Boko Haram had in fact infiltrated not only the army and police, but also the executive, parliamentary and legislative arms of government. Boko Haram's spokesman also claimed responsibility for the assassination outside his home in Maiduguri of the politician Abba Anas Ibn Umar Garbai, the younger brother of the Shehu of Borno, who was the second most prominent Muslim in the country after the Sultan of Sokoto. He added that "We are doing what we are doing to fight injustice, if they stop their satanic ways of doing things and the injustices, we would stop what we are doing."

This was one of several political and religious assassinations carried out by Boko Haram that year, presumably with the overall intention of correcting injustices in the group's home state of Borno; meanwhile, the scale of massacres continued relentlessly, apparently intended to provoke a full-scale ethnic and religious civil war. By the start of 2012, these contradictory strategies and thus the apparent lack of cohesion within the group led to inevitable comparisons being drawn with the disparate factions of the militants of the Niger Delta, whose motivations ranged between ideology and greed. Adding to the confusion, in November the State Security Service claimed to have identified four criminal syndicates operating under the name 'Boko Haram'.

The common theme throughout the north-east was the targetting of police, who were regularly massacred at work or followed home and gunned down in drive-by shootings, perhaps in revenge for the murder of Yusuf, or as representatives of an illegitimate state apparatus, or for no particular reason. The arrest of 5 officers for the extra-judicial killing of Yusuf in 2009 had no noticeable effect. Opportunities for criminal enterprise flourished. By October 2012 hundreds of police officers had been killed in attacks on more than 60 police stations. The government's response to this self-reinforcing trend towards insecurity was not to restructure or reorientate the security services, but rather to invest heavily in security equipment, spending US $5.5 billion, 20 per cent of their overall budget, on bomb detection units, communication and transport, and US $470 million on a Chinese CCTV system for the capital Abuja.

State of emergency

President Jonathan's 2011 election victory had been the cause of widespread grievance, as it broke the terms of a tacit agreement whereby after two terms the presidency was expected to change hands to a northern, Muslim candidate, thus spreading the country's oil wealth more equitably, through the customary corrupt channels. The subsequent campaign of violence by Boko Haram culminated in a series of attacks across the country on Christmas Day. A church in the outskirts of Abuja was bombed, killing 37; in Niger State, in the north-west, a suicide car-bomb outside a church killed 43. On New Year's Eve the president declared a state of emergency in the most troubled areas of the country, and closed the borders with Cameroon, Chad and Niger in the northeast. On the following day he announced that he was scrapping fuel subsidies. The IMF had pushed for the move, but Nigerians believed the savings of $8 billion a year would be stolen. Fuel prices quickly doubled, leading to widespread strikes and protests which were quelled a fortnight later with army checkpoints throughout the commercial capital Lagos and police firing live ammunition and teargas.

In 2011, Boko haram had carried out 115 attacks, killing 550. The state of emergency ushered in an intensification of violence: the first three weeks of the year alone accounted for more than half the deaths of the preceeding year. Two days after the state of emergency was declared, Boko Haram released an ultimatum to southern Nigerians living in the north, giving them three days to leave. Three days later they began a series of mostly small-scale attacks on Christians and members of the Igbo ethnic group, causing many to flee their home state. On the 20th January, 2012, they launched by far their most deadly attack yet. More than 180 were killed in Kano in an assault on police buildings. The dead included a Nigerian TV reporter; information on events is scarce. The Al-Qaida style tactics involved a combination of car bombs, IEDs, suicide bombers and gunmen wearing army and police uniforms.

Amnesty International and Human Rights Watch released detailed reports in 2012, widely quoted by US and UK government agencies and in the international media, based on research conducted over the course of the conflict in the worst affected regions of the country. The NGOs were critical of the actions of both Boko Haram and government security forces. HRW said "Boko Haram should immediately cease all attacks, and threats of attacks, that cause loss of life, injury, and destruction of property. The Nigerian government should take urgent measures to address the human rights abuses that have helped fuel the violent militancy." Summarised in a (2012) US Department of State review, violations "committed by the security services with impunity" included:

- "Extrajudicial killings by security forces, including summary executions; security force torture, rape, and other cruel, inhuman, or degrading treatment of prisoners, detainees, and criminal suspects; harsh and life-threatening prison and detention center conditions; arbitrary arrest and detention; prolonged pretrial detention; denial of fair public trial; executive influence on the judiciary; infringements on citizens' privacy rights; restrictions on freedom of speech, press, assembly, religion, and movement; official corruption...
- On October 9, witnesses in Maiduguri claimed members of the JTF "Restore Order," based in Maiduguri, went on a killing spree after a suspected Boko Haram bomb killed an officer. Media reported the JTF killed 20 to 45 civilians

and razed 50 to 100 houses in the neighbourhood. The JTF commander in Maiduguri denied the allegations. On November 2, witnesses claimed the JTF shot and killed up to 40 people during raids in Maiduguri. The army claimed it dismissed some officers from the military as a result of alleged abuses committed in Maiduguri, but there were no known formal prosecutions in Maiduguri by year's end."

Corruption in the security forces was further documented in a December 2013 analysis by the UK Home Office:

- "The NPF, SSS, and military report to civilian authorities; however, these security services periodically act outside of civilian control. The government lack effective mechanisms to investigate and punish abuse and corruption. The NPF remain susceptible to corruption, commit human rights abuses, and generally operate with impunity in the apprehension, illegal detention, and sometimes execution of criminal suspects. The SSS also commit human rights abuses, particularly in restricting freedom of speech and press. In some cases private citizens or the government brought charges against perpetrators of human rights abuses in these units. However, most cases lingered in court or went unresolved after an initial investigation."

Boko Haram has increasingly ventured across the national border, often evading the Nigerian army by retreating into Cameroon, whose army is apparently unwilling to confront them.

The US Bureau of Counterterrorism has summarised the group's overseas operations:

- In February 2013, Boko Haram was responsible for kidnapping seven French tourists in the Far North of Cameroon. In November 2013, Boko Haram members kidnapped a French priest in Cameroon. In December 2013, Boko Haram gunmen reportedly attacked civilians in several areas of northern Cameroon. Security forces from Chad and Niger also reportedly partook in skirmishes against suspected Boko Haram members along Nigeria's borders. In 2013, the group also kidnapped eight French citizens in northern Cameroon and obtained ransom payments for their release.

TIMELINE OF BOKO HARAM ATTACKS

Between 2009 and beginning of 2012, Boko Haram was responsible for over 900 deaths.

On 14 May 2013, President Goodluck Jonathan declared a state of emergency in the states of Borno, Yobe, and Adamawa in a bid to fight the activities of Boko Harâm. He ordered the Nigerian Armed Forces to the three areas around Lake Chad. As of 17 May, Nigerian armed forces' shelling in Borno resulted in at least 21 deaths. A curfew was imposed in Maiduguri as the military used air strikes and shellings to target Boko Harâm strongholds. The Nigerian state imposed a blockade on the group's traditional base of Maiduguri in Borno in order to re-establish Nigeria's "territorial integrity".

On 21 May, the Defence Ministry issued a statement that read it had "secured the environs of New Marte, Hausari, Krenoa, Wulgo and Chikun Ngulalo after destroying all the terrorists' camps". Armed Forces Spokesman in Borno Lieutenant Colonel Sagir Musa said that the curfew that had been imposed was not relaxed with the curfew timings being 18:00 to 7:00, however there was minimal traffic in Maiduguri.

On 29 May, Boko Harâm's leader Abubakar Shekau, following military claims that the group had been halted, released a video in which he said the group had not lost to the Nigerian armed forces. In the video he showed charred military vehicles and bodies dressed in military fatigues.

While he called on Muslims from Iraq, Pakistan, Afghanistan and Syria to join his jihad, he said in Arabic and Hausa:

- My fellow brethren from all over the world, I assure you that we are strong, hale and hearty since they launched this assault on us following the state of emergency declaration. When they launch any attack on us you see soldiers fleeing and throwing away their weapons like a rabbit that is been hunted down.

On the same day, Nigeria's Director of Defence Information Brigadier-General Chris Olukolade said that Shekau's unnamed deputy was found dead near Lake Chad and that two others from Boko Harâm were arrested in the area. However, the military's claims were not verified.

Satellite photos raise questions about the government's retaliatory attack on Boko Harâm on April 16–17, 2013. Over 180 died, mostly from fires that appeared to be deliberately set during the government attack. Boko Harâm fighters and civilians died in the attack. The people of Maiduguri were unhappy with the declaration of war on the group and instead said the issues of poverty and inequality needed to be tackled first.

It was reported in August 2013 that Shekau had been shot and deposed by members of his sect, but he survived. He had been described as "the most dreaded and wanted" Boko Harâm leader and the United States had recently offered a US$7m bounty for information leading to his arrest. He has taken responsibility for the April 2014 kidnapping of over 200 school girls. On 6 May 2014, eight more girls were kidnapped by suspected Boko Harâm gunmen. In a videotape, Shekau threatened to sell the kidnapped girls into slavery. On May 12, 2014 Boko Harâm released a video which shows the kidnapped girls and alleging that the girls had converted to Islam and would not be released until all militant prisoners were freed. On May 17, 2014, Nigerian President Goodluck Jonathan and the presidents of Benin, Chad, Cameroon and Niger met in Paris and agreed to combat Boko Harâm on a coordinated basis, sharing in particular surveillance and intelligence gathering. Chad President Idriss Deby said after the meeting African nations were determined to launch a total war on Boko Harâm. Westen nations, including Britain, France, Israel, and the United States had also pledged support.

On 22 May 2014 Boko Harâm was officially declared a terrorist group affiliated to Al-Qaeda and Al-Qaeda in the Islamic Maghreb by the United Nations Security Council. International sanctions including asset freeze, travel ban and arms embargo were imposed against the Islamist extremist group.

On May 2014, Nigerian soldiers shot at the car of their divisional commander whom they suspected of colluding with Boko Harâm and it was reported that nine Nigerian generals were being investigated for suspected sale of weapons to Boko Harâm. Amnesty

International accused the Nigerian government of human rights abuses after 950 suspected Boko Harâm militants died in detention facilities run by Nigeria's military Joint Task Force in the first half of 2013.

Timeline of incidents:

- *7 September 2010:* Bauchi prison break
- *31 December 2010:* December 2010 Abuja attack
- *12 March 2011:* Assassinated Muslim Cleric Imam Ibrahim Ahmed Abdullahi for criticizing the violent groups in northeast Nigeria
- *22 April 2011:* Boko Harâm frees 14 prisoners during a jailbreak in Yola, Adamawa State
- *29 May 2011:* May 2011 northern Nigeria bombings
- *16 June 2011:* The group claims responsibility for the 2011 Abuja police headquarters bombing
- *26 June 2011:* Bombing attack on a beer garden in Maiduguri, leaving 25 dead and 12 injured
- *10 July 2011:* Bombing at the All Christian Fellowship Church in Suleja, Niger State
- *11 July 2011:* The University of Maiduguri temporarily closes down its campus citing security concerns
- *12 August 2011:* Prominent Muslim Cleric Liman Bana is shot dead by Boko Harâm.
- *26 August 2011:* 2011 Abuja bombing
- *4 November 2011:* 2011 Damaturu attacks
- *25 December 2011:* December 2011 Nigeria bombings
- *5–6 January 2012:* January 2012 Nigeria attacks
- *20 January 2012:* January 2012 Kano bombings
- *28 January 2012:* Nigerian army says it killed 11 Boko Harâm insurgents
- *8 February 2012:* Boko Harâm claims responsibility for a suicide bombing at the army headquarters in Kaduna.
- *16 February 2012:* Another prison break staged in central Nigeria; 119 prisoners are released, one warden killed.
- *8 March 2012:* During a British hostage rescue attempt to

free Italian engineer Franco Lamolinara and Briton Christopher McManus, abducted in 2011 by a splinter group Boko Harâm, both hostages were killed.

- *31 May 2012:* During a Joint Task Force raid on a Boko Harâm den, it was reported that 5 sect members and a German hostage were killed.
- *3 June 2012:* 15 church-goers were killed and several injured in a church bombing in Bauchi state. Boku Harâm claimed responsibility through spokesperson Abu Qaqa.
- *17 June 2012:* Suicide bombers strike three churches in Kaduna State. At least 50 people were killed.
- *17 June 2012:* 130 bodies were found in Plateau State. It is presumed they were killed by Boko Harâm terrorists.
- *18 September 2012:* Family of four murdered
- *18 September 2012:* Murder of six at an outdoor party
- *19 September 2012:* Nigerian Military arrests Boko Harâm militants, reported death of Abu Qaqa
- *3 October 2012:* Around 25–46 people were massacred in the town of Mubi in Nigeria during a night-time raid.
- *18 March 2013:* 2013 Kano Bus bombing: At least 22 killed and 65 injured, when a suicide car bomb exploded in Kano bus station.
- *19 April 2013:* Deadliest attack since 2009: gun battle with security forces leaves 260 dead and nearly 1000 injured
- *7 May 2013:* At least 55 killed and 105 inmates freed in coordinated attacks on army barracks, a prison and police post in Bama town.
- *6 July 2013:* Yobe State school shooting: 42 people, mostly students, were killed in a school attack in northeast Nigeria.
- *29 September 2013:* College of Agriculture in Gujba: 40 male students killed.
- *14 January 2014:* At least 31 people killed, over 50 people injured by suicide bombing in Maiduguri, Borno State.
- *16 February 2014:* Izghe massacre: 106 villagers are killed, 105 of whom were boys and men.

- *25 February 2014:* Federal Government College attack: Fury at military over Yobe deaths. At least 29 teenage boys dead at Federal Government College Buni Yadi.
- *14 April 2014:* 2014 Chibok kidnapping: Government properties, including the only girls' secondary school, attacked. At least 16 killed or missing, and 234 female students kidnapped. The Boko Harâm militants said it would treat them as slaves as part of the "war booty".
- *14 April 2014:* April 2014 Abuja bombing: Two bombs explode at a crowded bus station in Abuja, Nigeria, killing at least 90 people and injuring more than 200.
- *1 May 2014:* A car bomb exploded killing at least 19 people and injured at least 60 in the same area of Abuja as the April bomb.
- *5 May 2014:* 2014 Gamburu attack: Boko Harâm attacked the twin towns of Gamboru and Ngala in Borno State, Nigeria. They started shooting in a busy marketplace, set houses on fire, and gunned down anyone who tried to flee. The death toll of the massacre has been set as high as 336.
- *13 May 2014:* Menari, Tsangayari and Garawa: Boko Harâm attacked three villages, killing around 60 people in Menari. Vigilantes fought back, killing over 200 Boko Harâm militants.
- *17 May 2014:* Paris summit: A summit in Paris has declared Boko Harâm is part of al-Qaeda as leaders from West African nations resolved to mount a region-wide offensive against the group that is holding more than 200 schoolgirls hostage in a dense jungle. Western nations have pledged to provide technical expertise and training to the new regional African effort against the Islamic extremists.
- *18 May 2014:* Kano: Suicide car bomb kills five people.
- *20 May 2014:* Jos: Twin bomb explosions kill 118 people.
- *30 May 2014:* Assassination of Muslim leader Alhaji Idrissa Timta the Emir of Gwoza in Borno state.
- *1 June 2014:* Mubi bombing: An attack at a football field in Mubi, Adamawa state kills at least 40 people.

- *2 June 2014:* Militants dressed as soldiers slaughtered at least 200 civilians in three communities in northeastern Nigeria's Borno state, in the Gwoza local government district. A community leader who witnessed the Monday killings had said that local residents had pleaded for help from the military, but it did not arrive in time. It took a few days for word from survivors to reach the provincial capital of Maiduguri, because the roads are extremely dangerous and phone connections are poor or non-existent. The slaughter was confirmed by both Mohammed Ali Ndume, a senator representing Borno and whose hometown is Gwoza, and by a top security official in Maiduguri who insisted on anonymity.
- *29 May - June 5:* 6 attacks, killing 506 civilians, 5 military; 20 women and 3 men abducted. 60 Boko Haram killed by Cameroon's military
- *June 6 - June 12:* 4 attacks, killing 5 civilians, 6 military; military kill 50 Boko Haram
- *June 13 - June 19:* 2 attacks, 46 civilians killed; 8 Boko Haram killed by Borno vigilante group
- *June 20 - June 26:* 4 attacks, 93 civilians killed, 60 abducted. A military fighter jet bombed unknown number of Boko Haram in counterattack; 25 Boko Haram and 16 soldiers killed in attack on military base. Cameroon military killed 10 Boko Haram near border
- *June 27 - July 3:* 2 attacks, 112 killed
- *July 4 - July 10:* 4 Boko Haram attacks, 11 civilians, 1 vigilante, 33 soldiers, 4 police killed. 53 Boko Haram were killed while capturing a military base and police station in Borno on the 4th of July. On the 6th, soldiers killed a Boko Haram kingpin and his brother at their home in Kaduna; also on the 6th, 44 Boko Haram were killed in 2 military operations in Borno
- *July 11 - July 17:* 4 attacks, 81 civilians killed, many of these shot by fighter jet in a failed counter-attack. German teacher kidnapped and 2 vigilantes killed on July 16 in Adamawa, presumably by Boko Haram

- *July 25 - July 27:* 2 attacks in Kolofata, Cameroon, including the kidnapping of the wife of the Vice Prime Minister, Amadou Ali, as well as local religious leader and mayor, Seini Boukar-Lamine.
- 11 August 2014: 28 civilians killed, 97 kidnapped, all men and boys, in attacks on villages in Borno State in rural northeast Nigeria. Many homes torched in the raid.
- 29 October 2014: Several people were killed after clashes with the armed forces resulted in Boko Haram taking over the second largest city in Adamawa, Mubi. It followed the overrunning of Uba in Borno. Kukawa local government chairman Modu Musa said that several people were killed especially around the market.
- 25 November 2014: Suicide bombing in the Maiduguri market by two women killed at least 45 people. Other sources count 78 deaths.
- 28 November 2014: 120 people were killed in Kano, where a local mosque was bombed by Boko Haram.
- 1 December 2014: In Damaturu, during a Boko Haram attack, two female suicide bombers detonated bombs at the central Maiduguri market, killing dozens.
- 3 December 2014: Boko Haram abducted 20 women, mostly young girls, during an attack on Lassa in Borno State.
- 4 December 2014: Boko Haram raided Bajoga, in Gombe State, occupying buildings briefly before leaving with stolen vehicles and motorbikes.
- 10 December 2014: Boko Haram raided Gaji-gana, north of Borno State, killing at least 14 people.
- 1 January 2015: Boko Haram abducted 40 boys and young men from the village of Malari in Borno State, Nigeria.
- 9 January 2015: 40 boys kidnapped by Boko Haram in Kukawa, northeast Nigeria

2015 BAGA MASSACRE

The 2015 Baga massacre is a series of mass killings and attacks believed to have been committed and, according to some reports, still ongoing in the Nigerian town of Baga and its environs, in the state of Borno, between 3 January and 7 January 2015 by the Islamist militiaBoko Haram. The attack began on 3 January when Boko Haram overran a military base that was the headquarters of the Multinational Joint Task Force, which consisted of troops fromChad, Niger, and Nigeria, after which the militants forced thousands of locals from the region, before carrying out widespread mass killings that culminated on the 7th.

Fatalities have been reported to be "heavy" but their extent is presently unclear; local officials and residents who have fled have been quoted as saying that "over 2,000" people are thought to have been killed or "unaccounted for", but others report "at least a hundred" fatalities. Several government officials denied that the fatalities were as extensive as reported, with some even claiming that the massacre had never taken place or that the Nigerian military had repelled the militants from the region, a claim that was refuted by local officials, survivors, and the international media.

Baga and at least 16 other towns are thought to have been destroyed as over 35,000 people are reported to have been displaced, with many feared to have drowned while trying to cross Lake Chad and others trapped on islands in the lake. The attacks are said to have resulted in Boko Haram extending its control to over 70% of Borno State.

Background

Baga, in Borno State, was the location of a Nigerian Army base that was the headquarters of the Multinational Joint Task Force (MNJTF), an international force of soldiers from Nigeria, Niger and Chad that was formed in 1994 to deal with cross-border security issues and, more recently, combating the Boko Haram insurgency. For that reason, the town is believed to have been of strategic importance to Boko Haram, as the last major town in Northern Borno State under the control of the Nigerian governmentand a key military base for government and international forces.

Massacre and attacks

The attacks began on 3 January, when a large number of Boko

Haram militants captured the town of Baga and overran the MNJTF headquarters and army base in town.

Attack on MNJTF headquarters

According to Senator Ahmed Zanna, who represents the district of Borno Central, government forces—despite being the joint headquarters only Nigerian Army forces were stationed there at the time—resisted the militants, who "attacked from all sides", for several hours, but eventually "joined civilians fleeing into the bush". They reportedly seized a large number of weapons and vehicles, according to Zanna.

In the days following the assault, the militants forced Baga's residents into the surrounding area villages. On the evening of Tuesday, 6 January, two local residents reported that the militants began to burn local buildings using petrol bombs and explosives, and according to survivors proceeded to kill those left. On 9 January, a resident described the extent of the damage by reporting, "There is not any single house that is standing there." According to Musa Bukar, head of the Kukawa local government area, all 16 villages in the LGA were razed as well, and their residents either killed or forced to flee.

Extent of fatalities

The extent of the killings is as of yet unknown, and reports vary wildly. Over two thousand people were thought to have been killed, according to Bukar. Zanna said that two thousand were "unaccounted for", but other sources said that "dozens" or "over a hundred" had been killed. At least 100 were killed in the initial attack on 3 January, according to Baba Abba Hassan, the district head, later adding that "hundreds of corpses still lay on the streets" of the town and that many women and children were among the victims, having been pursued into the bush by the militants.

Hassan, however, denied that the attack on 7 January had ever occurred and that the figure of 2,000 deaths was "outrageous". Several government sources allegedly rejected claims of such a high number of fatalities, suggesting that it was considerably lower. However, the Nigerian government has downplayed the extent of, and frequently outright denied the existence of, Boko

Haram attacks several times in the past, including a prior massacre in Baga in 2013 where both Boko Haram and the Nigerian military were implicated in the death of over 200 citizens.

Aftermath and response

Government security officials quickly denied that any attack had taken place in Baga, and stated that "base troops had held their positions". One pro-government newspaper, citing a local fisherman, went as far to claim that Boko Haram had instead been dealt a "heavy defeat" by the Nigerian military in Baga and that the town was firmly under government control. Air Chief Marshal Alex Badeh, theChief of the Defence Staff, initially denied that the MNJTF headquarters had been captured but later admitted that it had.

One government spokesperson gave the atypically precise figure of 1,636 people as having been displaced as a result of the attack, and "brushed aside" claims that it had been more severe. According to independent reports and local officials, however, least 35,000 people are thought to have fled the region. "Bodies lay strewn on the streets", according to survivors, as the entire population of Baga is thought to have fled, some into Cameroon and Chad. Approximately 20,000 sought shelter at camp near Maiduguri, the state capital, and another 10,000 in Monguno were waiting to be transported. Bukar said that the town was now "virtually non-existent". Local human rights activists said that they had been told by women who had escaped the town that their daughters, some as young as 10, had been kidnapped.

Chadian Prime Minister Kalzeubet Pahimi Deubet said that at least 2,500 Nigerians and 500 Chadians had sought refuge in the neighbouring country following the attacks, some of whom were trying to cross Lake Chad in flimsy and overloaded canoes. Many of those trying to cross the lake are feared to have drowned, while hundreds of others, over five hundred by one account, have been trapped on islands in the lake. According to local officials who had communicated with the refugees via telephone, refugees were "dying from lack of food, cold and malaria" on one "mosquito-infested island."

Maina Maaji Lawan, a former Governor of Borno state and the

current Senator representing the district of Borno North, questioned why the soldiers had reportedly fled the base, saying "[t]here is definitely something wrong that makes our military abandon their posts each time there is an attack from Boko Haram". This followed a spate of Nigerian troops, numbering in the hundreds, fleeing Boko Haram in battle. According to Lawan, the attack meant that 70% of Borno State would now be under the control of Boko Haram.

2013 BAGA MASSACRE

The Baga massacre began on 16 April 2013 in the village of Baga, Nigeria, in Borno State, when as many as 200 civilians were killed, hundreds wounded, and over 2,000 houses and businesses worth millions of Naira were destroyed. Conflicting media reports suggest the massacre may have continued for a number of days.

Refugees, civilians officials, and human rights organizations accused the Nigerian Military of carrying out the massacre; some military officials blamed the insurgent groupBoko Haram.

Background

Thousands of people have died in fighting in Nigeria since the beginning of 2009 Boko Haram Uprising, which began in northern Nigeria. The leader of 2009 Boko Haram Uprising, Mohammed Yusuf (Boko Haram), was killed in Maiduguri of Borno State in 2009.

According to *The New York Times*, the Nigerian military has employed "scorched-earth standards" in their fight against Boko Haram, with civilians routinely killed during operations in poor neighborhoods. Massacres prior to the Baga massacre were commonly employed as punitive measures against the civilian population, without legal consequences in Nigeria.

Baga is a small fishing village on the banks of lake Chad, near the borders of Chad and Niger. Prior to the massacre, Boko Haram controlled some or all of the village.

Events

On the evening of 16 April, members of Boko Haram engaged government soldiers at a military post outside Baga, killing one of them. According to residents, soldiers returned with reinforcements supported by armored vehicles.

Soldiers doused homes in Baga with gasoline and set fire to the village, shooting villagers who attempted to flee. Some attempting to escape into lake Chad drowned there, while others were able to escape into the surrounding bush. Casualties were especially high among children and the elderly.

According to some villagers, the massacre took place over a number of days.

By Wednesday, 193 wounded victims had been admitted to a local health clinic. Journalists attempting to access the village have been blocked by the Nigerian military.

Reactions

Following the massacre, the Nigerian government came under intense pressure from international governments and media, leading the Nigerian national assembly to call for an investigation.

Nigerian army denial

Brigadier General Austin Edokpaye stated that only six civilians were killed in the event, while the army was able to kill 30 "Boko Haram terrorists." Brigadier General Chris Olukolade stated that anyone blaming Nigerian soldiers sympathized with Boko Haram, which he said was responsible for the massacre, and had shot at government soldiers from the village.

U.S. Government condemnation

The United States's acting deputy State Department spokesman Patrick Ventrell on Monday 22 April condemned the clash between members of the Armed Forces' Joint Task Force (JTF) and militants in Baga, urging authorities to respect human rights.

Nigeria orders probe

Nigeria's President Goodluck Jonathan through his special adviser on media and publicity, Reuben Abati has ordered a full-scale investigation into the civilian casualties in the war between Boko Haram and Nigeria's soldiers at the weekend.

Assessment

The U.S. State Department designated Boko Haram and Ansari as terrorist organisations in November 2013, citing various reasons, including links with AQIM, "thousands of deaths in northeast and central Nigeria over the last several years, including targeted killings of civilians", and Ansaru's 2013 kidnapping and execution of seven international construction workers.

In the statement from the Department it was noted, however, "These designations are an important and appropriate step, but only one tool in what must be a comprehensive approach by the Nigerian government to counter these groups through a combination of law enforcement, political, and development efforts." Boko Haram is not currently (June 2014) believed by the US government to be affiliated to Al Qaeda.

Boko Haram gets funding from bank robberies and kidnapping ransoms. In February 2012, recently arrested officials revealed that "while the organization initially relied on donations from members, its links with Al-Qaeda in the Islamic Maghreb, AQIM, opened it up to more funding from groups in Saudi Arabia and the UK".

They went on to say that other sources of funding included the Al Muntada Trust Fund and the Islamic World Society. The group also extorts local governments. A spokesman of Boko Haram claimed that Kano state governor Ibrahim Shekarau and Bauchi state governor Isa Yuguda had paid them monthly. In the past, Nigerian officials have been criticized for being unable to trace much of the funding that Boko Haram has received.

The Nigerian military is, in the words of a former British military attache speaking in early 2014, "a shadow of what it's reputed to have once been. It's fallen apart." They are short of basic equipment including radios and armoured vehicles; morale is said to be low. The defence budget accounts for more than a third of the country's security budget of $5.8 billion, but only 10 per cent is allocated to capital spending. In a 2014 US DOD assessment, funds are being "skimmed off the top"; troops are "showing signs of real fear," and are "afraid to even engage."

In a [illegible] S. report, Boko Haram was ranked as the second deadliest terrorist group in the world after the Taliban in

Afghanistan. In July 2014, Nigeria was estimated to have had the highest number of terrorist killings in the world over the past year: 3477 deaths reported in 146 attacks.

The governor of Borno State, Kashim Shettima, of the opposition All Nigeria Peoples Party, announced to journalists in February 2014:

- "Boko Haram are better armed and are better motivated than our own troops. Given the present state of affairs, it is absolutely impossible for us to defeat Boko Haram."

12

Hamas

Hamas is a Palestinian Sunni Islamic organization, with an associated military wing, the Izz ad-Din al-Qassam Brigades, in the Palestinian territories and elsewhere in the Middle East including Qatar. Since 2007, it has governed the Gaza Strip, after it won a majority of seats in the Palestinian Parliament in the 2006 Palestinian parliamentary elections and defeated the Fatah political organization in a series of violent clashes. Hamas is designated as a terrorist organization by Israel, the United States, the United Kingdom, Canada, the European Union, Jordan, Egypt and Japan. However it is not considered a terrorist organisation by several other states, including Iran, Russia, Turkey, China and many Arab nations.

Based on the principles of Islamism gaining momentum throughout the Arab world in the 1980s, Hamas was founded in 1987 (during the First Intifada) as an offshoot of the Egyptian Muslim Brotherhood. Co-founder Sheik Ahmed Yassin stated in 1987, and the Hamas Charter affirmed in 1988, that Hamas was founded to liberate Palestine from Israeli occupation and to establish an Islamic state in the area that is now Israel, the West Bank and the Gaza Strip. In July 2009, Khaled Mashal, Hamas's political bureau chief, said that the organization was willing to cooperate with "a resolution to the Arab-Israeli conflict which included a Palestinian state based on 1967 borders", provided that Palestinian refugees held the right to return to Israel and that East Jerusalem be the new nation's capital. In 2014, however, Mousa Mohammed Abu Marzook, deputy chairman of Hamas's political bureau, said: "Hamas will not recognize Israel... this is a red line that cannot be crossed".

The Izz ad-Din al-Qassam Brigades, the Hamas-affiliated military wing, has launched attacks on Israel, against both civilian and military targets. Attacks on civilian targets have included rocket attacks and, from 1993 to 2006, suicide bombings. Attacks on military targets have included small-arms fire and rocket and mortar attacks.

In the January 2006 Palestinian parliamentary elections, Hamas won a decisive majority in the Palestinian Parliament, defeating the PLO-affiliated Fatah party. Following the elections, the Quartet (the United States, Russia, United Nations and European Union) made future foreign assistance to the PA conditional upon the future government's commitment to non-violence, recognition of the state of Israel, and acceptance of previous agreements. Hamas resisted such changes, which led to the Quartet suspending its foreign assistance programme and Israel imposing economic sanctions on the Hamas-led administration. In March 2007, a national unity government headed by Prime Minister Ismail Haniyeh of Hamas was briefly formed, but this failed to restart international financial assistance. Tensions over control of Palestinian security forces soon erupted in the 2007 Battle of Gaza, after which Hamas retained control of Gaza, while its officials were ousted from government positions in the West Bank. Israel and Egypt then imposed an economic blockade of the Gaza Strip, on the grounds that Fatah forces were no longer providing security there.

In June 2008, as part of an Egyptian-brokered ceasefire, Hamas ceased rocket attacks on Israel and made some efforts to prevent attacks by other organizations. After a four-month calm, the conflict escalated when Israel carried out a military action with the stated aim of preventing an abduction planned by Hamas, using a tunnel that had been dug under the border security fence, and killed seven Hamas operatives. In retaliation, Hamas attacked Israel with a barrage of rockets. In late December 2008, Israel attacked Gaza, withdrawing its forces from the territory in mid-January 2009. After the Gaza War of 2008 and 2009, Hamas continued to govern the Gaza Strip and Israel maintained its economic blockade.

On May 4, 2011, Hamas and Fatah announced a reconciliation agreement that provides for "creation of a joint caretaker Palestinian government" prior to national elections scheduled for 2012. According to Israeli news reports quoting Fatah leader Mahmoud Abbas, as a condition of joining the PLO, Khaled Meshaal agreed to discontinue the "armed struggle" against Israel and accept Palestinian statehood within the 1967 borders, alongside Israel. Hostilities resumed between November 14–21, 2012. On 12 June 2014, three Israeli teenagers were kidnapped and murdered. The IDF initiated an operation in the West Bank aimed to find them (not until June 30 were their bodies found). Israeli authorities have named two Hamas members as prime suspects: Amer Abu Aysha and Marwan Kawasm. The increased tensions soon escalated, and a full military operation began on July 8.

HISTORY

The History of Hamas is an account of the Palestinian Islamist fundamentalist socio-political organization with an associated paramilitary force, the Izz ad-Din al-Qassam Brigades. Hamas is an acronym of Aarakat al-Muqawamat al-Islamiyyah, meaning "Islamic Resistance Movement".

Hamas was established in 1987, and has its origins in Egypt's Muslim Brotherhood movement, which had been active in the Gaza Strip since the 1950s and gained influence through a network of mosques and various charitable and social organizations. In the 1980s the Brotherhood emerged as a powerful political factor, challenging the influence of the PLO, and in 1987 adopted a more nationalist and activist line under the name of Hamas. During the 1990s and early 2000s, the organization conducted numerous suicide bombings and other attacks against Israel.

In the Palestinian legislative election of January 2006, Hamas gained a large majority of seats in the Palestinian Parliament, defeating the ruling Fatah party. After the elections, conflicts arose between Hamas and Fatah, which they were unable to resolve. In June 2007, Hamas defeated Fatah in a series of violent clashes, and since that time Hamas has governed the Gaza portion of the Palestinian Territories, while at the same time they were ousted from government positions in the West Bank. Israel and Egypt then imposed an economic blockade on Gaza and largely sealed their borders with the territory.

After acquiring control of Gaza, Hamas-affiliated and other militias launched rocket attacks upon Israel, which Hamas ceased in June 2008 following an Egyptian-brokered ceasefire. The ceasefire broke down late in 2008, with each side accusing the other of responsibility. In late December 2008, Israel attacked Gaza, withdrawing its forces in mid-January 2009.

Early Islamic activism in Gaza

With its takeover of Gaza after the 1967 war with Egypt, Israel hunted down secular Palestinian Liberation Organization factions but dropped the previous Egyptian rulers' harsh restrictions against Islamic activists. In fact, Israel for many years tolerated and at times encouraged Islamic activists and groups as a counterweight to the secular nationalists of the PLO and its dominant faction, Fatah.

Among the activists benefited was Sheikh Ahmed Yassin, leader of the Muslim Brotherhood in Gaza, who had also formed the Islamist group Mujama al-Islamiya in 1973, a charity recognized by Israel in 1979. Israel allowed the organization to build mosques, clubs, schools, and a library in Gaza.

Yitzhak Segev, the acting governor of Gaza in 1979, said he had no illusions about Yassin's intentions, having watched an Islamist movement topple the Shah as Israel's military attache in Iran. According to Segev, Yassin and his charity were completely peaceful towards Israel during this time, and Segev and other Israeli officials feared being viewed as an enemy of Islam. Segev maintained regular contact with Yassin, met with him around a dozen times, and arranged for Yassin to be taken to Israel for hospital treatment.

Also, Segev said, Fatah was "our main enemy". Islamists frequently attacked secular and leftist Palestinian movements, including Fatah, but the Israeli military avoided getting involved in those quarrels. It stood aside, for example, when Mujama al-Islamiya activists stormed the Red Crescent charity's headquarters in Gaza, but Segev did send soldiers to prevent the burning down of the home of the head of the organization.

In 1984 the Israeli army received intelligence that Sheikh Yassin's followers were collecting arms in Gaza. Israeli troops raided mosques and found a cache of weapons. Yassin was arrested, but told his interrogators the weapons were meant to be used against secular Palestinians, not Israel. The cleric was released a year later and allowed to continue to develop his movement in Gaza.

Around the time of Yassin's arrest, Avner Cohen, an Israeli religious affairs official, sent a report to senior military officers and civilian leadership in Gaza advising them of the dangers of the Islamic movement, but this report and similar ones were ignored. Former military intelligence officer Shalom Harari said the warnings were ignored out of neglect, not a desire to fortify the Islamists: "Israel never financed Hamas. Israel never armed Hamas."

1987—The founding of Hamas

In 1987, several Palestinians were killed in a traffic accident involving an Israeli driver, and the events that followed—a Palestinian uprising (now known as the First Intifada) against Israel's West Bank and Gaza occupation—led Yassin and six other Palestinians to found Hamas as an offshoot of the Muslim Brotherhood movement. The new group was supported by Brotherhood-affiliated charities and social institutions that had already gained a strong foothold in the occupied territories. The acronym "Hamas" first appeared in 1987 in a leaflet that accused the Israeli intelligence services of undermining the moral fibre of Palestinian youth as part of Mossad's recruitment of what Hamas termed collaborators. Nonetheless, Israeli military and intelligence was still focused on Fatah, and continued to maintain contacts with Gaza's Islamic activists. Numerous Islamist leaders, including senior Hamas founder Mahmoud Zahar, met with Yitzhak Rabin as part of "regular consultations" between Israeli officials and Palestinians not linked to the PLO.

Hamas carried out its first attack against Israel in 1989, abducting and killing two soldiers. The Israel Defence Forces immediately arrested Yassin and sentenced him to life in prison, and deported 400 Hamas activists, including Zahar, to South

Lebanon, which at the time was occupied by Israel. During this time Hamas built a relationship with Hezbollah.

1990s

Hamas's military branch, the Izz ad-Din al-Qassam Brigades, was created in 1991. During the 1990s the al-Qassam Brigades conducted numerous attacks on Israel, with both civilian and military victims. In April 1993, suicide bombings in the West Bank began. After the February 1994 massacre by Baruch Goldstein of 30 Muslim civilians in a Hebron mosque, the al-Qassam Brigades began suicide attacks inside Israel.

In December 1992 Israel responded to the killing of a border police officer by deporting 415 leading figures of Hamas and Islamic Jihad to Lebanon, which provoked international condemnation and a unanimous UN Security Council resolution condemning the action.

Although the suicide attacks by the al-Qassam Brigades and other groups violated the 1993 Oslo accords (which Hamas opposed), Palestinian Authority President Yasir Arafat was reluctant to pursue the attackers and may have had inadequate means to do so. Some analysts state that the Palestinian Authority could have stopped the suicide and other attacks on civilians but refused to do so.

According to the Congressional Research Service, Hamas admitted to having executed Palestinians accused of collaborating with Israeli authorities in the 1990s. A transcript of a training film by the al-Qassam Brigades tells how Hamas operatives kidnapped Palestinians accused of collaboration and then forced confessions before executing them.

In 1996, Yahya Ayash, the chief bombmaker of Hamas and the leader of the West Bank battalion of the Izz ad-Din al-Qassam Brigades, was assassinated by the Israeli secret service.

In September 1997, Israeli agents in Jordan attempted but failed to assassinate Hamas leader Khaled Mashal, leading to chilled relations between the two countries and release of Sheikh Yassin, Hamas's spiritual leader, from Israeli prison. Two years later Hamas was banned in Jordan, reportedly in part at the request of the United States, Israel, and the Palestinian Authority. Jordan's

King Abdullah feared the activities of Hamas and its Jordanian allies would jeopardize peace negotiations with Israel, and accused Hamas of engaging in illegitimate activities within Jordan. In mid-September 1999, authorities arrested Hamas leaders Khaled Mashal and Ibrahim Ghosheh on their return from a visit to Iran, and charged them with being members of an illegal organization, storing weapons, conducting military exercises, and using Jordan as a training base. Hamas leaders denied the charges. Mashal was exiled and eventually settled in Syria.

Second Intifada

Al-Qassam Brigades militants were among the armed groups that launched both military-style attacks and suicide bombings against Israeli civilian and military targets during the Second Intifada (also known as the Al-Aqsa Intifada, which began in late September 2000. This Palestinian uprising against Israeli rule in the occupied territories was much more violent than the First Intifada. The military and civilian death toll is estimated at 5500 Palestinians and more than 1100 Israelis, as well as 64 foreigners. A 2007 study of Palestinian suicide bombings during the second intifada (September 2000 through August 2005) found that about 40 per cent were carried out by the al-Qassam Brigades.

The immediate trigger for the uprising is disputed, but a more general cause, writes U.S. political science professor Jeremy Pressman, was "popular Palestinian discontent [that] grew during the Oslo peace process because the reality on the ground did not match the expectations created by the peace agreements". Hamas would be the beneficiary of this growing discontent in the 2006 Palestinian Authority legislative elections.

In January 2004, Hamas leader Sheikh Ahmed Yassin said that the group would end armed resistance against Israel in exchange for a Palestinian state in the West Bank, Gaza Strip, and east Jerusalem, and that restoring Palestinians' "historical rights" (relating to the 1948 Palestinian exodus) "would be left for future generations". On January 25, 2004, senior Hamas official Abdel Aziz al-Rantissi offered a 10-year truce, or *hudna,* in return for the establishment of a Palestinian state and the complete withdrawal by Israel from the territories captured in the 1967 Six Day War.

Al-Rantissi stated that Hamas had come to the conclusion that it was "difficult to liberate all our land at this stage, so we accept a phased liberation". Israel immediately dismissed al-Rantissi's statements as insincere and a smokescreen for military preparations. Yassin was assassinated on March 22, 2004, by a targeted Israeli air strike, and al-Rantisi was assassinated by a similar air strike on April 18, 2004.

Hamas–Fatah conflict

After the formation of the Hamas-led cabinet on March 20, 2006, tensions between Fatah and Hamas militants progressively rose in the Gaza strip as Fatah commanders refused to take orders from the government while the Palestinian Authority initiated a campaign of demonstrations, assassinations and abductions against Hamas, which led to Hamas responding. Israeli intelligence warned Mahmoud Abbas that Hamas had planned to kill him at his office in Gaza. According to a Palestinian source close to Abbas, Hamas considers president Abbas to be a barrier to its complete control over the Palestinian Authority and decided to kill him. In a statement to Al Jazeera, Hamas leader Mohammed Nazzal, accused Abbas of being party to besieging and isolating the Hamas-led government.

On June 9, 2006, during an Israeli artillery operation, an explosion occurred on a busy Gaza beach, killing eight Palestinian civilians. It was assumed that Israeli shellings were responsible for the killings, but Israeli government officials denied this. Hamas formally withdrew from its 16-month ceasefire on June 10, taking responsibility for the subsequent Qassam rocket attacks launched from Gaza into Israel.

On June 25, two Israeli soldiers were killed and another, Gilad Shalit, abducted following an incursion by the Izz ad-Din al-Qassam Brigades, Popular Resistance Committees and Army of Islam. In response, the Israeli military launched Operation Summer Rains three days later, to secure the release of the kidnapped soldier, arresting 64 Hamas officials. Among them were 8 Palestinian Authority cabinet ministers and up to 20 members of the Palestinian Legislative Council, The arrests, along with other events, effectively prevented the Hamas-dominated legislature from functioning during most of its term. On February 2007 Saudi-sponsored negotiations in Mecca produced agreement on a signed by Mahmoud Abbas on behalf of Fatah and Khaled Mashal on behalf of Hamas. The new government was called on to achieve Palestinian national goals as approved by the Palestine National Council, the clauses of the Basic Law and the National Reconciliation Document (the "Prisoners' Document") as well as the decisions of the Arab summit.

In March 2007, the Palestinian Legislative Council established a national unity government, with 83 representatives voting in favour and three against. Government ministers were sworn in by Mahmoud Abbas, the chairman of the Palestinian Authority, at a ceremony held simultaneously in Gaza and Ramallah.

In June that year, renewed fighting broke out between Hamas and Fatah. In the course of the June 2007 Battle of Gaza, Hamas exploited the near total collapse of Palestinian Authority forces in Gaza, to seize control of Gaza, ousting Fatah officials. President Mahmoud Abbas then dismissed the Hamas-led Palestinian Authority government. and outlawed the Hamas militia. At least 600 Palestinians died in fighting between Hamas and Fatah. Human Rights Watch, a U.S.-based group, accused both sides in the conflict of torture and war crimes.

Human Rights Watch estimates several hundred Gazans were "maimed" and tortured in the aftermath of the Gaza War. 73 Gazan men accused of "collaborating" had their arms and legs broken by "unidentified perpetrators" and 18 Palestinians accused of collaborating with Israel, who had escaped from Gaza's main prison compound after Israel bombed the facility, were executed by Hamas security officials in the first days of the conflict.

Hamas security forces attacked hundreds Fatah officials who supported Israel.

Human Rights Watch interviewed one such person:

- "There were eight of us sitting there. We were all from Fatah. Then three masked militants broke in. They were dressed in brown camouflage military uniforms; they all had guns. They pointed their guns at us and cursed us, then they began beating us with iron rods, including a 10-

year-old boy whom they hit in the face. They said we were "collaborators" and "unfaithful".

- They beat me with iron sticks and gun butts for 15 minutes. They were yelling: "You are happy that Israel is bombing us!" until people came out of their houses, and they withdrew.

In March 2012 Mahmoud Abbas stated that there were no political differences between Hamas and Fatah as they had reached agreement on a joint political platform and on a truce with Israel. Commenting on relations with Hamas, Abbas revealed in an interview with Al Jazeera that "We agreed that the period of calm would be not only in the Gaza Strip, but also in the West Bank," adding that "We also agreed on a peaceful popular resistance [against Israel], the establishment of a Palestinian state along the 1967 borders and that the peace talks would continue if Israel halted settlement construction and accepted our conditions."

Gaza War

On June 17, 2008, Egyptian mediators announced that an informal truce had been agreed to between Hamas and Israel. Hamas agreed to cease rocket attacks on Israel, while Israel agreed to allow limited commercial shipping across its border with Gaza, barring any breakdown of the tentative peace deal; Hamas also hinted that it would discuss the release of Gilad Shalit. Israeli sources state that Hamas also committed itself to enforce the ceasefire on the other Palestinian organizations. Even before the truce was agreed to, some on the Israeli side were not optimistic about it, Shin Bet chief Yuval Diskin stating in May 2008 that a ground incursion into Gaza was unavoidable and would more effectively quell arms smuggling and pressure Hamas into relinquishing power.

While Hamas was careful to maintain the ceasefire, the lull was sporadically violated by other groups, sometimes in defiance of Hamas. For example, on June 24 Islamic Jihad launched rockets at the Israeli town of Sderot; Israel called the attack a grave violation of the informal truce, and closed its border crossings with Gaza. On November 4, 2008, Israeli forces, in an attempt to stop construction of a tunnel, killed six Hamas gunmen in a raid inside the Gaza Strip. Hamas responded by resuming rocket attacks, a total of 190 rockets in November according to Israel's military.

With the six-month truce officially expired on December 19, Hamas launched 50 to more than 70 rockets and mortars into Israel over the next three days, though no Israelis were injured. On December 21, Hamas said it was ready to stop the attacks and renew the truce if Israel stopped its "aggression" in Gaza and opened up its border crossings.

On December 27 and 28, Israel implemented Operation Cast Lead against Hamas. Egyptian President Hosni Mubarak said "We warned Hamas repeatedly that rejecting the truce would push Israel to aggression against Gaza." According to Palestinian officials, over 280 people were killed and 600 were injured in the first two days of airstrikes. Most were Hamas police and security officers, though many civilians also died. According to Israel, militant training camps, rocket-manufacturing facilities and weapons warehouses that had been pre-identified were hit, and later they attacked rocket and mortar squads who fired around 180 rockets and mortars at Israeli communities. Chief of Gaza police force Tawfiq Jabber, head of the General Security Service Salah Abu Shrakh, senior religious authority and security officer Nizar Rayyan, and Interior Minister Said Seyam were among those killed during the fighting. Although Israel sent out thousands of cell-phone messages urging residents of Gaza to leave houses where weapons may be stored, in an attempt to minimise civilian casualties, some residents complained there was nowhere to go because many neighbourhoods had received the same message. Israeli bombs landed close to civilian structures such as schools, and some alleged that Israel was deliberately targeting Palestinian civilians.

Israel declared a unilateral ceasefire on January 17, 2009. Hamas responded the following day by announcing a one-week ceasefire to give Israel time to withdraw its forces from the Gaza Strip. Israeli, Palestinian, and third-party sources disagreed on the total casualty figures from the Gaza war, and the number of Palestinian casualties who were civilians. In November 2010, a senior Hamas official acknowledged that up to 300 fighters were killed and "In addition to them, between 200 and 300 fighters from the Al-Qassam Brigades and another 150 security forces were martyred."

These new numbers reconcile the total with those of the Israeli military, which originally said were 709 "terror operatives" killed.

After the Gaza War

On August 16, 2009, Hamas leader Khaled Mashal stated that the organization is ready to open dialogue with the Obama administration because its policies are much better than those of former U.S. president George W. Bush: "As long as there's a new language, we welcome it, but we want to see not only a change of language, but also a change of policies on the ground. We have said that we are prepared to cooperate with the US or any other international party that would enable the Palestinians to get rid of occupation." Despite this, an August 30, 2009 speech during a visit to Jordan in which Mashal expressed support for the Palestinian right of return was interpreted by David Pollock of the Washington Institute for Near East Policy as a sign that "Hamas has now clearly opted out of diplomacy." In an interview on May 2010, Mashal said that if a Palestinian state with real sovereignty was established under the conditions he set out, on the borders of 1967 with its capital Jerusalem and with the right of return, that will be the end of the Palestinian resistance, and then the nature of any subsequent ties with Israel would be decided democratically by the Palestinians.

In July 2009, Khaled Mashal, Hamas's political bureau chief, stated Hamas's willingness to cooperate with a resolution to the Arab-Israeli conflict, which included a Palestinian state based on 1967 borders, provided that Palestinian refugees be given the right to return to Israel and that East Jerusalem be recognized as the new state's capital.

In 2011, after the outbreak of the Syrian Civil War, Hamas distanced itself from the Syrian regime and its members began leaving Syria. Where once there were "hundreds of exiled Palestinian officials and their relatives", that number shrunk to "a few dozen". In 2012, Hamas publicly announced its support for the Syrian opposition. This prompted Syrian state TV to issue a "withering attack" on the Hamas leadership. Khaled Mashal said that Hamas had been "forced out" of Damascus because of its disagreements with the Syrian regime. In late October, Syrian

Army soldiers shot dead two Hamas leaders in Daraa refugee camp. On November 5, 2012, the Syrian state security forces shut down all Hamas offices in the country. In January 2013, another two Hamas members were found dead in Syria's Husseinieh camp. Activists said the two had been arrested and executed by state security forces. In 2013, it was reported that the military wing of Hamas had begun training units of the Free Syrian Army.

In 2013, after "several intense weeks of indirect three-way diplomacy between representatives of Hamas, Israel, and the Palestinian Authority", no agreement was reached. Also, intra-Palestinian reconciliation talks stalled and, as a result, during Obama's visit to Israel, Hamas launched five rocket strikes on Israel. In November, Isra Almodallal was appointed the first spokeswoman of the group.

HAMAS OF IRAQ

Hamas in Iraq is a Sunni militia group based in Iraq, which split from the 1920 Revolution Brigade on 18 March 2007. The group claims to have released videos of its attack on US troops. The 1920 Revolution Brigade insists that Hamas in Iraq was involved in assisting US troops in their recent Diyala operations against Al-Qaeda in Iraq. Iraqi Prime Minister Nuri al-Maliki has feared the US-armed 'concerned local citizens' are an armed Sunni opposition in the making, and has argued that such groups should be under the command of the Iraqi Army or police. On October 11, 2007, the militia group joined a political council that embraced armed insurgency against American forces.

Political program

Hamas in Iraq released a political program in April 2007 with some of the following provisions:

- "The movement believes in armed jihad as a means for expelling the occupier, and calls on public opinion and agencies and international institutions to respect this right... of all peoples to resist occupation, and to distinguish between that and armed crimes which target innocent civilians."
- "We believe in a necessary link between military efforts

and political action as two mutually supportive instruments for achieving the goals of resistance for liberation and salvation and preventing the fundamentalist movements from harvesting the fruits of the resistance."

- "We confirm the necessity of continuing the killing until the exit of the last soldier from the occupying armies, and to not negotiate with the enemy except with an agreement of the factions of the jihad and the Iraqi resistance; and under the appropriate circumstances and conditions."

In July 2007, *The Guardian* reported that the group participated with other insurgent groups in an alliance called the Political Council for the Iraqi Resistance, which includes a range of Islamist and nationalist-leaning groups which was formed to negotiate with the Americans in anticipation of an early US withdrawal. Main planks of the joint political program included a commitment to free Iraq from foreign troops, rejection of cooperation with parties involved in political institutions set up under the occupation and a declaration that decisions and agreements made by the US occupation and Iraqi government are null and void."

Operations in Diyala in August 2007

The 1920 Revolution Brigades insists that Hamas in Iraq was involved in assisting US troops in their recent Diyala operations against al-Qaeda in Iraq in August 2007.

The insistences occurred when *The Washington Post* reported in a telephone interview with Lt. Col. Joseph Davidson, executive officer of the 2nd Infantry Division, U.S. forces were now "partnering with Sunni insurgents from the 1920 Revolution Brigades, which includes former members of ousted president Saddam Hussein's disbanded army." The 1920 Revolution Brigades replied that: "We say to ... the occupation and to your followers and agents that you made a very big lie" in linking us with the Diyala anti-al Qaida campaign. The group maintains that the US military spokesman should have referred to "Iraqi Hamas", which consisted of Brigades before the operations.

HAMAS COVENANT

The Hamas Covenant also known as Hamas Charter, refers to

the Charter of the Hamas, issued on 18 August 1988, outlining the movement founding identity, stand, and aims.

The Charter identified Hamas as the Muslim Brotherhood in Palestine and declares its members to be Muslims who "fear God and raise the banner of Jihad in the face of the oppressors." The charter states that "our struggle against the Jews is very great and very serious" and calls for the eventual creation of an Islamic state in Palestine, in place of Israel and the Palestinian Territories, and the obliteration or dissolution of Israel. It emphasizes the importance of jihad stating in article 13, "There is no solution for the Palestinian question except through Jihad. Initiatives, proposals and international conferences are all a waste of time and vain endeavors." The charter also states that Hamas is humanistic, and tolerant of other religions as long as they "stop disputing the sovereignty of Islam in this region". The Charter adds that "renouncing any part of Palestine means renouncing part of the religion" of Islam.

In 2010 Hamas leader Khaled Meshaal stated that the Charter is "a piece of history and no longer relevant, but cannot be changed for internal reasons." Hamas have moved away from its charter since it decided to go for political office. In 2009 interviews with the BBC,Tony Blair claimed that Hamas does not accept the existence of Israel and continues to pursue its objectives through terror and violence;Sir Jeremy Greenstock however argued that Hamas has not adopted its charter as part of its political program since it won the Palestinian legislative election, 2006. Instead it has moved to a more secular stance. In 2008, the Hamas leader in Gaza, Ismail Haniyeh, stated that Hamas would agree to accept a Palestinian state along the 1967 borders, and to offer a long-term truce with Israel. In contrast to this, Hamas leader Mahmoud al-Zahar stated that any talk of the 1967 lines is "just a phase" until Hamas has a chance to "regain the land...even if we [Hamas] have to do so inch by inch." Other Hamas leaders, including Ismail Haniyah and Khaled Meshaal have also stated repeatedly that "Palestine – from the [Jordan] River to the [Mediterranean] Sea, from its north to its south – is our land, our right, and our homeland. There will be no relinquishing or forsaking even an inch or small part of it," and that "we shall not relinquish the Islamic waqf on the land of Palestine, and Jerusalem shall not be divided into Western and Eastern Jerusalem. Jerusalem is a single united [city], and Palestine stretches from the Mediterranean Sea to the Jordan River, and from Naqoura [Rosh Ha-Niqra] to Umm Al-Rashrash [Eilat] in the south."

BACKGROUND

In 1987, 20 years after the 1967 war, the First Intifada (1987–1993) had begun. In the late 1980s, the PLO sought a negotiated solution with Israel in the form of a two-state solution. This was not acceptable to Hamas, the Palestinian wing of the Muslim Brotherhood, and the covenant was written to bridge the ideological gap between the PLO and Muslim Brotherhood. According to Hamas's Deputy Foreign Minister Dr. Ahmed Yousef, the Charter "was ratified during the unique circumstances of the Uprising in 1988 as a necessary framework for dealing with a relentless occupation".

While the PLO was nationalistic, it was more secular in nature, while Hamas subscribed to a neo-Salafi jihadi theology and nationalism. Hamas was a shift from the Muslim Brotherhood's more universal Islamic vision to a focus on Palestinian nationalism and a strategy of armed struggle, or violent jihad. Its political goals were identical to those of the PLO's charter and was essentially an armed struggle to retrieve the entire land of Palestine as an Islamic waqf.

RELEVANCE OF THE CHARTER IN THE 21ST CENTURY

Dr. Ahmed Yousef, an adviser to Ismail Haniyeh (the senior political leader of Hamas) claimed that Hamas has changed its views with time since the charter was issued in 1988. In 2010 Hamas leader Khaled Meshaal stated that the Charter is "a piece of history and no longer relevant, but cannot be changed for internal reasons."

In 2006, Hamas proposed government programme, which stated that "the question of recognizing Israel is not the jurisdiction of one faction, nor the government, but a decision for the Palestinian people." However many remain sceptical of Hamas's new stance, and view it as a ploy to hide its true agenda, "but it is equally true that the "new" discourse of diluted religious content—to say nothing of the movement's increasing pragmatism and flexibility in the political domain—reflects genuine and cumulative changes within Hamas."

HAMAS CONDEMNS PARIS ATTACKS AS HAVING NO JUSTIFICATION

The Hamas group that controls the Gaza Strip on Saturday issued a condemnation of the deadly attacks by Islamist gunmen in France this week, saying there was no "justification for killing innocents".

In the worst assault on France's homeland security for decades, 17 victims lost their lives in three days of violence that began with an attack on the Charlie Hebdo satirical newspaper on Wednesday and ended with Friday's dual sieges at a print works outside Paris and a kosher supermarket in the city.

- "[Hamas] stresses that its position on the latest events in Paris is in line with the statement issued by the International Union of Muslim Scholars which condemned the attack on the Charlie Hebdo newspaper and that any differences in opinion are no justification for killing innocents," Hamas said in a rare statement in French.

On Friday, the leader of Lebanon's Shia group Hezbollah said the attacks in France had done more harm to Islam than any cartoon or book, a reference to the attack on Charlie Hebdo.

LEADERSHIP AND STRUCTURE

Hamas comprises three interrelated wings – the social welfare and political wings, which are responsible for the social, administrative, political, and propaganda activities of Hamas, and the military wing, which is engaged in covert activities, such as acting against suspected collaborators, gathering intelligence on potential targets, procuring weapons, and carrying out military attacks.

Consultative councils

The Majlis al-Shura (consultative council) is the group's

overarching political and decision making body. It includes representatives from Gaza, the West Bank, Israeli prisons, and the exiled external leadership, the Political Bureau. Under this Shura council are committees responsible for supervising Hamas activities, from media relations to military operations. In the West Bank and Gaza, local Shura committees answer to the Shura council and carry out its decisions.

Hamas's highest decision-making body is its Political Bureau, which consists of 15 members. Before the beginning of the Syrian Civil War, it operated in exile in Damascus, Syria. The bureau is elected by members who select their representatives in local Consultative Councils in specific geographic regions. The councils then nominate representatives to the General Consultative Council, and the Political Bureau is elected by members of the General Consultative Council.

Military wing

The Izz ad-Din al-Qassam Brigades, Hamas's military wing formed in 1992, is named in commemoration of influential Palestinian nationalist Sheikh Izz ad-Din al-Qassam. Armed Hamas cells sometimes refer to themselves as "Students of Ayyash", "Students of the Engineer", or "Yahya Ayyash Units", to commemorate Yahya Ayyash, an early Hamas bomb-maker killed in 1996. Since its establishment, the military capability of Hamas has increased markedly, from rifles to Qassam rockets and more.

While the number of members is known only to the Brigades leadership, Israel estimates the Brigades have a core of several hundred members who receive military style training, including training in Iran and in Syria (before the Syrian Civil War). Additionally, the brigades have an estimated 10,000 operatives "of varying degrees of skill and professionalism" who are members of Hamas or their supporters and the internal security forces. These operatives can be expected to reinforce the Brigades in an "emergency situation".

Although the Izz al-Din al-Qassam Brigades are an integral part of Hamas, they also operate independently of Hamas, and at times contrary to Hamas' stated aims. Most analysts agree that although differences of opinion between the Hamas military and political wing exist, Hamas's internal discipline is strong enough to contain them. Political scientists Ilana Kass and Bard O'Neill liken Hamas's relationship with the Brigades to the political party Sinn Féin's relationship to the military arm of the Irish Republican Army. To further explain the relationship, they quote a senior Hamas official: "The Izz al-Din al-Qassam Brigade is a separate armed military wing, which has its own leaders who do not take their orders from [Hamas] and do not tell us of their plans in advance." However, according to former U.S. Department of Treasury official and terrorism expert Matthew Levitt, the Hamas Political Bureau operates as the highest ranking leadership body determining the policy of the Hamas organization and has responsibility for directing and coordinating terrorist acts. Hamas' founder, Sheikh Ahmad Yassin, stated in 1998: "We can not separate the wing from the body. If we do so, the body will not be able to fly. Hamas is one body."

Social welfare

Hamas is popular among Palestinians in the Gaza Strip, though it also has a following in the West Bank, and to a lesser extent in other Middle Eastern countries. Its popularity stems in part from its welfare wing providing social services to Palestinians in the occupied territories. Such services are not generally provided by the Palestinian Authority. Israeli scholar Reuven Paz estimates that 90 per cent of Hamas activities revolve around "social, welfare, cultural, and educational activities". Social services include running relief programmes and funding schools, orphanages, mosques, health care clinics, soup kitchens, and sports leagues.

In particular, Hamas funded health services where people could receive free or inexpensive medical treatment. Hamas greatly contributed to the health sector, and facilitated hospital and physician services in the Palestinian territory. On the other hand, Hamas's use of hospitals is sometimes criticised as purportedly serving the promotion of violence against Israel. Charities affiliated with Hamas are known to financially support families of those who have been killed or imprisoned while carrying out militant actions or supporting such actions. Families typically receive a one time grant of $500 to $5,000, and those whose homes have been destroyed by the Israel Defence Forces have their rent paid for temporary housing. Families of militants not affiliated with Hamas sometimes receive less.

Hamas has funded education and built Islamic charities, libraries, mosques and education centers for women. They also built nurseries, kindergartens and supervised religious schools that provide free meals to children. When children attend their schools and mosques, parents are required to sign oaths of allegiance. Refugees, as well as those left without homes, are able to claim financial and technical assistance from Hamas.

The work of Hamas in these fields supplements that provided by the United Nations Relief Works Agency (UNRWA). Hamas is also well regarded by Palestinians for its efficiency and perceived lack of corruption compared to Fatah. Since the 2008–2009 Israeli military operation in Gaza, Palestinian public opinion polls have shown Hamas steadily increasing in popularity with 52 per cent support compared to 13 per cent for Fatah. All public opinion surveys conducted recently have supported this trend.

Despite building materials needing to be smuggled into the territory, luxury beach resorts and tourist facilities operated by the interior ministry have been constructed by Hamas government-linked charities, including gardens, playgrounds, football fields, a zoo and restaurants aimed to provide employment and low cost entertainment for citizens. Some Palestinians have complained about the admission fee, criticizing Hamas for charging them to use "government-owned" property.

ISLAMIZATION EFFORTS

In the Gaza Strip

From 1987 to 1991, during the first intifada, Hamas campaigned for the wearing of the hijab alongside other measures, including insisting women stay at home and be segregated from men, and the promotion of polygamy. In the course of this campaign, women who chose not to wear the hijab were verbally and physically harassed, with the result that the hijab was being worn 'just to avoid problems on the streets'.

Since Hamas took control of the Gaza Strip in 2007, some of its members have attempted to impose Islamic dress or the hijab head covering on women. Also, the government's "Islamic Endowment Ministry" has deployed Virtue Committee members to warn citizens of the dangers of immodest dress, card playing, and dating. However, there are no government laws imposing dress and other moral standards, and the Hamas education ministry reversed one effort to impose Islamic dress on students. There has also been successful resistance to attempts by local Hamas officials to impose Islamic dress on women.

Hamas officials deny having any plans to impose Islamic law, one legislator stating that "What you are seeing are incidents, not policy," and that Islamic law is the desired standard "but we believe in persuasion". The Hamas education ministry reversed one effort to impose Islamic dress on students. In March 2010, the BBC interviewed five "middle-class" women in Gaza City in March 2010, and all indicated there had been little or no change towards more conservative dress and mores.

In 2013, UNRWA canceled its annual marathon in Gaza after Hamas rulers prohibited women from participating in the race.

In the West Bank

In 2005, the human rights organization Freemuse released a report titled "Palestine: Taliban-like attempts to censor music", which said that Palestinian musicians feared that harsh religious laws against music and concerts will be imposed since Hamas group scored political gains in the Palestinian Authority local elections of 2005.

The attempt by Hamas to dictate a cultural code of conduct in the 1980s and early 1990s led to a violent fighting between different Palestinian sectors. Hamas members reportedly burned down stores that stocked videos they deemed indecent and destroyed books they described as "heretical".

In 2005, an outdoor music and dance performance in Qalqiliya were suddenly banned by the Hamas led municipality, for the reason that such an event would be forbidden by Islam, or "Haram". The municipality also ordered that music no longer be played in the Qalqiliya zoo, and mufti Akrameh Sabri issued a religious edict affirming the municipality decision. In response, the Palestinian national poet Mahmoud Darwish warned that "There are Taliban-type elements in our society, and this is a very dangerous sign."

The Palestinian columnist Mohammed Abd Al-Hamid, a resident of Ramallah, wrote that this religious coercion could cause the migration of artists, and said "The religious fanatics in Algeria destroyed every cultural symbol, shattered statues and rare works of art and liquidated intellectuals and artists, reporters and authors, ballet dancers and singers – are we going to imitate the Algerian and Afghani examples?"

Tayyip Erdoðan's Turkey as a role model

Some Hamas members stated that the model of Islamic government that Hamas seeks to emulate is that of Turkey under the rule of Tayyip Erdoðan. The foremost members to distance Hamas from the practices of Taliban and to publicly support the Erdoðan model were Ahmad Yousef and Ghazi Hamad, advisers to Prime Minister Hanieh. Yusuf, the Hamas deputy foreign minister, reflected this goal in an interview to a Turkish newspaper, stating that while foreign public opinion equates Hamas with the Taliban or al-Qaeda, the analogy is inaccurate. Yusuf described the Taliban as "opposed to everything," including education and women's rights, while Hamas wants to establish good relations between the religious and secular elements of society and strives for human rights, democracy and an open society. According to professor Yezid Sayigh of the King's College in London, how influential this view is within Hamas is uncertain, since both Ahmad Yousef and Ghazi Hamad were dismissed from their posts as advisers to Hamas Prime Minister Ismail Hanieh in October 2007. Both have since been appointed to other prominent positions within the Hamas government. Khaled al-Hroub of the West Bank-based and anti-Hamas Palestinian daily Al Ayyam added that despite claims by Hamas leaders that it wants to repeat the Turkish model of Islam, "what is happening on the ground in reality is a replica of the Taliban model of Islam."

POLITICAL VIOLENCE AND TERRORISM

Hamas uses both political activities and violence in pursuit of its goals. For example, while politically engaged in the 2006 Palestinian Territories parliamentary election campaign, Hamas stated in its election manifesto that it was prepared to use "armed resistance to end the occupation".

From 2000 to 2004, Hamas was responsible for killing nearly 400 Israelis and wounding more than 2,000 in 425 attacks, according to the Israeli Ministry of Foreign Affairs. From 2001 through May 2008, Hamas launched more than 3,000 Qassam rockets and 2,500 mortar attacks into Israel.

Attacks on civilians

In the first years of the First Intifada (1987–93), Hamas violence was directed first at collaborators with Israel and at individuals it considered moral deviants, and then later at the Israeli military. A new direction began with the formation of the al-Qassam Brigades militia in 1992, and in 1993 suicide attacks began against Israeli targets on the West Bank.

The first such attack occurred on April 16, 1993, when an al-Qassam Brigades operative detonated explosives in a car he parked next to two buses, one military and one civilian, in the West Bank town of Mehola, killing a Palestinian civilian and wounding 8 Israeli soldiers.

After the February 1994 massacre by Baruch Goldstein of 30 Muslim civilians in a Hebron mosque, the al-Qassam Brigades expanded suicide attacks to target primarily civilians. The first of the suicide bombings that targeted civilians was at Afula on April 16, 1994, when a suicide bomber detonated an explosives-laden car next to a bus, killing nine (including the bomber) and wounding 50. The most deadly suicide bombing was an attack on a Netanya hotel on March 27, 2002, in which 30 people were killed and 140 were wounded. The attack has also been referred to as the Passover massacre since it took place on the first night of the Jewish festival of Passover at a Seder.

Hamas defended suicide attacks as a legitimate aspect of its asymmetric warfare against Israel, but they are consideted as crimes against humanity under international law. Hamas renounced suicide attacks in April 2006. In a 2002 report, Human Rights Watch stated that Hamas leaders "should be held accountable" for "war crimes and crimes against humanity" committed by the al-Qassam Brigades.

In May 2006 Israel arrested a top Hamas official, Ibrahim Hamed, who Israeli security officials alleged was responsible for dozens of suicide bombings and other attacks on Israelis. Hamed's trial on those charges has not yet concluded.

While the suicide attacks ceased in 2005, al-Qassam Brigades rocket and mortar attacks on towns and settlements near Gaza continued. Since 2002, paramilitary soldiers of al-Qassam Brigades and other groups have used homemade Qassam rockets to hit Israeli towns in the Negev, such as Sderot. Al-Qassam Brigades was estimated in 2007 to have launched 22 per cent of the rocket and mortar attacks, which killed fifteen people between the years 2000 and 2009. The introduction of the *Qassam*-2 rocket in 2008 enabled Palestinian paramilitary groups to reach, from Gaza, such Israeli cities such as Ashkelon.

In 2008, Hamas leader Khaled Mashal, offered that Hamas would attack only military targets if the IDF would stop causing the deaths of Palestinian civilians. Following a June 19, 2008 ceasefire, the al-Qassam Brigades ended its rocket attacks and arrested Fatah militants in Gaza who had continued sporadic rocket and mortar attacks against Israel. The al-Qassam Brigades resumed the attacks after the November 4 Israeli incursion into Gaza.

On 15 June, 2014, Israeli Prime Minister Benjamin Netanyahu accused Hamas of involvement in the kidnapping of three Israeli teenagers (including one who held American citizenship), saying "This has severe repercussions." On 20 July 2014, nearly two weeks into Operation Protective Edge, Netanyahu in an interview with CNN described Hamas as "genocidal terrorists."

Rocket attacks on Israel

According to Human Rights Watch, Hamas and other Palestinian armed groups have launched thousands of rockets into Israel since 2001, killing 15 civilians, wounding many more, and posing an ongoing threat to the nearly 800,000 Israeli civilians who live and work in the weapons' range. Hamas officials have said that the rockets were aimed only at military targets, saying that civilian casualties were the "accidental result" of the weapons' poor quality. According to Human Rights Watch, statements by

Hamas leaders suggest that the purpose of the rocket attacks was indeed to strike civilians and civilian objects. From January 2009, following Operation Cast Lead, Hamas largely stopped launching rocket attacks on Israel and has on at least two occasions arrested members of other groups who have launched rockets, "showing that it has the ability to impose the law when it wants". In February 2010, Hamas issued a statement regretting any harm that may have befallen Israeli civilians as a result of Palestinian rocket attacks during the Gaza war. It maintained that its rocket attacks had been aimed at Israeli military targets but lacked accuracy and hence sometimes hit civilian areas. Israel responded that Hamas had boasted repeatedly of targeting and murdering civilians in the media.

Attempts to derail 2010 peace talks

In 2010, Hamas, who have been actively sidelined from the peace talks by Israel, spearheaded a coordinated effort by 13 Palestinian militant groups, in attempt to derail the stalled peace talks between Israel and Mahmoud Abbas, President of the Palestinian Authority. According to the Israeli Coordinator of Government Activities in the Territories Major Gen. Eitan Dangot, Israel seeks to work with Salam Fayyad, to help revive the Palestinian economy, and hopes to ease restrictions on the Gaza Strip further, "while somehow preventing the Islamic militants who rule it from getting credit for any progress". According to Dangot, Hamas must not be seen as ruling successfully or be allowed to "get credit for a policy that would improve the lives of people". The campaign consists of attacks against Israelis in which, according to a Hamas declaration in early September, "all options are open." The participating groups also include Palestinian Islamic Jihad, the Popular Resistance Committees and an unnamed splinter group of Fatah.

As part of the campaign, on August 31, 2010, 4 Israeli settlers, including a pregnant woman, were killed by Hamas militants while driving on Route 60 near the settlement Kiryat Arba, in the West bank. According to witnesses, militants opened fire on the moving vehicle, but then "approached the car" and shot the occupants in their seats at "close range". The attack was described by Israeli sources as one of the "worst" terrorist acts in years. A senior Hamas official said that Israeli settlers in the West Bank are legitimate targets since "they are an army in every sense of the word."

Themes of martyrdom

According to a translation by Palestinian Media Watch, in 2008, Fathi Hamad, a member of the Palestinian Legislative Council, stated on Al-Aqsa TV, "For the Palestinian people death became an industry, at which women excel and so do all people on this land: the elderly excel, the Jihad fighters excel, and the children excel. Accordingly (Palestinians) created a human shield of women, children, the elderly and the Jihad fighters against the Zionist bombing machine, as if they were saying to the Zionist enemy: 'We desire death as you desire life.'"

In 2010, Hamas speaker Ahmad Bahr praised the virtues of martyrdom and Jihad, and said that 2.5 million black-eyed virgins were waiting in the Garden of Eden, which could be entered only by prophets, by the righteous, and by martyrs. He continued by saying that nobody on Earth "will be able to confront the resistance, or to confront the mujahideen, those who worship Allah and seek martyrdom".

Guerrilla warfare

Hamas has made great use of guerrilla tactics in the Gaza Strip and to a lesser degree the West Bank. It has successfully adapted these techniques over the years since its inception. According to a 2006 report by rival Fatah party, Hamas had smuggled between several hundred and 1,300 tons of advanced rockets, along with other weaponry, into Gaza.

Hamas has used IEDs and anti-tank rockets against the IDF in Gaza. The latter include standard RPG-7 warheads and home-made rockets such as the Al-Bana, Al-Batar and Al-Yasin. The IDF has a difficult, if not impossible time trying to find hidden weapons caches in Palestinian areas — this is due to the high local support base Hamas enjoys.

Extrajudicial executions of rivals

In addition to killing Israeli civilians and armed forces, Hamas has also murdered suspected Palestinian Israel collaborators and Fatah rivals. In the wake of the 2006 Israeli conflict with Gaza, Hamas was accused of systematically rounding up, torturing and summarily executing Fatah supporters suspected of supplying information to Israel. Human Rights Watch estimates several hundred Gazans were "maimed" and tortured in the aftermath of the conflict. Seventy-three Gazan men accused of "collaborating" had their arms and legs broken by "unidentified perpetrators" and 18 Palestinians accused of helping Israel were executed by Hamas security officials in the first days of the conflict. In November 2012, Hamas' Izzedine al-Qassam brigade publicly executed six Gaza residents accused of collaborating with Israel. According to the witnesses, six alleged informers were shot dead one by one in Gaza City, while the corpse of the sixth victim was tied by a cable to the back of a motorcycle and dragged through the streets. In 2013, Human Rights Watch issued a statement condemning Hamas for not investigating and giving a proper trial to the 6 men. Their statement was released the day before Hamas issued a deadline for "collaborators" to turn themselves in, or they will be pursued "without mercy".

Frequent killings of unarmed people have also occurred during Hamas-Fatah clashes. NGOs have cited a number of summary executions as particular examples of violations of the rules of warfare, including the case of Muhammad Swairki, 28, a cook for Palestinian Authority Chairman Mahmoud Abbas's presidential guard, who was thrown to his death, with his hands and legs tied, from a 15-story apartment building in Gaza City. Hamas security forces reportedly shoot and torture Palestinians who opposed Hamas rule in Gaza. In one case, a Palestinian had criticized Hamas in a conversation on the street with some friends. Later that day, more than a dozen armed men with black masks and red kaffiyeh took the man from his home, and brought him to a solitary area where they shot him three times in the lower legs and ankles. The man told Human Rights Watch that he was not politically active.

On August 14, 2009, Hamas fighters stormed the Mosque of cleric Abdel-Latif Moussa. The cleric was protected by at least 100 fighters from Jund Ansar Allah ("Army of the Helpers of God"), an Islamist group with links to Al-Qaeda. The resulting battle left at least 13 people dead, including Moussa and 6 Hamas fighters, and 120 people injured.

2011–2013 Sinai insurgency

Hamas has been accused of providing weapons, training and fighters for Sinai-based insurgent attacks, although Hamas strongly denies the allegations, calling them a smear campaign aiming to harm relations with Egypt. According to the Egyptian Army, since the ouster of Egypt's Muslim-Brotherhood president Mohamed Morsi, over 600 Hamas members have entered the Sinai Peninsula through smuggling tunnels. In addition, several weapons used in Sinai's insurgent attacks are being traced back to Hamas in the Gaza Strip, according to the army. Hamas is also accused of helping Morsi and other high-ranking Egyptian Muslim Brotherhood members break out of the Wadi Natroun prison in Cairo during the 2011 revolution. Hamas called the accusation a "dangerous development".

Activities in the United States

Hamas is believed to have conducted a number of illegal activities on American soil. In 2004, three suspected Hamas operatives, Mohammed Salah, Abdelhaleem Ashqar and Ismail Elbarasse were arrested by American authorities and charged with providing material support to Hamas including racketeering and money laundering.

Debate whether to attack America

Hamas officials have publicly debated whether or not to attack American interests in the Middle East in response to US support of Mahmoud Abbas preceding the 2006 Gaza elections.

13

Haqqani Network

The Haqqani Network is an Islamist insurgent group using asymmetric warfare to fight against US-led NATO forces and the government of Afghanistan. Maulvi Jalaluddin Haqqani and his son Sirajuddin Haqqani lead the group. The group operates on both sides of the Afghanistan-Pakistan border, and U.S. officials believe it is based in Pakistan's Waziristan tribal frontier. The Haqqani network is allied with the Taliban.

JALALUDDIN HAQQANI

Mawlawi Jalaluddin Haqqani (born 1939) is the leader of theHaqqani network, a insurgent group fighting, initially against US-led NATO forces, and the present government of Afghanistan they support. He distinguished himself as an American-sponsored insurgent fighter in the 1980s during the Soviet war in Afghanistan, including Operation Magistral. By 2004, he was directing pro-Taliban militants to launch a holy war in Afghanistan and hit government targets inside Pakistan. Steve Coll, author of *Ghost Wars*, claims that Haqqani introduced suicide bombing in the Afghanistan-Pakistan region.

Early life

Haqqani was born, the son of a wealthy landowner and trader, in 1939 in the village of Karezgay in the Zadran district of Paktia Province, Afghanistan, though the family later moved to Sultankhel. He is an ethnic Pashtun from the Zadran tribe of Khost. He undertook advanced religious studied at the Dar-al-'Ulam Haqqaniya Deobandi seminary in 1964 and was graduated with a doctorate which entitled him to the status of mawlawi in Peshawar in 1970. After King Zahir Shah's exile and President Daoud Khan rise to power in 1973, the political situation in Afghanistan was slowly beginning to change. A number of parties such as the People's Democratic Party of Afghanistan (PDPA) and others were seeking power. Haqqani was one of them, and after being suspected of plotting against the government he went into exile and based himself in and around Miranshah, Pakistan. From there he began to organise a rebellion against the government of Daoud Khan in 1975. After the 1978 Marxist revolution by the PDPA, Haqqani joined the Hezb-i Islami of Mawlawi Mohammad Yunus Khalis. It was during this time that Haqqani began to build a relationship with theInter-Services Intelligence (ISI) spy network.

Mujahideen commander

In the 1980s, Jalaluddin Haqqani was cultivated as a "unilateral" asset of the CIA and received tens of thousands of dollars in cash for his work in fighting the Soviet-led Afghan forces in Afghanistan, according to an account in *The Bin Ladens*, a 2008 book by Steve Coll. He reputedly attracted generous support from prosperous Arab countries compared to other resistance leaders. At that time, Haqqani helped and protected Osama bin Laden, who was building his own militia to fight Soviet-backed Afghanistan.

The influential U.S. Congressman Charlie Wilson, who helped to direct tens of millions of dollars to the Afghan resistance, was so taken by Haqqani that he referred to him as "goodness personified". He was a key US and Pakistani ally in resisting the Soviet-backed Afghanistan. Some news media outlets report that Haqqani even received an invitation to, and perhaps even visited, President Ronald Reagan's White House, although the photographs used to support the allegation of such a meeting have cast doubt that Haqqani ever visited the US. (The pictures originally purporting to show this meeting are, in fact, of Mohammad Yunus Khalis.)

During the rule of Najibullah in 1991, Haqqani captured the city of Khost, which became the first communist city to fall to the Afghan resistance. After the fall of Kabul to the Mujahideen forces in 1992, he was appointed Justice Minister of the Islamic State of Afghanistan, and refrained from taking sides in the fratricidal conflict that broke out between Afghani factions during the 1990s, a neutrality that was to earn him respect.

Relations with the Taliban

Haqqani was not originally a member of the Taliban. In 1995, just prior to the Taliban's occupation of Kabul, he switched his allegiance to them. In 1996-97, he served as a Taliban military commander north of Kabul, and was accused of ethnic cleansing against local Tajik populations. During the Taliban government, he served as the Minister of Borders and Tribal Affairs and governor of Paktia Province.

In October 2001, Haqqani was named the Taliban's military commander. He may have had a role in expediting the escape of Osama Bin Laden. Initially the Americans tried to woo him away from the Taliban. He refused their offers on the grounds that, as a Muslim, he was duty-bound to resist them, as "infidel invaders" just as he had the Soviets in earlier decades. With his base in Khost under repeated American air attack, it is believed that in November or December of that year he crossed the Durand Line border into the Waziristan region of Pakistan. Four Guantanamo detainees — Abib Sarajuddin, Khan Zaman, Gul Zaman and Mohammad Gul — were captured and held because American intelligence officials received a report that one of them had briefly hosted Haqqani shortly after the fall of the Taliban. After the Karzai administration was formed in December 2001, in which many former warlords, mujahideen, and others took part, Interim-President Hamid Karzai decided to offer Haqqani a position in government but was rejected by Haqqani.

In 2008, CIA officials confronted Pakistani officials with evidence of ties between Inter-Services Intelligence and Jalaluddin Haqqani but the ISI denied the allegations. A September 2008 airstrike which targeted Haqqani, resulted in the deaths of between ten and twenty-three people. The US missile strike hit the house of Haqqani in the village Dandi Darpa Khail in North Waziristan and a close-byseminary. The madrasah, however, was closed and Haqqani had previously left the area. Haqqani has been accused by the United States of involvement in the 2008 Indian embassy bombing in Kabul and the February 2009 Kabul raids.

Role in the Taliban insurgency

The success of the mujahideen fighters in the two-year Waziristan Conflict against the Pakistani para-military forces pressured the government to agree to the 2006 Waziristan Accord. In the absence of political will to confront militants with regular Pakistan Army units, a cease-fire agreement (allowing Taliban fighters to operate with impunity in Waziristan as long as Pakistani law is followed and the Taliban do not launch raids into neighboring Afghanistan) was reached. The local Taliban, identified by some as the Islamic Emirate of Waziristan, appear to have been strengthened by the cease-fire agreement, as well as the release of some fighters detained by the Pakistani government at the start of hostilities.

Haqqani along with son Sirajuddin are currently the commanders of the Haqqani network, which is believed to be based in Waziristan, Pakistan. The network is made up of resistance forces waging a jihad against US-led NATO forces and the Islamic republic of Afghanistan. On 16 October 2011, "Operation Knife Edge" was launched by NATO and Afghan forces against the Haqqani network in south-eastern Afghanistan. Afghan Defense Minister, Abdul Rahim Wardak, explained that the operation will "help eliminate the insurgents before they struck in areas along the troubled frontier". Both he and his son, Sirajuddin appear to have been the first Taliban to adopt the Iraqi tactic of using suicide bombers, and their network is accused of engaging in kidnappings, beheadings, the killing of women, and assassinations. George Gittoes, the Australian maker of Pashto-language films at his Yellow House in Jalalabad says Haqqani, who has befriended him, would be ready to support Ashraf Ghani in future Afghan elections.

TOP COMMANDER OF FEARED HAQQANI NETWORK KILLED IN US DRONE STRIKE

A US drone strike in the South Waziristan region of Pakistan on Thursday killed at least seven militants, including Abdullah Haqqani, a top commander for the Haqqani Network, an Islamist insurgent group allied with the Afghan Taliban.

The strike occurred early Thursday about 18 miles (30 km) west of Wana, near the Afghan border, according to AFP.

Both Pakistan officials and a militant source confirmed that four foreign fighters and a top commander believed to be Abdullah Haqqani perished in the attack.

"At least seven militants were killed in the drone strike," including a top Haqqani leader and four foreigners, an intelligence official in Wana told AFP.

Haqqani is known to have coordinated and sent suicide bombers to Afghanistan, the official added.

Another official in the nearby town of Bannu confirmed the number of fatalities and the commander's death.

A militant source told AFP a vehicle full of arms and ammunition was also destroyed by the drone missile.

The Haqqani Network has been a consistent thorn in the side of NATO forces during the Afghan War, sending fighters over the border from their base in the Waziristan tribal areas of Pakistan. The group has also allied with Al-Qaeda, Tehreek-e-Taliban Pakistan, and other militant groups against NATO.

Top members of the Haqqani Network, a subgroup of the Afghan Taliban, have been targeted for death by the United States' unmanned drone regime. The group's former third-in-command Badruddin Haqqani - son of Haqqani Network founder and former mujahideen commander Jalaluddin Haqqani, and brother of the Network's operational leader, Sirajuddin Haqqani - was confirmed by the Talibanone year ago to have perished in a US drone strike in the summer of 2012.

The US has also successfully targeted top members of the Pakistani Taliban, including Hakimullah Mehsud.

Like Al-Qaeda, the Haqqani Network was borne out of the Soviet occupation of Afghanistan in the 1980s. Both groups, among others, can credit US INVESTMENT in militant fighters opposed to Soviet forces as a springboard for their rise ever since. The group has consistently targeted Western forces in the region during the US occupation of Afghanistan following the attacks of Sept. 11, 2001.

The Haqqani Network was responsible for capturing American Army Sgt. Bowe Bergdahl in 2009. Bergdahl was released earlier this year in exchange for 18 US-held Taliban fighters.

The United States has operated clandestine, CIA-run unmanned drone strikes in Pakistan since 2004. The US justifies this violation of Pakistani sovereignty with the Authorization for the Use of Military Force, a law the US Congress signed days after the 9/11 strikes that granted the US President the right to use *"all necessary and appropriate force"* against those behind the attacks on America. In May 2013, nearly 12 years after the law's signing, US President Obama - in promising reforms to the drone program that are difficult to verify based on the government's secrecy - clarified who falls into that category as *"Al-Qaeda, the Taliban and its associated forces."*

Pakistan has denounced US drone activity, claiming it is illegal and counterproductive. Yet many believe the two nations collude in their mutual desire to eradicate Islamist militants from the semi-autonomous tribal areas on the Afghan border.

In June, Islamabad launched its own offensive in North Waziristan, site of many US drone strikes. The Pakistani military claims to have killed more than 1,100 extremist fighters since its assault began, with 100 of their own soldiers dying along the way, according to AFP. The offensive began after peace talks between the government and the Pakistani Taliban fell through.

This still image provided on December 7, 2010 by IntelCenter shows the Taliban associated video production group Manba al-Jihad December 7, 2010 release of someone that appears to be US soldier Bowe Bergdahl (L), who has been held hostage by the Taliban since his disappearance from his unit on June 30, 2009. (AFP/IntelCenter)

Observers cite a pause in US drone strikes during those government-Taliban negotiations as proof of the collaboration between Washington and Islamabad, though Pakistan government and military officials deny these allegations.

US drone strikes have killed as many as 3,858 people, including as many as 957 civilians, according to The Bureau of Investigative Journalism, which conducts the most comprehensive accounting of drone activity in Pakistan, Yemen, and Somalia. US officials avoid acknowledging CIA drone strikes, instead preferring to assure that any strikes are used against top Islamist militants when capture is not available. The New York Times reported in May 2012 that those targeted for strikes - Obama's *"kill list"* - are cleared through the White House during weekly meetings dubbed *"Terror Tuesdays."*

PAKISTAN DECLARES WAR ON HAQQANI NETWORK

Last week, Pakistan's chief military spokesman said something extraordinary — something that could signal a sea change in the country's security policy. Which makes it all the more perplexing that the international media has given scant coverage to what the spokesman had to say.

"There is no discrimination among different Tehreek-i-Taliban Pakistan groups or the Haqqani network," Gen. Asim Bajwa toldjournalists at military headquarters in a briefing about Pakistan's military offensive in North Waziristan. "[The] Army will crush them all."

If this is in fact true, then it is great news.

The Haqqani network, formally designated by the U.S. as a terrorist organization, is a formidable Taliban-linked entity. It regularly launches high-profile attacks in Afghanistan, including assaults on the U.S. embassy. Some believe the Haqqani network introduced suicide bombing to Afghanistan. It also has extensive links to al-Qaeda; a West Point study has concluded that it operates with al-Qaeda "as an interdependent system."

Pakistan's security establishment has long refused to act against the Haqqani network. It has regarded the group — as it does other militant organizations that don't launch attacks in Pakistan — as a strategic asset, in that it helps limit the activities of archenemy India in Afghanistan (Haqqani fighters have frequently targeted Indians in Afghanistan). In 2011, Mike Mullen, the then-Chairman of the Joint Chiefs of Staff — and hence the top U.S. military official — famously stated that the Haqqani network "acts as a veritable arm" of Pakistan's main intelligence agency, the ISI.

By declaring war on the Haqqani network, Pakistan could seriously degrade one of the most destabilizing forces in Afghanistan. It could also be a tremendous boost to India-Pakistan relations (New Delhi has long criticized Pakistan for not cracking down on the various Pakistan-based organizations — from Lashkar-e-Taiba to the Haqqani network — that mount attacks on Indians). And, of course, it could also greatly improve U.S.-Pakistan ties (it bears mentioning that just days before Bajwa's announcement, high-level Pakistani military officials held meetings at the Pentagon).

Still, let's not get too excited.

First, U.S. officials allege that Haqqani network commanders were tipped off by Pakistan about the North Waziristan offensive, and have fled the area. If true, this suggests the military's announcement could be mere spin, and that its policy toward the group hasn't changed. It's easy to talk tough about targeting your strategic asset if you've already ensured it won't be harmed.

Second, Bajwa's language was telling. "Whoever challenges the writ of the state will be taken to task," he said. In fact, the Haqqani network doesn't do this because it doesn't target the Pakistani state. This language is reminiscent of Pakistani threats earlier this year to launch operations in North Waziristan against "anti-state groups" — clearly a reference to the likes of the Pakistani Taliban, not the Haqqani network.

Third, from a strategic perspective, it's a strange time for Pakistan to turn on the Haqqani network. With much uncertainty (and more instability) likely to set in amid the NATO troop drawdown in Afghanistan, wouldn't Pakistan want to tighten its ties with its old reliables? And particularly those long-time assets used to project influence and promote Pakistani interests in Afghanistan?

IDEOLOGY AND GOALS

The Haqqani Network's root values are Islamic and Nationalistic. They seek to re-establish sharia law, a law derived from Islamic moral and religious values, as the nation's pillar of government. They are ideologically aligned with the Taliban, who has worked to eradicate Western influence and restructure the government into a strictly Sharia-following state. This was exemplified in the government that formed after Soviet Troops were driven from Afghanistan. Both groups have the common goal of disrupting the Western military and political efforts in Afghanistan and driving them from the country permanently. Currently the group demands that US and Coalition Forces, made up mostly of NATO Nations, withdraw from Afghanistan and no longer interfere with the politics or educational systems of Islamic nations.

History

Originating in Afghanistan during the mid-1970s, it was nurtured by the U.S. Central Intelligence Agency (CIA) and Pakistan's Inter-Services Intelligence (ISI) during the 1980s Soviet war in Afghanistan.

Haqqani family

The Haqqani family hails from southeastern Afghanistan and belongs to the Mezi Clan of the Zadran Pashtun tribe. Jalalludin Haqqani rose to prominence as a senior military leader during the Soviet occupation of Afghanistan. Like Gulbuddin Hekmatyar, Haqqani was more successful than other resistance leaders at forging relationships with outsiders prepared to sponsor resistance to the Soviets, including the CIA, Pakistan's Inter-Services Intelligence (ISI), and wealthy Arab private donors from the Persian Gulf.

Al-Qaeda affiliation

Jalaluddin Haqqani commanded the Mujahideen Army from 1980-1992, he is credited with recruiting foreign fighters. Two notable jihadist are two well known Arabs, Abdullah Azzam and Osama bin Laden, both began their careers as volunteers for the Haqqani's and trained to fight the Soviets. "Al-Qa'ida and the Haqqani network, in other words, evolved together, and they have remained intertwined throughout their history. They remain so to this day. The Haqqani Network's relationship with Al-Qaeda dates back to the founding of AQ. The significant difference between the two organizations is that Al-Qaeda's goals are global and use global means; whereas Haqqani is solely interested in Afghanistan and the Pashtun Tribal regions. To Jalaluddin Haqqani he is more interested in the influence of Islamic Law over Afghanistan than the global Jihad. Nonetheless the Haqqani Network has always been fully aware of Al-Qaeda's intentions and goals.

Al-Qaeda and Haqqani evolved together

These two groups are intertwined in tactics, strategy, and Islamic extremism; J. Haqqani realized the importance of Azzam's "foundational Islamic legal decisions declaring the Afghan jihad a universally and individually binding duty borne by all Muslims worldwide." Though many Muslim leaders asked for aid from oil wealthy Arab nations in 1978 when Afghan Communists with the backing of the Soviet Union conquered Kabul. J. Haqqani was the only Afghan Islamic Resistance leader to also request foreign Muslim fighters, and was the only group to welcome non-Afghan's into its ranks. Thus "linking it to the broader Jihad struggles and giving birth to the following decade to what would come to be known as global jihadism." Its the Haqqani Network's use of the Saudi Arabian financiers and other Arab investors in his mission that clearly highlights the groups understand of Global Jihad. A major difference between the Haqqani Network and Al-Qaeda is the spheres of influence they both seek to control. Al-Qaeda's is global, Haqqani's is regional.

Taliban affiliation

Foreign jihadists recognized the network as a distinct entity as early as 1994, but Haqqani was not affiliated with the Taliban until they captured Kabul and assumed de facto control of Afghanistan in 1996. After the Taliban came to power, Haqqani accepted a cabinet-level appointment as Minister of Tribal Affairs. Following the U.S.-led invasion of Afghanistan in 2001 and the subsequent overthrow of the Taliban government, the Haqqanis fled to the Pakistani bordering tribal regions and regrouped to fight against coalition forces across the border. As Jalaluddin has grown older his son Sirajuddin has taken over the responsibility of military operations. Journalist Syed Saleem Shahzad reported that President Hamid Karzai had invited the elder Haqqani to serve as Prime Minister in an attempt to bring "moderate" Taliban into the government. However, the offer was refused by Jalaluddin.

Aiding Al-Qaeda and Bin Laden's escape into Pakistan

Many sources believe Jalaluddin Haqqani and his forces assisted with the escape of Al-Qaeda into safe-havens in Pakistan. Considering how closely the two groups are inter-twined it is not a stretch. It is well documented that the Haqqani Network did assist with the establishment of safe-havens. Analyst Peter Bergen argues this point in his book "The Battle for Tora Bora" Judging by the possibilities and the amount of US Military assets focused on such a small region, the theory that the Haqqani Network most certainly aided in the escape seems reasonable. Regardless of exactly what occurred in those mountains, the Haqqanis played a role. And their actions of providing safe-havens for Al-Qaeda and Osama Bin Laden shows the strength of bond and some role in or knowledge of Al-Qaeda and Bin Laden's escape.

United States

According to US military commanders, it is "the most resilient enemy network" and one of the biggest threats to the U.S.-led NATO forces and the Afghan government in the current war in Afghanistan. It is also the most lethal network in Afghanistan. Presently, the United States is offering a reward for information leading to the capture of their leader, Sirajuddin Haqqani, in the amount of $5,000,000.00.

Obama administration

In September 2012, the Obama administration labeled the network as a foreign terrorist organization. After this announcement, Taliban issued a statement arguing that there is "no separate entity or network in Afghanistan by the name of Haqqani" and that Jalaluddin Haqqani is a member of the Quetta Shura, Taliban's top leadership council.

Leadership

- Jalaluddin Haqqani-Following his time as a commander in the Mujahideen Army (1980–1992), the Network was founded under Haqqani during the insurgency against Soviet forces in Afghanistan during the 1980s. Haqqani himself was trained in Pakistan during the 1970s, in order to fight Prime Minister Mohammad Daud Kahn, an Afghan policeman who had overthrown the previous Prime Minister. During the Soviet invasion, the Pakistani government's Inter-Services Intelligence Agency became close with Haqqani and his organization, allowing them to become a main benefactor of American weapons, intelligence, and training. In the 1990s, Haqqani agreed to join the Taliban, arising to the position of Interior Minister. The United States attempted to convince Haqqani to sever ties with the Taliban, which he refused to do. Since Hamid Karzai's leadership began in Afghanistan, he has approached Haqqani and offered him the position as Minister of Tribal Affairs in his cabinet, which Haqqani has also refused. Since the emergence of the Haqqani Network, Haqqani and his family have thrived off of the contacts made by Haqqani during the Cold War.

- Sirajuddin Haqqani - one of the sons of Jalaluddin Haqqani.
- Badruddin Haqqani – younger brother of Sirajuddin. (He was reported dead on 25 August 2012. Some Taliban commanders claimed the reports of his death were true while others claimed the reports were inaccurate. However, on 29 August 2012, Pakistani officials confirmed his death in a US drone strike on 24 August 2012. The next day, this claim was backed by US officials as well. The Taliban officially confirmed Badruddin's death a year later)
- Sangeen Zadran (killed 6 September 2013)– According the US State Department, he was a senior lieutenant to Sirajuddin and the shadow governor for Paktika province in Afghanistan. He was also one of the captors of U.S. soldier Bowe Bergdahl.
- Nasiruddin Haqqani – He was Siraj's brother and a key financier and emissary of the network. As the son of Jalaluddin's Arab wife, he spoke fluent Arabic and traveled to Saudi Arabia and the United Arab Emirates for fundraising. He was killed by unknown assailants in Islamabad, Pakistan, on 11-November-2013.
- Maulvi Ahmad Jan (killed November 21, 2013) The network's spiritual leader who was also responsible for

organizing some of the network's most deadly attacks in Afghanistan. He was subjected to UN sanctions in March 2010 and had also served the Taliban government of Mullah Omar as federal minister for water and power, before being appointed the Governor of the Zabul Province in 2000. At the time of his death, Jan was thought be Sirajuddin Haqqani's chief deputy.

- Abdul Aziz Abbasin – According to the U.S. Treasury, he is "a key commander in the Haqqani Network" and serves as the "Taliban shadow governor of Orgun District, Paktika Province, Afghanistan."
- Haji Mali Khan – According to NATO, he is "the senior Haqqani commander in Afghanistan" and is uncle to Sirajuddin and Badaruddin. ISAF also reported that he acted as an emissary between Baitullah Mehsud and the Haqqanis. He was captured by ISAF forces on 27 September 2011.

Following Wikileaks' July 2010 publication of 75,000 classified documents the public learned that Sirajuddin Haqqani was in the tier one of the International Security Assistance Force's Joint Prioritized Effects List – its "kill or capture" list.

Activities

Anand Gopal of the *Christian Science Monitor*, citing unnamed US and Afghan sources, reported in June 2009 that the leadership is based in Miranshah, North Waziristan in the Federally Administered Tribal Areas of Pakistan along the Afghan border.

It operates from at least three compounds: a Miranshah bazaar camp containing a madrassa and computer facilities, a compound in the nearby suburb of Sarai Darpa Khel and another compound in Danday Darpa Khel, where some of Jalaluddin's family stay.

The network is active in Afghanistan's southeastern areas of Paktia Province, Paktika Province, Khost Province, Wardak Province, Logar Province, and Ghazni Province.

In September 2011, Sirajuddin Haqqani told Reuters that the group feels "more secure in Afghanistan besides the Afghan people."

Funding

Some of Sirajuddin's brothers travel to the Persian Gulf region to raise funds from wealthy donors. *The New York Times* reported in September 2011 that the Haqqanis have set up a "ministate" in Miranshah with courts, tax offices and madrassas, and that the network runs a series of front companies selling automobiles and real estate. They also receive funds from extortion, kidnappings and smuggling operations throughout eastern Afghanistan. In an interview a former Haqqani commander called the extortion "the most important source of funding for the Haqqanis." According to a tribal elder in Paktia, "Haqqani's people ask for money from contractors working on road construction. They are asking money or goods from shopkeepers… District elders and contractors are paying money to Afghan workers, but sometimes half of the money will go to Haqqani's people."

Military strength

Haqqani is reported to run his own training camps, to recruit his own foreign fighters, and to seek out financial and logistic support on his own, from his old contacts. Estimates of the Haqqanis's numbers vary. A 2009 *New York Times* article indicates that they are thought to have about 4,000 to 12,000 Taliban under their command while a 2011 report from the Combating Terrorism Center places its strength roughly at 10,000-15,000. During a September 2011 interview, Sirajuddin Haqqani said the figure of 10,000 fighters, as quoted in some media reports, "is actually less than the actual number." Throughout its history the network's operations have been conducted by small, semi-autonomous units organized according to tribal and sub-tribal affiliations often at the direction of and with the logistical support of Haqqani commanders.

The network is comprised broadly of four groups: those who have been with Jalalludin since the Soviet-era jihad, those from Loya Paktiya who have joined since 2001, those from North Waziristan who have joined in more recent years, and foreign militants of primarily Arab, Chechen and Uzbek origins. Leadership roles are mostly filled with personnel from the first group while the relative neo-phytes from Loya Paktia and non-Pushtuns are not part of this inner circle. The Haqqani network pioneered the use of suicide attacks in Afghanistan and tend to use mostly foreign bombers whereas the Taliban tend to rely on locals in attacks.

The network, according to the *National Journal*, supplies much of the potassium chlorate used in bombs employed by the Taliban in Afghanistan. Also, the network's bombs use more sophisticated remote triggering devices than the pressure-plated activators used elsewhere in Afghanistan. Sirajuddin Haqqani told MSNBC in April 2009 that his fighters had, "acquired the modern technology that we were lacking, and we have mastered new and innovative methods of making bombs and explosives."

In late 2011, a 144-page book attributed to Sirajuddin Haqqani began circulating in Afghanistan and Pakistan. Described by *Newsweek* as a "manual for guerrillas and terrorists," the Pashto-language book details instructions on setting up a jihadi cell, receiving financing, recruiting and training. The manual advises recruits that parental permission is not necessary for jihad, that all debts should be paid before joining, and that suicide bombings and beheadings are allowed by Islam.

Attacks and alleged attacks:

- *14 January 2008:* The 2008 Kabul Serena Hotel attack is thought to have been carried out by the network.
- *March 2008:* Kidnapping of British journalist Sean Langan was blamed on the network.
- *27 April 2008:* Assassination attempts on Hamid Karzai.
- *7 July 2008:* US intelligence blamed the network for 2008 Indian embassy bombing in Kabul.
- *10 November 2008:* The Kidnapping of David Rohde was blamed on Sirajuddin Haqqani.
- *30 December 2009:* Camp Chapman attack is thought to have been carried out by the network.
- *18 May 2010:* May 2010 Kabul bombing was allegedly carried out by the network.
- *19 February 2011:* Kabul Bank in Jalalabad, Afghanistan.
- *28 June 2011:* According to ISAF, elements of the Haqqani network provided "material support" in the 2011 attack

on the Hotel Inter-Continental in Kabul. The Taliban claimed responsibility.

- *10 September 2011:* A massive truck bomb exploded outside Combat Outpost Sayed Abad in Wardak province, Afghanistan, killing five Afghans, including four civilians, and wounding 77 U.S. soldiers, 14 Afghan civilians, and three policemen. The Pentagon blamed the network for the attack.
- *12 September 2011:* US Ambassador Ryan Crocker blamed the Haqqani network for an attack on the US Embassy and nearby NATO bases in Kabul. The attack lasted 19 hours and resulted in the deaths of four police officers and four civilians. 17 civilians and six NATO soldiers were injured. Three coalition soldiers were killed. Eleven insurgent attackers were killed.
- *October 2011:* Afghanistan's National Directorate of Security said that six people arrested in an alleged plot to assassinate President Karzai had ties to the Haqqani network.
- *15 April 2012:* Haqqani Network fighters initiate the summer fighting season, conducting a complex attack across Kabul, Logar and Paktia provinces. Several western embassies in Kabul were attacked in the Say Wallah district.
- *1 June 2012:* A massive suicide truck bomb breaches the southern perimeter wall of US Forward Operating Base Salerno in Khost province. A dozen Haqqani fighters wearing suicide vests entered the breach, but were isolated and killed by US Forces.

Links with Pakistan

Abdul Rashid Waziri, a specialist at Kabul's Center for Regional Studies of Afghanistan, explains that links between the Haqqani network and Pakistan can be traced back to the mid-1970s, before the 1978 Marxist revolution in Kabul. During the rule of President Daoud Khan in Afghanistan (1973–78), Jalaluddin Haqqani went into exile and based himself in and around Miranshah, Pakistan. From there he began to form a rebellion against the government of Daoud Khan in 1975. The network allegedly maintains ties with the Inter-Services Intelligence (ISI), and Pakistan's army has been reportedly reluctant to move against them. The ISI spy network had links with the Haqqanis since at least the 1979 Soviet invasion of Afghanistan. They provided CIA funds and assistance to the group during the Afghan resistance. While Pakistan has declared the Tehrik-i-Taliban Pakistan (TTP) as an enemy which engages in attacks against civilians and the state, the Haqqani group refrains from attacking the Pakistani state and thus, has traditionally been considered to be in the Pakistani sphere of what some analysts call the "good" Taliban. According to a July 2011 report published by West Point's Combating Terrorism Center, the network acts as a key facilitator of negotiations between the Pakistani government and the TTP and as the "primary conduit" of many Pakistani Taliban fighters into Afghanistan. *The News International* also reported in October 2011 that the Haqqanis were urging the TTP to not fight Pakistani forces.

14

Liberation Tigers of Tamil Eelam

The Liberation Tigers of Tamil Eelam was a separatist militant organisation that was based in northern Sri Lanka. Founded in May 1976 by Velupillai Prabhakaran, it waged a secessionist nationalist campaign to create an independent state in the north and east of Sri Lanka for Tamil people. This campaign evolved into the Sri Lankan Civil War, which ran from 1983 until 2009, when the LTTE was defeated by the Sri Lankan Military.

At the height of its power, the LTTE possessed a well-developed militia and carried out many high-profile attacks, including the assassinations of several high-ranking Sri Lankan and Indian politicians. The LTTE was the only militant group to assassinate two world leaders: former Indian Prime Minister Rajiv Gandhi in 1991 and Sri Lankan President Ranasinghe Premadasa in 1993 The LTTE used suicide belts and women in suicide attacks. It was the first militant group to acquire air power and used light aircraft in some of its attacks. It is currently proscribed as a terrorist organisation by 32 countries, including India, but has support amongst Tamils in Tamil Nadu in India. University Teachers for Human Rights (Jaffna) alleges that the LTTE has killed at least 8,000 fellow Tamils they accused of being traitors. Velupillai Prabhakaran headed the organization from its inception until his death in 2009.

Historical inter ethnic imbalances between majority Sinhalese and minority Tamil populations created the background for the origin of the LTTE. Post independent Sri Lankan governments attempted to rectify the disproportionate favoring and empowerment of Tamil minority by the colonial rulers led to exclusivist ethnic policies including the 3Sinhala only act3 and gave rise to separatist ideologies among many Tamil leaders. By the 1970s, initial non- violent political struggle for an independent mono ethnic Tamil state, gave away to a violent secessionist campaign led by the LTTE. Over the course of the conflict, the Tamil Tigers frequently exchanged control of territory in north-east Sri Lanka with the Sri Lankan military, with the two sides engaging in fierce military confrontations. It was involved in four unsuccessful rounds of peace talks with the Sri Lankan government over the course of the conflict. At its peak in 2000, the LTTE was in control of 76 per cent of the landmass in the Northern and Eastern provinces of Sri Lanka.

At the start of the final round of peace talks in 2002, the Tamil Tigers, with control of 15,000 km area, ran a virtual mini-state. After the breakdown of the peace process in 2006, the Sri Lankan military launched a major offensive against the Tigers, defeating the LTTE militarily and bringing the entire country under its control. Victory over the Tigers was declared by Sri Lankan President Mahinda Rajapaksa on 16 May 2009, and the LTTE admitted defeat on 17 May 2009. Prabhakaran was killed by government forces on 19 May 2009 and Selvarasa Pathmanathan succeeded Prabhakaran as leader of the LTTE, who was later arrested in Malaysia and handed over to the Sri Lankan government in August 2009.

VELUPILLAI PRABHAKARAN

Thiruvenkadam Velupillai Prabhakaran (November 26, 1954 – May 18, 2009) was the founder and leader of the Liberation Tigers of Tamil Eelam (the LTTE or the Tamil Tigers), a militant organization that sought to create an independent Tamil state in the north and east of Sri Lanka. For over 25 years, the LTTE waged a violent secessionist campaign in Sri Lanka that led to it being designated a terroristorganization by 32 countries. Founded in 1976, the LTTE rocketed to prominence in 1983 afterthey ambushed a patrol of the Sri Lanka Army outside Jaffna, resulting in the deaths of 13 soldiers. This ambush, along with the subsequent rioting which resulted in the deaths of hundreds of Tamil civilians, is generally considered the start of the Sri Lankan Civil War. After years of fighting, including the unsuccessful intervention of the Indian Army, the conflict was halted after international mediation in 2001. By then, the Tamil Tigers controlled large swaths of land in the north and east of the country, running virtually a mini-state with Prabhakran serving as its unquestioned leader. Peace talks eventually broke down, and the Sri Lanka Armylaunched a military campaign to defeat the Tamil Tigers in 2006. Prabhakaran was killed in fighting with the Army on May 18, 2009. It was alleged that his 12-year old son was executed a short time later. His death brought an immediate end to the Civil War.

Early life

Velupillai Prabhakaran was born in the northern coastal town of Valvettithurai on November 26, 1954, as the youngest of four children to Thiruvenkadam Velupillai and his wife Vallipuram Parvathy. Thiruvenkadam Velupillai was the District land Officer in the Ceylon Government Angered by what he saw as discrimination against Tamil people by successive Sri Lankan governments, he joined the student group TIP during the standardization debates. In 1972 Prabhakaran founded the Tamil New Tigers (TNT) which was a successor to many earlier organizations that protested against the post-colonial political direction of the country, in which the minority Sri Lankan Tamils were pitted against the majority Sinhalese people.

In 1975, after becoming heavily involved in the Tamil movement, he carried out the first major political murder by a Tamil group, assassinating the mayor of Jaffna, Alfred Duraiappah, by shooting him at point-blank range when he was about to enter the Hindu temple at Ponnaalai. The assassination was in response to the 1974 Tamil conference incident, for which the Tamil radicals had blamed Duraiappah, because he backed the then ruling Sri Lanka Freedom Party.

Tamil Tigers

Founding of the LTTE

In the early 1970s, United Front government of Sirimavo

Bandaranaike introduced the Policy of standardization to rectify the low numbers of Sinhalese being accepted into university in Sri Lanka. A student named Satiyaseelan formed Tamil Manavar Peravai (Tamil Students League) to counter this biased move. This group comprised Tamil youth who advocated the rights of students to have fair enrollment. Inspired by the failed 1971 insurrection of Janatha Vimukthi Peramuna, it was the first Tamil insurgent group of its kind. It consisted of around 40 Tamil youth, including Ponnuthurai Sivakumaran (later, the leader of the Sivakumaran group), K. Pathmanaba (one of the founder members of EROS) and Velupillai Prabhakaran, an 19 years old youth from single caste oriented Valvettithurai (VVT). In 1972, Prabhakaran teamed up with Chetti Thanabalasingam, Jaffna to form the Tamil New Tigers (TNT), with Thanabalasingham as its leader. After he was killed, Prabhakaran took over. At the same time, Nadarajah Thangathurai and Selvarajah Yogachandran (better known by his nom de guerre Kuttimani) were also involved in discussions about an insurgency. They would later (in 1979) create a separate organization named Tamil Eelam Liberation Organization (TELO) to campaign for the establishment of an independent Tamil Eelam. These groups, along with another prominent figure of the armed struggle, Ponnuthurai Sivakumaran, were involved in several hit-and-run operations against pro-government Tamil politicians, Sri Lanka Police and civil administration during the early 1970s. These attacks included throwing bombs at the residence and the car of SLFP Jaffna Mayor, Alfred Duraiyappah, placing a bomb at a carnival held in the stadium of Jaffna city (now "Duraiyappah stadium") and Neervely bank robbery. 1974 Tamil conference incident also sparked the anger of these militant groups. Both Sivakumaran and Prabhakaran attempted to assassinate Duraiyappah in revenge for the incident. Sivakumaran committed suicide on 5 June 1974 to evade capture by Police. But on 27 July 1975, Prabhakaran was able to assassinate Duraiyappah, who was branded as a "traitor" by TULF and the insurgents alike. Prabhakaran himself shot and killed the Mayor when he was visiting the Krishnan temple at Ponnalai

On May 5, 1976, the TNT was renamed the Liberation Tigers of Tamil Eelam (LTTE), commonly known as the *Tamil Tigers*.

Religion was not a major factor in his philosophy or ideology, indeed the ideology of the Tamil Tigers emerged from Marxist-Leninistthought, and was explicitly secular. Its leadership professed opposition to religion. Their focus was on a single-minded approach toward the attainment of an independent Tamil Eelam.

Prabhakaran's first and only major press conference was held in Killinochchi on April 10, 2002. It was reported that more than 200 journalists from the local and foreign media attended this event and they had to go through a 10-hour security screening before the event in which Anton Balasingham introduced the LTTE leader as the *"President and Prime minister of Tamil Eelam."*

A number of questions were asked about LTTE's commitment towards the erstwhile peace process and Prabhakaran and Dr. Anton Balasingham jointly answered the questions.

Repeated questions of his involvement in the Rajiv Gandhi assassination were only answered in a sober note by both Balasingham and Prabhakaran. They called it a "tragic incident" ("Thunbiyal Chambavam", as quoted in Tamil) they requested the press "not to dig into an incident that happened 10 years ago."

During the interview he stated that the right condition has not risen to give up the demand of Tamil Eelam. He further mentioned that "There are three fundamentals. That is Tamil homeland, Tamil nationality and Tamil right to self-determination. These are the fundamental demands of the Tamil people. Once these demands are accepted or a political solution is put forward by recognising these three fundamentals and our people are satisfied with the solutions we will consider giving up the demand for Eelam." He further added that Tamil Eelam was not only the demand of the LTTE but also the demand of the Tamil people.

Prabhakaran also answered a number of questions in which he reaffirmed their commitment towards peace process, quoted "We are sincerely committed to the peace process. It is because we are sincerely committed to peace that we continued a four month cessation of hostilities" was also firm in de-proscription of the LTTE by Sri Lanka and India, "We want the government of India to lift the ban on the LTTE. We will raise the issue at the appropriate time."

Prabhakaran also insisted firmly that only de-proscription would bring forth an amenable solution to the ongoing peace process mediated byNorway: "We have informed the government, we have told the Norwegians that de-proscription is a necessary condition for the commencements of talks."

Philosophy and ideology

Prabhakaran was fascinated by Napoleon and Alexander the Great. He was also highly influenced by prominent Indian nationalists Subhas Chandra Bose and Bhagat Singh who fought the British Empire. Prabhakaran never developed a systematic philosophy, but did declare that his goal was 'Revolutionary socialism and the creation of an egalitarian society'. He joined the Tamil nationalist movement in his youth and quickly established himself as a strong-willed militant leader by founding the LTTE. His rare interviews, his annual Tamil Eelam Heroes Day speeches and the policies and actions of the LTTE can be taken as indicators of Prabhakaran's philosophy and ideology. The following are important areas when considering the philosophy and ideology of Prabhakaran.

Sri Lankan Tamil nationalism

Prabhakaran's source of inspiration and direction was Sri Lankan Tamil nationalism. His stated and ultimate ideal was to get Tamil Eelamrecognised as a nation as per the U.N. Charter that guarantees the right of a people to political independence. The LTTE also proposed the formation of an Interim Self Governing Authority during Peace Negotiations in 2003. Former Tamil guerrilla and politician Dharmalingam Sithadthan has remarked that Prabhakaran's "dedication to the cause of the Tamil Eelam was unquestionable, he was the only man in Sri Lanka who could decide if there should be war or peace." Prabhakaran was also called "Karikalan" for his bravery and his administration (in reference to Karikala Chola, a famous Chola king who ruled in Sangam Age.)

Militarism of the LTTE

Prabhakaran explicitly stated that an armed struggle is the only way to resist asymmetric warfare, in which one side, that of the Sri Lankan government, is armed and the other comparatively unarmed. He argued that he chose military means only after observing that non–violentmeans have been ineffectual and obsolete, especially after the Thileepan incident. Thileepan, a colonel rank officer adopted Gandhianmeans to protest against the IPKF killings by staging a fast unto death from September 15, 1987, and by abstaining from food or water till 26 September, when he died in front of thousands of Tamils who had come there to fast along with him. This further strengthened Prabhakaran's resolve that peaceful protests would either be ignored or crushed but never heard.

Tactically, Prabhakaran perfected the recruitment and use of suicide bomber units. His fighters usually took no prisoners and were notorious for assaults that often left every single enemy soldier dead. Interpol described him as someone who was "very alert, known to use disguise and capable of handling sophisticated weaponry and explosives."

Death

When the Sri Lankan military rapidly advanced into the last LTTE held territory in the final days of 2008–2009 SLA Northern offensive, Prabhakaran and his top leadership retreated into Vellamullivaikkal, Mullaitivu. Fierce fighting occurred between LTTE and Sri Lanka Armyduring these last few days. At around 3:00 a.m. on 18 May 2009, Prabhakaran's son Charles Anthony tried to break the defenses of the Army, but was unsuccessful. He died along with around 100 other LTTE cadres. Troops found 12 million rupees in his possession. By the noon of that day, reports emerged that Prabhakaran was killed by a rocket attack while trying to flee the conflict zone in a captured ambulance and his body was badly burned. But this rumor was proven false in a short while. Skirmishes occurred also in the evening of 18 May around eastern bank of Nandikadal lagoon. A team of LTTE cadres consisting of 30 most loyal bodyguards of Prabhakaran and Prabhakaran himself tried to sneak through the mangrove islands of Nandikadal to its west bank. It has been alleged that one bodyguard had a can of gasoline with him to burn the Tiger leader's body if ever he was killed or committed suicide. This was to prevent the enemy seizing his body. Clearing and mopping-up operations were carried out by troops under Colonel G. V. Ravipriya from 3:30 pm to 6:30 pm that evening. But they did not encounter this last group of LTTE fighters that day. At 7:30 am next morning, mopping-up operations started again. This time, they were confronted by the fighters, led by Prabhakaran himself. Fighting went on till 9.30 am May 19, 2009. The firing stopped as all LTTE fighters died in the battle. Troops started collecting bodies again. This time, Sergeant Muthu Banda, attached to Sri Lanka Army Task Force VIII, reported to its commander, Colonel G. V. Ravipriya, that a body similar to Velupillai Prabhakaran had been found. After the body, which was floating among the mangroves, was brought ashore, Colonel Ravipriya positively identified it as that of the leader of the LTTE. A dog tag marked *001*, two pistols, a T56 rifle with telescopic sight, a satellite phone, and a canister filled with diabetic medicine were found along with the body.

At 12:15 pm army commander Sarath Fonseka officially announced Prabhakaran's death on TV. At around 1:00 pm his body was shown inSwarnavahini for the first time. Prabakaran's identity was confirmed by Karuna Amman, his former confidant, and through DNA testing against genetic material from his son, who had been killed earlier by the Sri Lankan military. Circumstantial evidence suggested that his death was caused by massive head trauma, perhaps due to a shot at close range. There are also allegations that he was executed, a claim vehemently denied by Sri Lankan authorities. A week later, the new Tamil Tiger leader, Selvarasa Pathmanathan, admitted that Prabhakaran was dead.

POLITICAL ACTIVITIES

The LTTE is one of several violent offshoots of the Tamil United Liberation Front (TULF), formerly the Tamil United Front (TUF). TUF was formed in the early 1970s from groups such as the Tamil Congress and the Federal Party. When it officially called for the formation of an independent Tamil state in 1976, the group's name was changed to the Tamil United Liberation Front. Several more radical militant Tamil groups, including Prabhakaran's LTTE, emerged from the TULF.

The LTTE formed its political front, The People's Front of Liberation Tigers, in 1989, during a time in which the LTTE was in negotiations with the Sri Lankan government. Yogaratnam Yogi was the party's General Secretary. It has, until recently, been a registered political party in Sri Lanka. However they have rarely been active in local politics. Although they were listed on a few local ballots in 2008, the government deregistered the party in 2011.

The LTTE demonstrated its willingness to negotiate with the Sri Lankan government on several occasions; although, the LTTE often used talks and agreements to enhance its own position, re-arm, and get rid of its competitors. The first set of talks with the government took place in 1985 in Bhutan, and was followed by an accord between India and Sri Lanka in 1987. The Indian government agreed to intervene in the Sri Lankan conflict and provide a peacekeeping force to ensure that the LTTE disarmed. The Indians were unable to subdue the LTTE and withdrew in 1990, giving the LTTE time to re-group and eliminate dissenters among the Tamil population. Peace talks continued throughout the 1990s and were largely unsuccessful. During this period, the LTTE adopted "hit-and-run" tactics wherein peace talks were alternated with bouts of violence and clashes between the LTTE and government forces. The most significant negotiation occurred in February 2002 when Norway, serving as a mediator, helped secure a ceasefire between the LTTE and the Sri Lankan government. However, after six rounds of additional talks in Thailand and Japan, the LTTE announced the suspension of further talks in 2003. Some experts believe this was a tactical move to garner further concessions from the Sri Lankan government. The LTTE has since cited the Sri Lankan government's exclusion of the group from an international aid conference, continued military occupation of Tamil-settled areas, and marginalization in government economic policies as the primary reasons for the breakdown of the ceasefire. After the breakdown of another round of peace talks in 2006, the Sri Lankan government launched an all-out offensive against the LTTE. On May 17, 2009, an LTTE representative conceded the defeat of the LTTE by government forces. Prabhakaran was killed by government forces on May 18, 2009, bringing an immediate end to the conflict and the LTTE.

Major Attacks

1. May 14, 1985: Gunfire attack on Sri Lankan Buddhist holy site in Anaradhapura. (146 killed (BBC) (GTD: 86 killed, 100 wounded)).
2. May 3, 1986: Bomb planted on Sri Lankan Air flight carrying British, French, and Japanese tourists, at the Colombo airport set to fly to the Maldives. (14-16 killed, 23-39 wounded).
3. April 21, 1987: Car bomb explodes at a bus station in Colombo, killing civilians. (113-150 killed, 200 wounded).
4. June 2, 1987: Aranthalawa massacre of Buddhist monks on a bus in Eastern Sri Lanka. (33 killed).
5. July 5, 1987: A soldier drove an explosive-filled truck into a Sri Lankan Army camp in Nelliady, northern Jaffna, followed by a ground attack by a group of LTTE soldiers. (40 killed (GTD: 20 dead, 27 wounded)).
6. October 10, 1988: Massacre in Mahakongaskada Village of civilians. (44-45 killed, 17 wounded).
7. June 11, 1990: Massacre of Police Officers in Kalmunai in eastern Sri Lanka. (144 killed (GTD); most other sources claim over 600).
8. August 3, 1990: Kattankudy mosque massacre; LTTE highly suspected but has not yet claimed official responsibility (112-150 killed).
9. May 21, 1991: Assassination of Rajiv Gandhi, Prime Minister of India, and 14-18 others by a female suicide bomber, in Sriperumbudur, Tamil Nadu. The LTTE did not officially claim responsibility. (15-19 killed).
10. October 16, 1992: Motorcycle-based suicide attack in Colombo killed Chief Sri Lankan Navy Commander Vice Admiral Fernando and four other Navy personnel. (5 killed).
11. May 1, 1993: Sri Lankan President Ranasinghe Premadasa is killed by a suicide bomber along with 23 others during a May Day rally in Colombo. (24 killed).
12. October 24, 1994: Female suicide bomber assassinates Gamini Dissanyake, Leader of the Opposition and United

National Party candidate for the Presidential Elections, during a Colombo elections rally, (59 dead).

13. October 20, 1995: Explosion in Orugodawatte crude oil company by a suicide unit of four, killing 23 soldiers and two civilians. Fourteen storage tanks were destroyed, causing $61 million in damage. (25 killed, 32 injured).
14. October 22, 1995: Attack in Thamanagama fishing village and three other Eastern Sri Lankan villages. (50-66 killed).
15. November 24, 1995: Two female suicide bombers attack the Sri Lankan army headquarters in Colombo. (16 killed, 52 wounded).
16. December 23, 1995: Army ambush in Batticaloa district that killed 32 Sri Lankan troops, and a government-reported 60 rebels. (92-93 killed, 34 wounded).
17. January 31, 1996: A suicide bomber detonates an explosives-loaded truck at the Central Bank in Colombo. (91 dead, 1400 injured).
18. July 18, 1996: LTTE took control of a Sri Lankan army camp in the northeastern town of Mullaitivu. (1200 soldiers killed (BBC and Guardian)/150+ troops and 34 rebels killed (Reuters)).
19. July 24, 1996: Explosive attack on a commuter train near Colombo. (60-61 killed, 391-600 wounded).
20. September 30, 1998: Major LTTE offensive on Sri Lankan Army at key city Kilinochchi, former LTTE base, near the Sri Lankan army's major Elephant Pass base, killing over 600-900 (varied estimates) Sri Lankan soldiers. (900 killed (varied estimates)).
21. July 29, 1999: Neelan Thiruchelvam, a moderate Tamil MP member of TULF and involved in the government-backed peace process, was killed in a suicide attack in Colombo. (3 killed, 5 injured).
22. September 18, 1999: Attack on three villages in Sri Lanka's Eastern Province in an apparent retaliation for Sri Lankan army attacks on Tamil civilians early that week. (50 killed).
23. December 18, 1999: Assasination attempt on Sri Lankan President Chandrika Kumaratunga, who was injured in

two bombings while campaigning for a second term during election rallies in Colombo. (15-34 killed).

24. April 23, 2000: Tigers take control of key Sri Lankan Army base in Jaffna, Elephant Pass, which they had been fighting to seek control since the Army takeover of the former LTTE stronghold in the Jaffna peninsula in 1995. (79 soldiers killed, 400+ injured, and 150 LTTE members injured).
25. June 7, 2000: Senior Sri Lankan Industry Minister CV Gooneratne assassinated in Colombo by a suicide bomber. (20-21 killed).
26. July 7, 2004: First suicide bombing in three years. LTTE female soldier in an apparent attempt to assassinate high-profile Hindu Affairs Minister Douglas Devananda, a voracious LTTE critic. (5 killed, 9 injured).
27. October 25, 2005: Foreign Minister Lakshman Kadirgamar, a key player in the peace process and close aide of President Chandrika Kumaratunga, was assassinated at his home in a suicide attack in Colombo. (1 killed).
28. April 9, 2006: Over 100 killed during a 2 week period, the most intensified fighting since the 2002 truce. (100+ killed).
29. June 15, 2006: Evidence suggests that the LTTE was responsible for a bus bombing in Aduradhapura district. (64 killed, 84 wounded).
30. October 16, 2006: Suicide bombing attack on Sri Lankan naval convoy buses in northeast region of Dambulla, one of the deadliest since 2002 peace. (95 killed).
31. May 9, 2009: Attack on civilians in Mullaitivu, Northern Province, Sri Lanka. (9 killed, 19 wounded).

Relationships With Other Groups

Tamil militant groups began to emerge in 1970s, the first of which was the "Tamil Students Movement" that protested the limited admission of Tamil students to universities. By 1972, the original student movement broke up into smaller, militant groups such as the Tamil New Tigers (TNT), the LTTE's predecessor, and the Tamil Eelam Liberation Organization (TELO). By the late 1980s, there were over thirty different Tamil militant groups. The most significant groups were the LTTE, the Eelam People's Revolutionary Liberation Front (EPRLF), TELO, the Eelam Revolutionary Organization of Students (EROS), and the People's Liberation Organization of Tamil Eelam (PLOTE). By 1987, the LTTE was the dominant group. TELO especially was repeatedly attacked by the LTTE during the 1987 war against India, as well as members of PLOTE and EPRLF.

In March 2004, Colonel Vinayagamoorthy Maralitharan, commonly known as "Karuna Amman," broke away from the LTTE and formed an underground organization and political party with a band of his supporters. His organization's military wing is called the Tamil National Front and its political wing is known as the Tamileela Makkal Viduthalai Pulligal (TMVP), allied with the Eelam National Democratic Liberation Front (ENDLF). By April 2004, the LTTE had essentially subdued the breakaway faction; however, Colonel Karuna escaped with a small group of supporters and regrouped in Colombo. In 2006, Colonel Karuna allied with the Sri Lankan government, delivering a huge blow to the LTTE.

The LTTE has developed relationships with various Islamist groups because of its criminal activities in the informal arms market, rather than any form of ideological affinity. By the 1990s, the LTTE had developed a close relationship with the Kurdish Support Group in France and had modeled their diaspora funding efforts after the Kurdish example. The LTTE's acquisition of 11 Greek surface to air missiles was reportedly a result of the LTTE's relationship with the PKK. Furthermore, it is believed that Otharad Cargo, an LTTE-operated cargo company based in Dubai, received military hardware from the Sharjah network, a large Taliban weapons-procurement operation. In Karachi, Pakistan, the LTTE registered a front company that obtained weapons for both the LTTE and Pakistani militant groups. An LTTE shipping fleet was also involved in providing logistical support for the Al Qaeda-affiliated Pakistani group Harakat-al Mujahideen.

The LTTE also established a presence in Eritrea, which is known to be a major shipment point in the informal arms market. It is suspected that the LTTE has interactions with Al Qaeda affiliated groups in the Eritrean Network. A US Senate Foreign Relations Committee report in December 2006 claims that the Eritrean government directly supports the LTTE. The LTTE also maintains relationships with the Moro Islamic Liberation Front (MILF) and Aby Sayyaf in the Philippines in activities related to fund transfers and training operations.

Community Relationships

Support for the LTTE was primarily based around the disenfranchised Tamil population in the north of Sri Lanka, and later the Tamils who escaped to the south. In the territory it controlled, the LTTE established some civil administration, including postal services, courts, police, banks, radio, etc. These structures collect taxes and administer the rule of law.

The LTTE was notorious for actively recruiting women and children from among the Tamil community. It was thought that women constituted 20-30% of the LTTE's fighting cadre and that an estimated 4,000 female members were killed during the 26 years of the Sri Lankan conflict. A female LTTE suicide bomber carried out the assassination of Indian Prime Minister Rajeev Gandhi. The LTTE also actively used children as part of their front-line troops. The LTTE's recruitment of child soldiers led to discontent among the Tamil community. According to UNICEF, the LTTE has recruited over 5,800 child soldiers since 2001. Many of these children were abducted from refugee camps and orphanages in Tamil-controlled areas.

Global network

LTTE had developed a massive international network since the days of N. S. Krishnan, who served as its first international representative. In the late 1970s, TULF parliamentarian and opposition leader A. Amirthalingam provided letters of reference for fundraising, and V. N. Navaratnam, who was an executive committee member of the Inter-Parliamentary Union (IPU), introduced many influential and wealthy Tamils living overseas to Tamil insurgent leaders. Navaratnam also introduced LTTE members to the members of Polisario Front, a national liberation movement in Morocco, at a meeting held in Oslo, Norway. In 1978, during the world tour of Amirthalingam (with London-based

Eelam activist S. K. Vaikundavasan), he formed the World Tamil Coordinating Committee (WTCC), which later turned out to be an LTTE front organization. The global contacts of LTTE grew steadily since then. At the height of its power, LTTE had 42 offices all over the world. The global network of LTTE engages in propaganda, fundraising, arms procurement, and shipping.

There were three types of organisations to do propaganda and fund raising—*i.e.,* Front, Cover, and Sympathetic. Prior to the ethnic riots of 1983, attempts to raise funds for a sustaining military campaign were not realised. It was the mass exodus of Tamil civilians to India and western countries following Black July ethnic riots, which made it possible. As the armed conflict evolved and voluntary donations dwindled, LTTE used force and threats to collect money. LTTE was worth US$200–300 million at its peak. The group's global network owned numerous business ventures in various countries. These include investment in real estate, shipping, grocery stores, gold and jewellery stores, gas stations, restaurants, production of films, mass media organisations (TV, radio, print), industries, etc. It was also in control of numerous charitable organisations including Tamils Rehabilitation Organisation, which was banned and funds were frozen by United States Treasury in 2007 for covertly financing terrorism.

Arms Procurement and shipping activities of LTTE were largely clandestine. Prior to 1983, it procured weapons mainly from Afghanistan via the Indo-Pakistani border. Explosives were purchased from commercial markets in India. From 1983 to 1987, LTTE acquired substantial amount of weapons from RAW and from Lebanon, Cyprus, Singapore, and Malaysia-based arms dealers. LTTE received its first consignment of arms from Singapore in 1984 on board the MV *Cholan,* the first ship owned by the organisation. Funds were received and cargo was cleared at Chennai Port with the assistance of M. G. Ramachandran, the Chief Minister of Tamil Nadu. In November 1994, LTTE was able to purchase whopping 60 tonnes of explosives (50 tonnes of TNT and 10 tonnes of RDX) from Rubezone Chemical plant in Ukraine, providing a forged Bangladeshi Ministry of Defence end-user certificate. Payments for the explosives were made from a Citibank account in Singapore held by Selvarasa Pathmanathan.

Consignment was transported on board MV Sewne. Same explosives were used for the Central Bank bombing in 1996. Myanmar, Thailand, Malaysia, Cambodia and Indonesia remained the most trusted outposts of LTTE, after India alienated it after the Rajiv Gandhi assassination.

Since late 1997, North Korea became the principal country to provide arms, ammunition, and explosives to the LTTE. The deal with North Korean government was carried out by Ponniah Anandaraja *alias* Aiyannah, a member of World Tamil Coordinating Committee of the United States and later, the accountant of LTTE. He worked at the North Korean embassy in Bangkok since late 1997. LTTE had nearly 20 second-hand ships, which were purchased in Japan, and registered in Panama and other Latin American countries. Most of the times, these ships transported general cargo, including paddy, sugar, timber, glass, and fertiliser. But when an arms deal was finalised, they travelled to North Korea, load the cargo and brought it to the equator. Then the ships are based there. Then on board merchant tankers, weapons were transferred to the sea of Alampil, just outside the territorial waters in Sri Lanka's Exclusive Economic Zone. After that, small teams of Sea Tigers brought the cargo ashore. Sri Lanka Navy, during 2005–08 destroyed at least 11 of these cargo ships belonged to LTTE in the international waters.

LTTE's last shipment of weapons came in March 2009, towards the end of the war. Merchant vessel *Princess Iswari* went from Indonesia to North Korea under captain Kamalraj Kandasamy *alias* Vinod, loaded the weapons and it came back to international waters beyond Sri Lanka. But due to the heavy naval blockades set up by Sri Lankan Navy, it could not deliver the arms consignment. Thus it dumped the weapons in the sea. The same ship, after changing its name to MV Ocean Lady, appeared in Vancouver with 76 migrants, in October-2009. In December 2009, Sri Lanka Navy apprehended a merchant vessel belonged to LTTE, "Princess Chrisanta" in Indonesia and brought it back to Sri Lanka.

The United States Senate Committee on Foreign Relations (USSFRC) and Ethiopian based Jimma Times claimed that the Eritrean government had provided direct military assistance, including light aircraft to LTTE, during the 2002–03 period when the LTTE was having negotiations with Sri Lankan government via the Norwegian mediators. It was also alleged that Erik Solheim, the chief Norwegian facilitator, helped LTTE to establish this relationship. None of these claims have since been verified. These allegations and a suspicion from within the Sri Lankan armed forces, that LTTE had considerable connections and assets in Eritrea and that its leader Prabhakaran may try to flee to Eritrea in the final stages of war, prompted the Sri Lankan government to establish diplomatic relations with Eritrea in 2009. None of the allegations nor suspicions have since materialised into verifiable fact.

Links to other designated terrorist organizations

LTTE was believed to have few connections with other terrorist groups, with no military association with al-Qaeda or other Islamic terrorist organisations. But the group maintained interactions with other terrorist organisations through illegal arms markets in Myanmar, Thailand, and Cambodia. It had also smuggled weapons from Pakistan-based Islamists to their counterparts in the Philippines. During the mid-1970s, LTTE rebels were known to have trained from the Popular Front for the Liberation of Palestine (PFLP) in Southern Lebanon.

LTTE also had connections with Maoist Naxalite movement, which is fighting to establish a Marxist Indian state, and Khalistan movement, which is fighting to create a separate Sikh state in India. LTTE's shipping fleet has provided logistics support to Harkat-ul-Mujahideen, a Pakistani group with al-Qaeda affiliations, to transport a consignment of weapons to the Abu Sayyaf Group (ASG) in the Philippines. They also maintain close contact with the Kurdistan Workers' Party (PKK). LTTE had also sent two combat tacticians and explosive experts to the southern Philippines to train members of the Moro Islamic Liberation Front.

The *Times of India,* in 2001, highlighted an alleged nexus between al-Qaeda and the LTTE, and claimed that "[al-Qaeda links with the LTTE] are the first instance of an Islamist group collaborating with an essentially secular outfit". The Maritime Intelligence Group, a U.S.-based research organization, said the Indonesian group Jemaah Islamiya, which has known links to al-Qaeda, had been trained in sea-borne guerrilla tactics by LTTE Sea Tiger veterans.

"Norwegians Against Terrorism" led by Falk Rune Rovik, described how the Tamil community in Norway, at the behest of the LTTE, sold fake and stolen Norwegian passports to al-Qaeda members. The LTTE itself acquired a fake passport for Ramzi Yousef, convicted mastermind of the 1993 attack on the World Trade Center in New York. He further alleged that funds from Government of Norway had been inadvertently diverted to the LTTE.

15

Revolutionary Armed Forces of Colombia

Established in 1964 as the military wing of the Colombian Communist Party, the Revolutionary Armed Forces of Colombia (Fuerzas Armadas Revolucionarios de Colombia) is Latin America's oldest, largest, most capable, and best-equipped insurgency of Marxist origin—although it only nominally fights in support of Marxist goals today. The FARC primarily operates in Colombia, with some activities—including extortion, kidnapping, weapons acquisition, and logistics—occuring in neighboring countries.

FARC tactics include bombings, murder, mortar attacks, kidnapping, extortion, and hijacking, as well as guerrilla and conventional military action against Colombian political, military, and economic targets. The FARC has well-documented ties to a range of drug trafficking activities including taxation, cultivation, and distribution. The group considers US persons to be legitimate military targets due to US support for the Colombian Government. FARC's most widely known operation was its kidnapping of three US contractors—Marc Gonsalves, Thomas Howes, and Keith Stansell; together with French politician Ingrid Betancourt—in February 2002. The four were freed by Colombian security forces in July 2008.

The group had a number of setbacks in 2010 highlighted by the September 2010 Colombian military raid that resulted in the death of the FARC's senior military commander Victor Julio Suarez Rojas, better known as Mono Jojoy. In addition, Bogota frustrated

FARC attempts to disrupt the March 2010 congressional and May 2010 presidential elections. However, the group in June 2011 conducted some small-scale attacks and kidnappings to demonstrate its continued relevance.

Juan Manuel Santos, elected as president in May 2010, has continued Bogota's policy of aggressive military operations—known as Democratic Security—against the FARC as evidenced by the raid that killed Mono Jojoy and continuing government raids targeting FARC Supreme Leader Alfonso Cano. Santos, a former defense minister, has publicly vowed to strengthen Colombia's military and police forces in order to defeat the FARC and end the conflict, now nearly 50 years long.

FARC

The Revolutionary Armed Forces of Colombia—People's Army (Spanish: *Fuerzas Armadas Revolucionarias de Colombia—Ejército del Pueblo*, FARC–EP and FARC) are a guerilla organization involved in the continuing Colombian armed conflict since 1964. It has been known to employ a variety of military tactics in addition to more unconventional methods including terrorism. The FARC-EP have a claim to be an army of peasant Marxist–Leninists with a political platform of agrarianism and anti-imperialism. The operations of the FARC–EP are funded by kidnap to ransom, illegal mining, extortion and/or taxation of various forms of economic activity and the production and distribution of illegal drugs. As of the early 21st century the organization has seemingly been returning to more traditional a methodology of guerilla warfare, including hit and run attacks while also having released all its kidnapped civilians.

The strength of the FARC–EP forces is indeterminate; in 2007, the FARC said they were an armed force of 18,000 men and women; in 2010, the Colombian military calculated that FARC forces consisted of approximately 13,800 members, 50 per cent of which were armed guerrilla combatants; and, in 2011, the President of Colombia, Juan Manuel Santos, said that FARC–EP forces comprised fewer than 10,000 members. In 2013 it was reported that 26,648 FARC and ELN members had decided to demobilize since 2002. According to a report from Human Rights Watch, approximately 20–30% of the recruits are minors, most of whom are forced to join the FARC. The greatest concentrations of FARC terrorist forces are in the south-eastern regions of Colombia's 500,000 square kilometers (190,000 sq mi) of jungle, in the plains at the base of theAndean mountain chain and in northwestern Colombia. However, the FARC and the *ELN* (National Liberation Army of Colombia) lost control of the territory, forcing them to hide primarily in remote areas in the jungle.

In 1964, the FARC–EP were established as the military wing of the Colombian Communist Party (Partido Comunista Colombiano, PCC), after the Colombian military attacked rural Communist enclaves in the aftermath of *The Violence* (La Violencia, ca. 1948–58). The FARC are a violent non-state actor (VNSA) whose formal recognition aslegitimate belligerent forces is disputed by some organizations. As such, the FARC has been classified as a terrorist organization by the governments of Colombia, the United States, Canada, Chile, New Zealand, and the European Union; whereas the governments of Venezuela, Brazil, Argentina, Ecuador, and Nicaragua do not. In 2008, Venezuelan President Hugo Chávez recognized the FARC-EP as a proper army. President Chávez also asked the Colombian government and their allies to recognize the FARC as a belligerent force, arguing that such political recognition would oblige the FARC to forgo kidnapping and terrorism as methods of civil war and to abide by the Geneva Convention. Juan Manuel Santos, the current President of Colombia, has followed a middle path by recognizing in 2011 that there is an "armed conflict" in Colombia although his predecessor, Alvaro Uribe, strongly disagreed. In 2012, FARC announced they would no longer participate in kidnappings for ransom and released the last 10 soldiers and police officers they kept as prisoners but it has kept silent about the status of hundreds of civilians still reported as hostages, but continued kidnapping soldiers and civilians. In February 2008, millions of Colombians demonstrated against the FARC.

In 2012, the FARC made 239 attacks on the energy infrastructure. However, the FARC have shown signs of fatigue. Also the FARC are, as of 2014, not seeking to engage in outright combat with the army, instead concentrating on small-scale ambushes against isolated army units. Meanwhile, since 2008, the FARC have opted to attack police patrols with home-made mortars, sniper rifles and explosives, as they are not considered strong enough to engage police units directly. This follows the trend of the 1990s during the strengthening of theGovernment forces. Currently the FARC and the Colombian Government are in peace talks in the city of Havana in Cuba, despite FARC failing to follow their own peace offers and ceasefires and repeatedly stating they won't stop their arms race.

JUAN MANUEL SANTOS'S PRESIDENCY

President Juan Manuel Santos began his term with a suspected FARC bomb-blast in Bogotá. This followed the resolution of the 2010 Colombia–Venezuela diplomatic crisis which erupted over outgoing President Álvaro Uribe's allegations of active Venezuelan support for FARC.

In early September 2010, FARC-EP attacks in the Nariño Department and Putumayo Department in southern Colombia killed some fifty policemen and soldiers in hit-and-run assaults.

According to a December report by the Corporación Nuevo Arco Iris NGO, 473 FARC-EP guerrillas and 357 members of the Colombian security forces died in combat between January and September 2010. An additional 1,382 government soldiers or policemen were wounded during the same period, with the report estimating that the total number of casualties could reach 2,500 by the end of the year. Nuevo Arco Iris head León Valencia considered that FARC guerrillas have reacted to a series of successful military blows against them by splitting up their forces into smaller groups and intensifying the offensive use of anti-personnel land mines, leading to what he called a further "degradation" of the conflict. Valencia also added that both coca crops and the drug trade have "doubled" in areas with FARC-EP presence. Researcher Claudia López considered that the Colombian government is winning the strategic and aerial side of the war but not the infantry front, where both the FARC-EP and ELN continue to maintain an offensive capacity.

Military offensives carried out under former President Alvaro Uribe and President Juan Manuel Santos have been able to reduce the number of FARC combattants to 7,000, which is much lower than the 20,000 combattants FARC employed in the early 2000s. This military offensive has also been able to reduce FARC territorial control and push guerillas to more remote and sparsely populated regions, often close to territorial or internal borders.

2010 death of Mono Jojoy

Colombian authorities announced the death of Víctor Julio Suárez Rojas, also known as *Mono Jojoy,* on 23 September 2010. President Juan Manuel Santos stated that the FARC commander was killed in an operation that began in the early hours of 21 September in the department of Meta, 200 miles (320 km) south of the capital Bogotá. According to Santos, he was "the impersonation of terror and a symbol of violence". After this event, the FARC-EP released a statement saying that defeating the group would not bring peace to Colombia and called for a negotiated solution, not surrender, to the social and political conflict.

January through October 2011

In January 2011 Juan Manuel Santos admitted that FARC-EP had killed 460 government soldiers and wounded over 2,000 in 2010. In April 2011 the Colombian congress issued a statement saying that FARC has a 'strong presence' in roughly one third of the municipalities in Colombia, while their attacks have increased. Overall FARC operations, including attacks against security forces as well as kidnappings and the use of land mines, have increased every year since 2005. In the first 6 months of 2011 the FARC carried out an estimated 1,115 actions, which constitutes a 10% increase over the same period in 2010.

By early 2011 Colombian authorities and news media reported that the FARC and the clandestine sister groups have partly shifted strategy from guerrilla warfare to 'a war of militias', meaning that they are increasingly operating in civilian clothes while hiding amongst sympathizers in the civilian population. In early January 2011 the Colombian army said that the FARC has some 18,000 members, with 9,000 of those forming part of the militias. The army says it has 'identified' at least 1,400 such militia members in the FARC strongholds of Valle del Cauca and Cauca in 2011. In June 2011 Colombian chief of staff Edgar Cely claimed that the FARC wants to 'urbanize their actions', which could partly explain the increased guerrilla activity in Medellín and particularly Cali. Jeremy McDermott, co-director of Insight Crime, estimates that FARC may have some 30,000 'part-time fighters' in 2011, consisting of both armed and unarmed civilian supporters making up the rebel militia network, instead of full-time fighters wearing uniforms.

According to Corporación Nuevo Arco Iris, FARC-EP killed 429 members of the Colombian government's security forces between January and October 2011. During this same period, the rebel group lost 316 of its own members. The year 2011 saw over 2,000 incidents of FARC activity, which was the highest figure recorded since 1998. The NGO has stated that while most of these incidents remain defensive in nature and are not like the large offensives from years past, FARC actions have been growing since 2005, and the rebel group is currently carrying out intense operations against small and medium-sized Colombian military units in vulnerable areas.

Death of Alfonso Cano

Colombian troops killed FARC leader Alfonso Cano in a firefight on 4 November 2011. The 6th Front of the FARC, which was in charge of Cano's security at the time of his death, retaliated by killing two policemen in Suarez and Jambalo some 24 hours after the death of Cano.

Death of captives in Operation Jupiter

On 26 November 2011, the FARC killed Police Captain Edgar Yesid Duarte Valero, Police Lieutenant Elkin Hernandez Rivas, Army Corporal Libio Jose Martinez Estrada and Police Intendant Alvaro Moreno after government troops approached the guerrilla camp where they were held. Police Sergeant Luis Alberto Erazo Maya managed to escape his captors and was later rescued.

The Colombian military had information indicating that there could be captives in the area and initiated Operation Jupiter in October 2011, using a 56 men Special Forces unit to carry out surveillance for preparing a future rescue mission that would involve additional troops and air support. According to the Colombian military, this same unit remained in the area for 43 days and did not find the captives until they accidentally ran into the FARC camp on the way back, which led to a shootout. Relatives of the captives, former victims and civil society groups blamed both the government and FARC for the outcome, questioning the operation as well as criticizing military rescues.

2012 release of last political hostages

On 26 February 2012, the FARC announced that they would release their remaining ten political hostages. The hostages were released on 2 April 2012. The president of Colombia, Juan Manuel Santos, said that this incident was "not enough", and asked the FARC to release the civilian hostages they possess.

Release of Chinese hostages

On 22 November 2012, the FARC released four Chinese oil workers. The hostages were working for the Emerald Energy oil company, a British-based subsidiary of China's Sinochem Group, when they were kidnapped on 8 June 2011. Their Colombian driver was also kidnapped, but released several hours later. Authorities identified the freed men as Tang Guofu, Zhao Hongwei, Jian Mingfu, and Jiang Shan.

Peace talks

Santos announced on 27 August 2012 that the Colombian government has engaged in exploratory talks with FARC in order to seek an end to the conflict:

Exploratory conversations have been held with the FARC to find an end to the conflict. I want to make very clear to Colombians that the approaches that have been carried out and the ones that will happen in the future will be carried out within the framework based on these principles: We are going to learn from the mistakes made in the past so that they are not repeated. Second, any process must lead to the end of the conflict, not making it longer. Third, operations and military presence will be maintained across the entire national territory.

He also said that he would learn from the mistakes of previous leaders, who failed to secure a lasting ceasefire with FARC, though the military would still continue operations throughout Colombia while talks continued. An unnamed Colombian intelligence source said Santos has assured FARC that no one would be extradited to stand trial in another country. *Al Jazeera* reported that the initiative began after Santos met with Venezuelan President Hugo Chavez and asked him to mediate. Former President Uribe has criticized Santos for seeking peace "at any cost" and rejected the idea of holding talks. *Telesur* reported that FARC and the Colombian government had signed a preliminary agreement in Havana the same day. The first round of the talks will take place in Oslo on 5 October and then return to Havana for approximately six months of talks before culminating in Colombia. However, Santos later ruled out a ceasefire pending the talks in Oslo and reiterated that offensive operations against FARC would continue.

ELN leader Nicolas Rodriguez Bautista, otherwise known as Gabino, added that his group was interested in joining the talks too: "Well we are open, it's exactly our proposal, to seek room for open dialogue without conditions and start to discuss the nation's biggest problems. But the government has said no! Santos says he has the keys to peace in his pocket, but I think he has lost them because there seems to be no possibility of a serious dialogue, we remain holding out for that."

Colombia's RCN Radio reported on 29 September that a preliminary draft of the proposals indicated that a resolution would involve answering FARC's historic grievances including rural development and agrarian reform; democracy development via an enhancement of the number of registered political parties; security and compensation for the victims of the conflict. In this regards, the Colombian government has alread passed a series of laws that entail compensation for the victims and a return of land to the displaced. FARC also indicated a willingness to give up their arms. Former M19 member Antonio Navarro Wolff said: "If the government wants a serious peace plan they will have to take control of the coca leaf plantations that are currently owned by the FARC because if not another criminal group will take over it." Santos later told *Al Jazeera* that peace was possible if there was "goodwill" on both sides. Santos told the General debate of the sixty-seventh session of the United Nations General Assembly on 26 September, that Venezuela and Chile were also helping in the discussion along with Cuba and Norway.

Peace talks were formally started on 18 October in a HOTEL 30 miles north of the Norwegian capital Oslo with a joint-press conference by both delegations. The representatives of the government, led by Humberto de la Calle and the FARC, led by Iván Márquez, said the so-called second phase of the peace process will be inaugurated in Oslo on 15 November, after which the delegations will go to Cuba to work on the negotiation of the peace accord, which will ultimately lead to a permanent agreement and ceasefire. The Colombian government has also stated that they expect that a post-Chavez government will continue to support the peace process. In late 2012, FARC declared a two-month unilateral cease-fire and said that they would be open to extending it as a bilateral truce afterwards during the rest of the negotiations. The Colombian government refused to agree to a bilateral cease-fire, alleging violations of the truce by FARC.

Shortly after lifting the ceasefire, FARC conducted attacks on a coal transport railway, which derailed 17 wagons and forced a suspension of operations and assaulted Milan, a town in the southern Caquetá, killing at least seven government soldiers and injuring five others.

Santos has been far more responsive to threats against social leaders than his predecessors. He has also been decisive in combatting the New Illegal Armed Groups that emerged as a result of the paramilitary process, especially in fighting threats and violence against human rights defenders and social leaders. During Santos' presidency, private security and proclaimed self-defense movements have also lost their legitimacy.

On 27 May 2013, it was announced that one of the most contentious issues had been resolved. Land reform and compensation was tackled with promises to compensate those who had lost land. This is the first time the government and FARC have reached an agreement on a substantive issue in four different negotiating attempts over 30 years. The peace process then moved on to the issue of "political participation", during which FARC insisted on its demand for an elected Constituent Assembly to rewrite Colombia's constitution. This demand has been forcefully rejected by Colombia's lead government negotiator, Humberto de la Calle.

On 1 July 2013, FARC and the second-largest guerrilla group in Colombia, ELN, announced that they would be working together to find a "political solution to the social and armed conflict."

The details of this partnership, however, are far from clear; Washington Office on Latin America's Adam Isacson explains that two issues central to peace accords with ELN—resource policy and kidnapping—are currently off the table in the talks in Havana with FARC, and the addition of these topics may complicate and slow down an already sluggish process.

On 6 November 2013 the Colombian government and FARC announced that they had come to an agreement regarding the participation of political opposition and would begin discussing their next issue, the illicit drug trade.

On 23 January 2014 Juan Fernando Cristo, the President of the Senate of Colombia, proposed a second Plan Colombia during a conference on the Colombian peace process in Washington, D.C. Cristo stated that this new plan should be "for the victims" and should redirect the resources from the original Plan Colombia towards supporting a post-conflict Colombia.

On May 16, 2014, the Colombian government and the FARC rebels agreed to work together against drug trafficking, added to the development of these peace talks.

FINANCING AND GOVERNANCE

FARC receives most of its funding—which has been estimated to average some $300 million per year—from taxation of the illegal drug trade and other activities, ransom kidnappings, bank robberies, and extortion of large landholders, multinational corporations, and agribusiness. From taxation of illegal drugs and other economic activity FARC has been estimated to receive approximately 60 to 100 million dollars per year. These funds are partly used to fund military operations and partly to keep the peace between peasants and traffickers, forcing the later to pay a livable wage, keeping crime at bay and sustaining social services where the government is absent

Role of FARC in the areas it controls

FARCs history is deeply rooted in its historical workers struggle for which its more peaceful members were persecuted and killed en massé during the period of *La Violencia*. It has continued to employ this ideology in the now mostly peasant dominated areas that it controls, attempting to follow the principles of FOCO. In acting as a vanguard it has often times forcefully instituted its rule of law in the areas that it controls as to bring an end to corruption and crime. In its struggle to provide social services it has succeeded delivering health care and education, and infrastructure in the form of roads and electricity. The people of these areas have become accustomed to accepting them as the local authority.

Means of financing

The guerillas main means of FINANCING is through the drug trade which includes both direct and indirect participation; taxation, administration or control of areas of production and trafficking. A large but often difficult to estimate portion of funding comes from the taxation of businesses and even local farmers, oftentimes lumped in or defined by its opponents as extortion. It is important to note that in areas in which this happens there rarely tends to be any government taxation or services and thus the absence of such provided by FARC would leave the population without any.

Drug trade

FARC-EP was not initially involved in direct drug cultivation, trafficking, or trans-shipment prior to or during the 1980s. Instead, it maintained a system of taxation on the production that took place in the territories that they controlled, in exchange for protecting the growers and establishing law and order in these regions by implementing its own rules and regulations. During the 1990s, FARC expanded its operations, in some areas, to include trafficking and production, which has provided a significant portion of its funding. Right-wing paramilitary groups also receive a large portion of their income from drug trafficking and production operations.

A 1992 Central Intelligence Agency report "acknowledged that the FARC had become increasingly involved in drugs through their 'taxing' of the trade in areas under their geographical control and that in some cases the insurgents protected trafficking infrastructure to further fund their insurgency", but also described the relationship between the FARC and the drug traffickers as one *"characterized by both cooperation and friction"* and concluded that *"we do not believe that the drug industry [in Colombia] would be substantially disrupted in the short term by attacks against guerrillas. Indeed, many traffickers would probably welcome, and even assist, increased operations against insurgents."*

In 1994, the DEA came to three similar conclusions. First, that any connections between drug trafficking organizations and Colombian insurgents were *"ad hoc 'alliances of convenience'"*. Second, that *"the independent involvement of insurgents in Colombia's domestic drug productions, transportation, and distribution is limited... there is no evidence that the national leadership of either the FARC or theELN has directed, as a matter of policy, that their respective organizations directly engage in independent illicit drug production, transportation, or distribution."* Third, the report determined that the DEA *"has no evidence that the FARC or ELN have been involved in the transportation, distribution, or marketing of illegal drugs in the United States. Furthermore it is doubtful that either insurgent group could develop the international transportation and logistics infrastructure necessary to establish independent drug distribution in the United States or Europe… DEA believes that the insurgents never will be major players in Colombia's drug trade."*

FARC has called for crop substitution programs that would allow coca farmers to find alternative means of income and subsistence. In 1999, FARC worked with a United Nations alternative development project to enable the transition from coca production to sustainable food production. On its own, the group has also implemented agrarian reform programs in Putumayo.

In those FARC-EP controlled territories that do produce coca, it is generally grown by peasants on small plots; in paramilitary or government controlled areas, coca is generally grown on large plantations. The FARC-EP generally makes sure that peasant coca growers receive a much larger share of profits than the paramilitaries would give them, and demands that traffickers pay a decent wage to their workers. When growers in a FARC-controlled area are caught selling coca to non-FARC brokers, they are generally forced to leave the region, but when growers are caught selling to FARC in paramilitary-controlled areas, they are generally killed. Lower prices paid for raw coca in paramilitary-controlled areas lead to significantly larger profits for the drug processing and trafficking organizations, which means that they generally prefer that paramilitaries control an area rather than FARC.

In 2000, FARC Spokesman Simon Trinidad said that taxes on drug laboratories represented an important part of the organization's income, although he didn't say how much it was. He defended this funding source, arguing that drug trade was endemic in Colombia because it had pervaded many sectors of its economy.

After the 21 April 2001 capture of Brazilian drug lord Luiz Fernando da Costa (aka Fernandinho Beira-Mar) in Colombia, Colombian and Brazilian authorities accused him of cooperating with FARC-EP through the exchange of weapons for cocaine. They also claimed that he received armed protection from the guerrilla group.

In Monday, 18 March 2002 the Attorney General of the United States John Ashcroft indicted leaders of the FARC after an 18-month investigation into their narcotics trafficking. Tomas Molina Caracas, the commander of the FARC's 16th Front, led the 16th Front's drug-trafficking activities together with Carlos Bolas and a rebel known as Oscar El Negro. Between 1994 and 2001, Molina and other 16th Front members controlled Barranco Minas, where they collected cocaine from other FARC fronts to sell it to international drug traffickers for payment in currency, weapons and equipment.

On 22 March 2006 the Attorney General Alberto Gonzales announced the indictment of fifty leaders of FARC for exporting more than $25 billion worth of cocaine to the United States and other countries. Several of the FARC leaders appeared on the Justice Department's Consolidated Priority Organization target list, which identifies the most dangerous international drug trafficking organizations. Recognizing the increased profits, the

FARC moved to become directly involved in the manufacture and distribution of cocaine by setting the price paid for cocaine paste and transporting it to jungle laboratories under FARC control. The charged FARC leaders ordered that Colombian farmers who sold paste to non-FARC buyers would be murdered and that U.S. fumigation planes should be shot down.

On 11 October 2012 Jamal Yousef, aka "Talal Hassan Ghantou", a native of Lebanon, was sentenced to 12 years in prison for conspiring to provide military-grade weapons to the Fuerzas Armadas Revolucionarias de Colombia (the FARC), in exchange for over a ton of cocaine. Yousef pled guilty in May 2012 to one count of providing material support to the FARC.

Kidnappings

The FARC-EP has carried out both ransom and politically motivated kidnappings in Colombia and has been responsible for the majority of such kidnappings carried out in the country.

The guerrillas initially targeted the families of drug traffickers, the wealthy upper-class and foreigners but the group later expanded its kidnapping and extortion operations to include the middle-class.

During the 1984 peace negotiations, FARC pledged to stop kidnapping and condemned the practice. However, hostage-taking by FARC increased in the years following this declaration. In a 1997 interview, FARC-EP Commander Alfonso Cano argued that some guerrilla units continued to do so for "political and economic reasons" in spite of the prohibition issued by the leadership.

In 2000, the FARC-EP issued a directive called "Law 002" which demanded a "tax" from all individuals and corporations with assets worth at least $1 million USD, warning that those who failed to pay would be detained by the group. In 2001, FARC Commander Simón Trinidad claimed that the FARC-EP does not engage in kidnapping but instead "retains [individuals] in order to obtain resources needed for our struggle". Commander Trinidad said he did not know how many people had been taken by FARC or how much money was collected by the organization in exchange for their freedom. In addition, FARC spokesperson Joaquín Gómez stated that the payment demanded was a tax which many people paid "voluntarily", with kidnapping undertaken because "those who have the resources must pay their share".

In 2002, Amnesty International sent a letter to FARC-EP Commander Manuel Marulanda condemning kidnapping and hostage-taking as well as rejecting the threats directed at municipal or judicial officials and their families, arguing that they are civilians who are protected byinternational humanitarian law as long as they do not participate in hostilities.

According to Amnesty International, the number of kidnappings has decreased in recent years but the human rights organization estimates that FARC and ELN guerrillas continue to be behind hundreds of cases. In 2008, press reports estimated that about 700 hostages continued to be held captive by FARC. According to the *Fundación País Libre* anti-kidnapping NGO, an estimated total of 6,778 people were kidnapped by FARC between 1997 and 2007. In 2009, the state's anti-kidnapping agency *Fondelibertad* reviewed 3,307 officially unsettled cases and removed those that had already been resolved or for which there was insufficient information. The agency concluded that 125 hostages remained in captivity nationwide of whom 66 were being held by the FARC-EP. The government's revised figures were considered "absurdly low" by *Fundación País Libre,* which has argued that its own archives suggest an estimated 1,617 people taken hostage between 2000 and 2008 remain in the hands of their captors, including hundreds seized by FARC. FARC claimed at the time that it was holding nine people for ransom in addition to hostages kept for a prisoner exchange.

In 2008, Venezuelan President Hugo Chávez expressed his disagreement with FARC-EP's resorting to kidnappings. Former President Fidel Castro of Cuba also criticized the use of hostage-taking by the guerrillas as "objectively cruel" and suggested that the group free all of its prisoners and hostages.

In February 2012, FARC announced that it would release ten members of the security forces, who it described as political prisoners, representing the last such captives in its custody. It further announced the repeal of Law 002, bringing to an end its support for the practice of kidnapping for ransom. However, it was not clear from the FARC statement what would happen to the civilians it still held in captivity. Colombian president Juan Manuel Santos used Twitter to welcome the move as a "necessary, if insufficient, step in the right direction".

ORGANIZATION AND STRUCTURE

FARC-EP remains the largest and oldest insurgent group in the Americas. According to the Colombian government, FARC-EP had an estimated 6,000–8,000 members in 2008, down from 16,000 in 2001, having lost much of their fighting force since President Álvaro Uribetook office in 2002. Political analyst and former guerrilla León Valencia has estimated that FARC's numbers have been reduced to around 11,000 from their 18,000 peak but cautions against considering the group a defeated force. In 2007 FARC-EP Commander Raúl Reyes claimed that their force consisted of 18,000 guerrillas.

The largest concentrations of FARC-EP guerrillas are located throughout the southeastern parts of Colombia's 500,000 square kilometers (190,000 sq mi) of jungle and in the plains at the base of the Andean mountains.

FARC's organized hierarchically into military units as follows:

- *Central High Command* – composed of a five-member Secretariat (one of them being the, Commander-in-Chief) and two "supplements". Coordinates the activities of the individual blocks, and determines overall strategy of FARC-EP.
- *Estado Mayor Central* – 25 members, who also coordinate activities of blocks
- *Block* – 5+ Fronts, with each block corresponding to one of Colombia's geographical regions: south, central, east, west, Middle Magdalena, Caribbean, and Cesar.
- *Front* – 1+ Columns. Within each Front, there are combat, support, and infrastructure elements.
- *Column* – 2+ Companies
- *Company* – 2+ Guerrillas
- *Guerrilla* – 2 Squads
- *Squad* – +/- 12 combatants

The FARC-EP secretariat was led by Alfonso Cano and six others after the death of Manuel Marulanda (Pedro Antonio Marín), also known as "Tirofijo", or Sureshot in 2008. The "international spokesman" of the organization was represented by "Raul Reyes", who was killed in a Colombian army raid against a guerrilla camp in Ecuador on 1 March 2008. Cano was killed in a military operation on 4 November 2011.

FARC-EP remains open to a negotiated solution to the nation's conflict through dialogue with a flexible government that agrees to certain conditions, such as the demilitarization of certain areas, cessation of paramilitary and government violence against rural peasants, social reforms to reduce poverty and inequality, and the release of all jailed (and extradited) FARC-EP rebels. It claims that until these conditions surface, the armed revolutionary struggle will remain necessary to fight against Colombia's elites. The FARC-EP says it will continue its armed struggle because it perceives the current Colombian government as an enemy because of historical politically motivated violence against its members and supporters including members of the Patriotic Union, a FARC-EP-created political party.

LIST OF ATTACKS ATTRIBUTED TO FARC

The following is a list of attacks attributed to the Revolutionary Armed Forces of Colombia (FARC). Since 1964, the Marxist-Leninistguerrilla organization has been fighting the Colombian government, and is the oldest insurgent group in the Americas. FARC is considered a terrorist group by the Colombian government, the United States Department of State, Canada and the European Union. There is a broader list of events related to the internal conflict in Colombia in Wikipedia en Español

This is an incomplete list that may never be able to satisfy particular standards for completeness. You can help by expanding it with entries that are reliably sourced.

2014

- November 16: Colombian General Ruben Dario Alzate Kidnapped by FARC in a small village close to the provincial capital of Quibdó.

- December 19: 5 soldiers were killed and 7 injured in the aftermath of a FARC ambush in the Cauca province.

2013

- July 20: Two rebel attacks on government positions killed 19 soldiers and an unspecified number of combatants. It was the deadliest day since peace talks began in November 2012.

2012

- January 1: FARC guerrillas attack police station in Norte de Santander, northern Colombia, injuring two policemen.
- January 3: Four army soldiers killed during hard combat with the FARCs 21 Front in southern Tolima. The soldiers were ambushed with landmines.
- January 4: FARC guerrillas from the 6th Front launch artillery pieces against several police stations in the Cauca department.
- January 4: FARC guerrillas attack the military close to the Pan-American highway between Cali and Popayán.
- January 5: One soldier and one member of FARC killed during intense combat between state forces and guerrillas in Caquetá.
- January 6: One policeman killed as guerrilla fighters from the FARC's Southern Bloc attacked police station in Putumayo, southern Colombia. One FARC member was also killed in the fighting.
- January 7: A group of 12 FARC guerrillas from the 26th Front attack a police station in Lejanías, Meta department.
- January 8: FARC guerrillas kill two policemen and wound one in a hit-and-run attack in Silvia municipality, Cauca Department.
- January 10: One soldier killed in western Antioquia as guerrillas from the 34th Front attacked a military patrol.
- January 13: One soldier wounded as FARC guerrilla throw grenades into a military office in San Vicente del Caguán. The office was the site of the 1998-2002 peace negotiations.

- January 14: Several FARC attacks in Norte de Santander leaves two policemen and three civilians wounded.
- January 15: FARC guerrillas attack military patrol with rockets and machine gun fire, killing one soldier and wounding three more. The attack took place in Nariño, near the Pacific Coast.
- January 18: One soldier killed by FARC guerrillas from the 45th Front in the Arauca Department
- January 19: Attack in El Mango, Cauca, leaves one soldier dead and two wounded. This was the 24th attack in El Mango municipality in less than one year.
- January 19–20: FARC guerrillas sabotage the El Limón oil pipeline, which runs through Colombia and transports much of the oil from several oil fields.
- January 20: Around 100 FARC guerrillas attack a police patrol in the Meta Department, killing one policeman and wounding another.
- January 20: FARC guerrillas launch a 25 minute attack with mortars and machine guns against police station in Toribío, Cauca.
- January 20: Between two and three soldiers killed as FARC guerrillas attack communication towers in Santa Ana, west of Popayán in the Cauca Department.
- January 21: FARC guerrillas from the 36th Front attack the army with a 'horse-bomb' in Toldeo, Antioquia, leaving one soldier dead and several wounded.
- January 22: FARC ambush in La Guajira, near the Venezuelan border, leaves one army soldier dead and four wounded.
- January 22: Guerrilla attack in El Tambo, Norte de Santander, leaves two policemen wounded. It is still unknown if the attackers were from ELN or FARC, as both guerrilla groups operate in the region.
- January 26: A police vehicle is attacked with small arms fire in the city of Neiva by presumed FARC guerrillas. The vehicle was transporting a captured female FARC member, and it is likely that the attack was a rescue attempt.

- January 28: Policeman killed by FARC militias in Antioquia.
- January 28: FARC guerrillas block road and burn an oil truck in the southern department of Guivare. No one was injured in the incident as the guerrillas told the driver to leave the truck before it was set on fire.
- January 29: Presumed FARC members attack police station in the Meta Department with a 'horse-bomb'.
- February 1: On policeman wounded by presumed FARC guerrillas from the 34th front in Antioquia.
- February 2: FARC guerrillas from the 36th front attack military checkpoint in the Caribbean part of the Antioquia department. No casualties.
- February 2: FARC guerrillas burn 8 oil trucks in the Catatumbo region of Norte de Santander.
- February 3: FARC or Los Rastrojos are accused of detonating a motorcycle bomb outside of a police station in Tumaco, Nariño. The attack killed nine or eleven people, both policemen and civilians, while some 70 people, the majority of them policemen, were wounded and taken to hospitals in Cali for treatment. Colombian media referred to the event as one of the most devastating attacks this year.
- February 3: Five policemen wounded as presumed FARC members detonated a bomb outside of a police station in Villarica, Cauca. The Army also reported ongoing skirmishes between FARC and the army in the municipality of Caloto in the same department.
- February 10: FARC attack in Corinto, Cauca, leaves two soldiers dead.
- February 11: FARC attack against military base in Jamundí, Valle del Cauca, leaves four soldiers killed and more than 18 wounded. This is the biggest attack the FARC guerrillas have launched in this municipality since August last year, according to press reports.
- February 18: Around 300 FARC guerrillas attack several locations, police stations and army units in the southwestern department of Cauca.

- February 22: FARC guerrillas kill three soldiers in the northern part of the Cauca department. Around eleven soldiers were also wounded in the attack.
- February 27: One soldier killed by FARC guerrillas in the northern department La Guijira.
- February 28: One soldier killed and four wounded in FARC offensive in southwest (Putumayo) Colombia.
- March 19: FARC guerrillas kill eleven soldiers in an ambush in Arauca, near the Venezuelan border.
- April 1: FARC attack in Antioquia leaves one policeman dead and six wounded.
- April 1: FARC guerrillas attack police station in Cauca, wounding two policemen.
- April 2: '[a]uthorities suspect that FARC guerrillas blew up two sections of the Rio Zulia-Ayacucho pipeline, forcing the Petroleos del Norte oil company to cease oil shipments and install protective barriers to prevent the contamination of the Catatumbo river'.
- April 3: One policeman killed by FARC's 15th front in Caquetá.
- April 3: FARC members in Cauca attack police station with explosives.
- April 4: Five soldiers killed in Orito, Putumayo, as presumed FARC members detonate a bomb next to a military patrol.
- April 7: At least seven soldiers killed and two wounded as FARC guerrillas from the 34th Front attack the military on the road between Quibdó and Medellín. The attack took place in the Chocó Department.
- April 7: FARC guerrillas in Cauca attack police station with 32 rounds of artillery.
- April 8: FARC guerrillas attack military base in Caquetá. No casualties reported.
- April 9: One Marine corps soldier killed by FARC militants from the 30th Front in Buenaventura municipality, Valle del Cauca

- April 9: One policeman killed and four wounded in FARC attack in El Bordo, southern Cauca. The guerrillas were from the 6th Front and 8th Front of the FARC.
- April 27: 5 soldiers killed by FARC guerrillas in Florida, Valle del Cauca, near the regional capital Cali.
- April 28: Between 15 and 21 soldiers killed by FARC guerrillas in northern Caquetá. The soldiers had just left their helicopters when they were ambushed by guerrillas. Also missing was a French journalist working for France 24 and four soldiers. Dozens of soldiers were also wounded in the defensive action. According to Caracol Radio at least 20 army soldiers were killed in the attack.

April 29: The 30th and 60th fronts of the FARC launch a series of attacks against police stations in the Cauca Department.

2011

Between January and early May 2011 the Colombian government claimed that FARC-EP killed 167 soldiers and policemen.

List of attacks since May 15, 2011:

- May 15: FARC attack on a highway close to Ibagué leaves three army soldiers wounded.
- May 16: 3 policemen wounded due to FARC attack in Tuluá, Valle del Cauca.
- May 17: 1 policeman killed in Pradera, Valle del Cauca, as a result of combat between the army and guerrillas.
- May 17: 1 policeman killed in Putumayo Department.
- May 19: Nine soldiers killed in Tumaco, Nariño as the soldiers stepped into camps that were mined by the guerrillas, according to information from the FARC. One FARC member was also killed in the fighting.
- May 20: FARC attack in Cauca on a helicopter transporting money leaves 1 policeman and 3 civilians wounded.
- May 22: 1 policeman dead and another wounded due to FARC attack near Popayán, Cauca.
- May 24: FARC attack near Cúcuta in Norte de Santander kills 2 army soldiers.

- May 26: Suspected FARC attack in Popayán in Cauca.
- May 28: Combat between FARC's 17:th Front and the army in the Huila Department leaves one soldier dead.
- May 28: 1 Soldier dies and 4 are injured due to a FARC attack in Buenos Aires, Cauca.
- May 30: FARC guerrillas assassinate two local politicians in Antioquia.
- May 30: FARC guerrillas rob a money transport in Cauca and kill 1 policeman.
- May 31: FARC attack in Arauca kills 3 soldiers and wounds 6 more.
- June 2: FARC 'bomb' leaves 3 soldiers injured in Tolima.
- June 2: FARC attack on the major highway La Línea between Cajamarca and Ibagué kills 3 soldiers from the Colombian army.
- June 3: Suspected FARC guerrillas of the 33:d Front destroy oil infrastructure in Norte de Santander.
- June 4: FARC sniper kills an army officer in Santander de Quilichao, Cauca.
- June 5: FARC attack on the highway between Cali and Popayán in Valle del Cauca closes the road for three hours.
- June 6: FARC defense action in Tolima Department leaves one soldier and one FARC guerrilla dead.
- June 7: FARC guerrillas killed 4 policemen and wounded 12 more in the Cauca Department near Popayán.
- June 9: 4 Chinese oil workers are kidnapped along with their driver in Caquetá by suspected FARC guerrillas. The driver was later released. The four Chinese oil workers were freed on November 22, 2012 in exchanage for $2 million.
- June 10: FARC guerrillas in Tolima activate several bombs. No casualties.
- June 10: FARC attack in Nóvita, Chocó kills 1 soldier and wounds 1 more.
- June 12: FARC attack in Cauca kills one soldier and wounds 7.

- June 12: Suspected FARC guerrillas burn a bus and destroy electricity towers in Tolima.
- June 13: FARC guerrillas attack police in Caquetá, killing 1 policeman.
- June 13: 2 army soldiers die and 1 more wounded as a result of suspected FARC landmines in Tolima.
- June 15: FARC ambush in Tolima leaves 1 army soldier dead.
- June 16: FARC guerrillas destroy electricity towers in Antioquia, leaving 12,000 people without electricity.
- June 19: Car bomb in Popayán kills one civilian and wounds several more. Authorities initially blamed FARC, but it is likely the perpetrators were from Ejército de Liberación Nacional.
- June 20: FARC guerrillas kidnap politicians in the Meta Department.
- June 20: Three policemen are injured by a bomb attack in Antioquia.
- June 21: FARC guerrillas ambushed and killed 3 policemen on the road between Cali and Buenaventura in Valle del Cauca.
- June 23: 3 army soldiers and 4 FARC or ELN members die during combat near Cúcuta in Norte de Santander. Press reports are conflicting and it remains unclear if the guerrillas were from ELN or FARC.
- June 24: 1 policeman killed and 3 wounded due to FARC attack against money transport in Nariño.
- June 27: FARC attack in Antioquia against the paramilitary group Los Rastrojos leaves 3 dead.
- June 29: FARC attack on a major highway in Antioquia linking Medellín to Cartagena leaves one police major dead and four officers wounded. The road was completely shut down for 24 hours.
- July 2: FARC Guerrillas attack military base in Boyacá.
- July 4: Guerrillas of the FARC launch attack against police station in Argelia, Cauca, killing one policeman and wounding three more.

- July 6: Guerrillas of the FARC attack the military in Norte de Santander, leaving one Colombian army soldier dead.
- July 7: FARC militias in Cauca launch attack against private property, destroying 7 buildings.
- July 8: 2 policemen wounded due to FARC attack in Argelia, Cauca.
- July 9: Simultaneous attacks against five different cities in the department of Cauca leaves two soldiers and four civilians dead, in addition to over 80 wounded.
- July 10: Another FARC attack in Cauca kills two policemen.
- July 10: FARC guerrillas plan and execute a successful jail break in Nariño. The prison was attacked with explosives. 18 presumed members of the FARC, including an important mid-level commander of the Western Bloc of the FARC-EP, were freed in the action.
- July 10: FARC guerrillas attack military transports in Caquetá, leaving two soldiers wounded.
- July 11: Guerrillas from the 5:th front of the FARC kill two policemen in Apartadó Antioquia.
- July 12: FARC attacks police station in Cauca with heavy mortars.
- July 13: Three Colombian army soldiers wounded by FARC mines in Arauca.
- July 14: FARC attack against electricity infrastructure in Catatumbo, Norte de Santander, leaves around 10,000 people without electricity.
- July 15: Three Colombian soldiers wounded in FARC ambush in Nariño, southern Colombia.
- July 16: FARC guerrillas of the Caribbean Bloc of the FARC-EP are suspected to be behind attack against oil infrastructure in La Guajira.
- July 17: Two policemen wounded due to attack by FARC militias in Norte de Santander.
- July 18: FARC guerrillas attack police station in Cauca with mortars.
- July 20: FARC guerrillas attack the Pan-American highway

between Popayán and Pasto in Cauca, leaving three policemen wounded.

- July 21: Around 80 FARC guerrillas from a mobile column attack a military post in Tuluá, Valle del Cauca.
- July 23: One casualty due to FARC attack on the highway between Popayán and Cali.
- July 24: One soldier dead and two more wounded due to minefield planted by guerrillas in Norte de Santander.
- July 28: Presumed FARC guerrillas fire mortars at police station in Santander de Quilichao, Cauca.
- July 28: FARC guerrillas in Valle del Cauca activate bomb by remote control.
- July 29: FARC militia members kill 2 soldiers in the town of Uribe, Meta.
- July 30: One policeman killed by FARC members armed with pistols near Popayán, Cauca.
- July 30: One soldier killed by FARC guerrillas in Norte de Santander.
- July 31: One soldier killed and one more wounded due to FARC attack in Cauqetá.
- July 31: FARC rebels kidnap 5 oil workers in Arauca, eastern Colombia. They worked for Occidental Petroleum.
- July 31: Two soldiers killed due to explosives in San Andrés de Cuerquia, Antioquia. The soldiers were ambushed as they entered an area with FARC presence.
- August 2: FARC attack leaves 1 dead and 6 injured in Puerto Rico, Caquetá.
- August 4: FARC attacks in Argelia and El Bordo in Cauca wounds one policeman and destroys one truck one the Pan-American highway.
- August 4: Six big oil trucks are set on fire in Guaviare, south-west Colombia. It is likely that the attack was a revenge for refusal to pay 'revolutionary tax' to the FARC.
- August 6: FARC guerrillas intercept a medical mission on a river between Meta Department and Guaviare

Department. The guerrillas are believed to have taken medical equipment and medicine from the group.

- August 7: Four army soldiers killed in combat with a mobile FARC column in Pradera, Valle del Cauca.
- August 7: FARC guerrillas launch attack against oil infrastructure in Tibú, Norte de Santander.
- August 8: One civilian killed and two policemen wounded due to FARC attack in Campamento, Antioquia.
- August 8: One policeman wounded as suspected FARC guerrillas attack police outpost with explosives in Valdivia, Antioquia.
- August 9: FARC attack in Cauca Department leaves one army soldier dead and three soldiers wounded. The fighting displaced more than 1,000 people from their homes.
- August 10: Five soldiers from the Colombian army die in rebel minefields in the municipalities of Toledo and Paramillo, * Antioquia.
- August 10: FARC guerrillas attack electricity towers in Taraza, Antioquia.
- August 10: Presumed FARC guerrillas attack the highway linking Popayán to Pasto with explosives.
- August 10: Two soldiers die in minefield planted by FARC guerrillas in Solano, Caquetá.
- August 10: FARC guerrillas are believed to be behind explosion in Neiva, Huila.
- August 11: Six Colombian soldiers killed and ten more wounded in combat with FARC's Miller Perdomo mobile column in Jamundí, Valle del Cauca. The bodies of the dead soldiers could not be recovered due to the fighting. The wounded soldiers were taken to the military hospital in Cali.
- August 11: Twelve Colombian soldiers wounded due to FARC mines in the Meta Department.
- August 11: Four Colombian soldiers killed and three wounded due to combat between the FARC and the army

in Puerto Rico, Meta, central Colombia. At least one guerrillero of the FARC confirmed killed in the fighting. The deaths occurred when an army transport was ambushed by members of the FARC's 27 and 43 Fronts.

- August 14: Three soldiers were killed and another was wounded when they triggered landmines planted by FARC guerrillas.
- August 17: Five policemen killed and two more wounded in FARC attack in Tumaco, Nariño. According to authorities the guerrillas were most likely from the 29th front or mobile column Daniel Aldana.
- August 18: FARC attack leaves three soldiers wounded in El Mango, Cauca.
- August 20: Two policemen wounded in FARC attack in Argelia, Cauca.
- August 26: Four soldiers 'gravely injured' due to FARC attack in Miranda, northern Cauca.
- August 26: Three soldiers, and three civilians, two of them minors, injured in an attack by the 29th front of FARC guerrillas in the municipality of Magüi Payan, Nariño.
- August 27: Five Soldiers from the Colombian army killed due to a FARC attack in Cesar Department.
- August 29: Yet another five soldiers killed, this time in Tumaco, Nariño, when their APC was intercepted by ambushing guerrillas of the FARC's 6th Front.
- September 1: One soldier killed and four civilians injured in FARC attack in Argelia, Cauca.
- September 1: Two soldiers killed and three more wounded in a FARC attack in the northern part of the Cauca Department, bordering on Valle del Cauca. "Following the attack, the military shut down transit routes between the north of Cauca and the south of Valle del Cauca for three hours to secure the area."
- September 2: One soldier killed and two more wounded due to FARC attack near Buenaventura, Valle del Cauca.

- September 11: Three soldiers die in a rebel minefield in Norte de Santander.
- September 12: Three policemen killed by FARC guerrillas in different municipalities of Valle del Cauca.
- September 13: One soldier killed and two more wounded due to combat between FARC and the Colombian army in Caquetá. Three FARC members were reportedly killed in the fighting.
- September 14: FARC guerrillas, reportedly from the 34th Front, attack police patrol escorting a politician, leaving one person wounded. The attack took place near Medellín, Antioquia.
- September 16: FARC attack on electricity towers in Antioquia.
- September 17: Two soldiers and one civilian killed in several FARC attacks in Caquetá.
- September 17: FARC guerrillas attack an oil transport convoy belonging to a Chinese oil company, Emerald Energy. The attack took place close to San Vicente del Caguán, Caquetá. One oil worker was killed.
- September 18: Six policemen and two soldiers wounded in a series of FARC attacks against the military and police in Sardinata andLas Mercedes, Norte de Santander. The attackers belong to the 33d Front, which forms a part of the Middle Magdalena Bloc of the FARC-EP.
- September 18: One soldier killed and around 14 soldiers wounded due to FARC attack in the Cauca Department. During midday a group from the FARC's 6th Front emerged from a mountain and attacked an army counter-guerrilla unit in the valley below with rockets, mortars and machine gun fire.
- September 19: FARC guerrillas from the 17th Front block a major highway just two hours drive from Neiva with a cattle truck, believed to be loaded with explosives. The truck had the text "Peligro - FARC-EP" written on it. The

highway is the only one linking Huila Department with Caquetá Department.

- September 19: Several FARC attacks in the Pacific department of Chocó. One of the attacks occurred close to the border with Panamá. One policeman was killed by FARC members in the capital of Quibdó.
- September 20: Two policemen killed and one policeman badly wounded in a FARC attack in El Mango, Cauca.
- September 20: Three army soldiers wounded in a FARC attack in Nariño, just 2 kilometers from the capital Pasto.
- September 21: Two policemen, one of them a high-ranking police chief, killed in a FARC or ELN attack in Norte de Santander, near Cúcuta.
- September 24: FARC guerrillas attack police station in Corinto, Cauca with mortars and rockets.
- September 24: One soldier wounded and one civilian killed due to combat between the 18th Front of the FARC and the army at a police station in Ituango, Antioquia.
- September 24 and 25: At least one soldier dead and several soldiers wounded in simultaneous FARC attacks in the municipalities of Jambaló, Caldono, Silvia, Siberia and Suárez, located in the Cauca Department.
- September 25: Two policemen kidnapped and later killed by presumed FARC guerrillas in Cauca, near Popayán.
- September 25: One soldier wounded as guerrillas from the Mobile Column Teófilo Forero launch attack against the military in the northern part of the Caquetá Department, near San Vicente del Caguán.
- September 25: Two policemen wounded during Sunday night in Buenaventura, Valle del Cauca, due to explosive devises thrown by alleged FARC militia members operating in the city.
- September 27: Three army soldiers die in a rebel minefield in Briceño, Antioquia.
- September 27: Four army soldiers wounded in Marquetalia,

southern Tolima, located in the municipality Planadas, due to an attack attributed to FARC guerrillas.

- September 28: FARC guerrillas attack police stations in Argelia and El Tambo, Cauca.
- September 29: An unidentified rebel group attack a main oil pipeline in northeastern Colombia. As of 29/9 it remained unclear if the guerrillas were from the FARC or ELN.
- September 29: One army soldier and one FARC member dead due to combat between the 29th front of the FARC and the army in Nariño.
- September 30: Two policemen killed in an attack by the FARC militia in Saravena Arauca. The attack coincided with an ELN attack against a nearby army base.
- September 30: FARC guerrillas burn buses on the main road connecting Boyacá with Casanare Department. This was the second such attack in the month of September, according to El Tiempo.
- October 3: FARC guerrillas are accused of being behind a car bomb attack in Florida, Valle del Cauca.
- October 4 and 5: FARC guerrillas in Cauca continue launching attacks against police stations with mortars and machine gun fire, this time in the municipality of Suárez.
- October 5: 1 soldier killed and 3 soldiers wounded in FARC attack near Fortul, Arauca.
- October 6: FARC guerrillas blow up a car bomb outside of the police station in San Vicente del Caguán, Caquetá.
- October 8: Combat between the army and the Central Bloc of the FARC-EP leaves one soldier and three guerilleros dead.
- October 9: Two policemen wounded in FARC attack in Norte de Santander.
- October 10: FARC militia members kill 7 soldiers from the Colombian army in Cauca.
- October 18: Three soldiers from the Colombian army killed,

two wounded and one 'missing in action' due to FARC attack in Putumayo, southern Colombia. The FARC members were from the 32nd Front, which together with other FARC Fronts operates in the area.

- October 18: FARC guerrillas bomb an oil pipeline on Putumayo.
- October 21: Between 9 and 10 soldiers from the Colombian army killed near Tumaco, Nariño, as they were ambushed by FARC guerrillas. 6 more soldiers were wounded in the attack. The attack is believed to have been carried out by the Mobile Column Danel Aldana The FARC guerrillas got away with 19 army rifles, a mortar and communications equipment.
- October 22: One soldier killed and three more injured as FARC guerrillas launch attack with explosives in the northern part of the southern Caquetá department.
- October 23: Another 10 soldiers killed, this time in Arauca, eastern Colombia, as their platoon was intercepted by several FARC groups from the 10th Front. In addition to the deaths some 13 army soldiers were wounded. This brings the total death toll on the behalf of the state forces to 21 in the past 48 hours.
- October 23: FARC guerrillas attack an oil pipeline in two different locations in Norte de Santander.
- October 28: Three soldiers from the Colombian army killed and eleven more wounded as they stepped into a minefield planted by FARC guerrillas in the northern part of the Cauca department. The action took place hours after the air force had bombed a presumed guerrilla camp in the area.
- November 2: Three soldiers killed and seven wounded due to combat with FARC guerrillas in the Huila Department, near the regional capital Neiva.
- November 5: One policeman killed due to FARC attack in Jambolo, Cauca. The attack came a few hours after the

army and air force killed FARC's top leader Alfonso Cano in the nearby municipality of Suarez.

- November 7: FARC guerrillas attack police station in Putumayo, injuring one policeman with small arms fire.
- November 9: One soldier killed due to FARC attack in Briceño, Antioquia, northern Colombia
- November 17: FARC guerrillas in Briceño and Yarumal (Antioquia) burn buses on the highway connecting with the Caribbean coast.
- November 19: One soldier killed by FARC guerrillas in Planadas, Tolima.
- November 22: FARC guerrillas are alleged to be behind an explosion in a military office in Popayán, Cauca.
- December 4: Six policemen wounded as FARC guerrillas set of a bomb in the city of Neiva, Huila Department.
- December 7: FARC guerrillas from the 13th Front ambush a police patrol in Caquetá, leaving four policemen wounded.
- December 10–12: Several FARC attacks against the police in the northern César department.
- December 11: FARC attacks military base in Meta Department, leaving 4 army soldiers wounded.
- December 11: FARC guerrilla en Tolima launch attack against the military, leaving one soldier and one civilian minor wounded.
- December 12: FARC milicianos install car bomb in Popayán.
- December 18: FARC guerrillas from the Caribbean Bloc attack railways and transport trains in the Caribbean La Guajira department.
- December 22: FARC guerrillas kill two policemen in the Arauca department.
- December 22: FARC guerrillas belonging to the 34th Front kill a high-ranking police chief in Antioquia.
- December 23: Two soldiers killed and one wounded in the northern part of the Antioquia department.

- December 25: Three soldiers wounded in FARC attack in Timbiqui, Valle del Cauca department.
- December 26: One soldier killed and more than six soldiers wounded in FARC attack in the Arauca department.
- December 30: FARC guerrillas attack military aircraft stationed at an airport in Tumaco, Nariño. The FARC members attacked the planes with artillery pieces. The attack did not cause damages.
- December 31: FARC guerrillas attack police station in Suarez, Cauca, with mortars and machine gun fire. Unknown casualties.

2010

In 2010 the FARC killed at least 460 members of the security forces, while wounding more than 2,000, according to state statistics.

Bibliography

Abha Avasthi: *Dimensions of Violence and Terrorism,* Bharat Publication, Delhi, 1998.

Ahmad, R.S. : *Al-Harakat Al-Islamiyya.* Cairo: Sina Linasr. Allport, G. 1958.

Allison, Graham: *Nuclear Terrorism: The Ultimate Preventable Catastrophe,* New York: Times Books, 2004.

Anil Bhat: Assam : *Terrorism and the Demographic Challenge,* Knowledge World, Delhi, 2009.

Arnab Goswami: *Combating Terrorism : The Legal Challenge,* Har Anand Publication, Delhi, 2002.

Aurobindo, Sri : *The Foundations of Islamic Culture and AlQaeda,* New York, 1973.

Ayesha Siddiqa-Agha: *Military Inc.: Inside Pakistan's Military Economy,* London: Pluto, 2007.

Bert Ruiz: *The Colombian Civil War.* McFarland & Company. 2001.

Choudhury, Golam W: *Pakistan: Transition from Military to Civilian Rule,* Scorpion, 1988.

Das. P.K.: *Jihad : Terrorist Strategies Against the West,* Sumit Enterprises, Delhi, 2009.

David Bushnell: *The Making of Modern Colombia, A Nation in Spite of Itself.* University of California Press. 2010.

Dekmejian, R. Hrair : *Islamic Revolution: Fundamentalism in the Arab World* Syracuse, New York: Syracuse University Press, 1995.

Friedman, G.: *The Future of War of Cyber Crimes,* N.Y., Random House, 1996.

Garry M. Leech: *Killing Peace: Colombia's Conflict and the Failure of U.S. Intervention.* Information Network of the Americas (INOTA). 2002

Hoffman, Bruce, *Inside Terrorism,* New York: Columbia University Press, 1998.

James J. Brittain: *Revolutionary Social Change in Colombia: The Origin and Direction of the FARC-EP.* Pluto Press. 2010.

Kaplan, David, *The Cult At the End of the World,* New York: Crown Publishers, 1996.

Kegley, C. W.: *The new global terrorism: Characteristics, causes, and controls,* Upper Saddle Creek, NJ: Prentice Hall, 2003.

Kline, H. F.: *Colombia: Democracy Under Assault,* Harper Collins, 1995.

Laquer, David: *Terrorism Attack from Computer Hacking,* Oxford: Oxford University Press, 1999.

Maullin, Richard L.: *The Fall of Dumar Aljure, a Colombian Guerrilla and Bandit.* The Rand Corporation, 1968

Osterling, Jorge P.: *Democracy in Colombia: Clientelist Politics and Guerrilla Warfare,* Transaction Publishers, 1989.

Oudha, Abdul Qadir : *Criminal Law of Islam,* Kitab Bhavan, New Delhi, 1999.

Qureshi, A. Iqbal : *Islam and the Theory of Interest,* Kitab Bhavan, New Delhi, 1994.

Rizvi, Hasan Askari : *Al Qaeda : a Socio Political Study,* Progressive Publishers, Lahore, 1981.

Robin Kirk: *More Terrible than Death: Massacres, Drugs, and America's War in Colombia.* PublicAffairs. 2003.

Schroeer, Dietrich, *Science, Technology, and the Nuclear Arms Race,* Ontario: John Wiley & Sons, 1984.

Sharma, Rajeev: *Global Jihad : Current Patterns and Future Trends,* Kaveri Books, Delhi, 2006.

Spindlove, J. R.: *Terrorism Today: The Past, the Players, the Future,* Upper Saddle Creek, NJ: Prentice Hall, 2000.

Steven Dudley: *Walking Ghosts: Murder and Guerrilla Politics in Colombia.* Routledge. 2004

Stout, C.: *The Psychology of Terrorism,* Westport, CT: Praeger, 2002.

Thomas Arnold: *The Spread of Islam in the World, A History of Peaceful Preaching,* Goodword Books, 2001.

Valliuddin, Mir : *The Quranic Sufism,* Motilal Banarsi Das Publishers, New Delhi, 1989.

Whitaker, D. J.: *The Terrorism Reader,* New York: Routledge, 2001.

Index

❑❑❑